FREE Study Skills Videos/D~~VD Offer~~

Dear Customer,

Thank you for your purchase from Mometrix! We consider it an honor and a privilege that you have purchased our product and we want to ensure your satisfaction.

As part of our ongoing effort to meet the needs of test takers, we have developed a set of Study Skills Videos that we would like to give you for <u>FREE</u>. These videos cover our *best practices* for getting ready for your exam, from how to use our study materials to how to best prepare for the day of the test.

All that we ask is that you email us with feedback that would describe your experience so far with our product. Good, bad, or indifferent, we want to know what you think!

To get your FREE Study Skills Videos, you can use the **QR code** below, or send us an **email** at <u>studyvideos@mometrix.com</u> with *FREE VIDEOS* in the subject line and the following information in the body of the email:

- The name of the product you purchased.
- Your product rating on a scale of 1-5, with 5 being the highest rating.
- Your feedback. It can be long, short, or anything in between. We just want to know your impressions and experience so far with our product. (Good feedback might include how our study material met your needs and ways we might be able to make it even better. You could highlight features that you found helpful or features that you think we should add.)

If you have any questions or concerns, please don't hesitate to contact me directly.

Thanks again!

Sincerely,

Jay Willis
Vice President
<u>jay.willis@mometrix.com</u>
1-800-673-8175

SCAN HERE

NASM CPT
Study Guide 2023-2024

NASM Personal Trainer Certification Exam Secrets Book

Full-Length Practice Test

Detailed Answer Explanations

3rd Edition

Copyright © 2022 by Mometrix Media LLC

All rights reserved. This product, or parts thereof, may not be reproduced, stored in a retrieval system, or transmitted in any form or by any means—electronic, mechanical, photocopy, recording, scanning, or other—except for brief quotations in critical reviews or articles, without the prior written permission of the publisher.

Written and edited by the Mometrix Personal Trainer Certification Test Team

Printed in the United States of America

This paper meets the requirements of ANSI/NISO Z39.48-1992 (Permanence of Paper).

Mometrix offers volume discount pricing to institutions. For more information or a price quote, please contact our sales department at sales@mometrix.com or 888-248-1219.

Mometrix Media LLC is not affiliated with or endorsed by any official testing organization. All organizational and test names are trademarks of their respective owners.

Paperback
ISBN 13: 978-1-5167-2160-3
ISBN 10: 1-5167-2160-8

DEAR FUTURE EXAM SUCCESS STORY

First of all, **THANK YOU** for purchasing Mometrix study materials!

Second, congratulations! You are one of the few determined test-takers who are committed to doing whatever it takes to excel on your exam. **You have come to the right place.** We developed these study materials with one goal in mind: to deliver you the information you need in a format that's concise and easy to use.

In addition to optimizing your guide for the content of the test, we've outlined our recommended steps for breaking down the preparation process into small, attainable goals so you can make sure you stay on track.

We've also analyzed the entire test-taking process, identifying the most common pitfalls and showing how you can overcome them and be ready for any curveball the test throws you.

Standardized testing is one of the biggest obstacles on your road to success, which only increases the importance of doing well in the high-pressure, high-stakes environment of test day. Your results on this test could have a significant impact on your future, and this guide provides the information and practical advice to help you achieve your full potential on test day.

Your success is our success

We would love to hear from you! If you would like to share the story of your exam success or if you have any questions or comments in regard to our products, please contact us at **800-673-8175** or **support@mometrix.com**.

Thanks again for your business and we wish you continued success!

Sincerely,
The Mometrix Test Preparation Team

Need more help? Check out our flashcards at:
http://mometrixflashcards.com/NASM

TABLE OF CONTENTS

Introduction

Thank you for purchasing this resource! You have made the choice to prepare yourself for a test that could have a huge impact on your future, and this guide is designed to help you be fully ready for test day. Obviously, it's important to have a solid understanding of the test material, but you also need to be prepared for the unique environment and stressors of the test, so that you can perform to the best of your abilities.

For this purpose, the first section that appears in this guide is the **Secret Keys**. We've devoted countless hours to meticulously researching what works and what doesn't, and we've boiled down our findings to the five most impactful steps you can take to improve your performance on the test. We start at the beginning with study planning and move through the preparation process, all the way to the testing strategies that will help you get the most out of what you know when you're finally sitting in front of the test.

We recommend that you start preparing for your test as far in advance as possible. However, if you've bought this guide as a last-minute study resource and only have a few days before your test, we recommend that you skip over the first two Secret Keys since they address a long-term study plan.

If you struggle with **test anxiety**, we strongly encourage you to check out our recommendations for how you can overcome it. Test anxiety is a formidable foe, but it can be beaten, and we want to make sure you have the tools you need to defeat it.

Copyright © Mometrix Media. You have been licensed one copy of this document for personal use only. Any other reproduction or redistribution is strictly prohibited. All rights reserved. This content is provided for test preparation purposes only and does not imply an endorsement by Mometrix of any particular political, scientific, or religious point of view.

Secret Key #1 – Plan Big, Study Small

There's a lot riding on your performance. If you want to ace this test, you're going to need to keep your skills sharp and the material fresh in your mind. You need a plan that lets you review everything you need to know while still fitting in your schedule. We'll break this strategy down into three categories.

Information Organization

Start with the information you already have: the official test outline. From this, you can make a complete list of all the concepts you need to cover before the test. Organize these concepts into groups that can be studied together, and create a list of any related vocabulary you need to learn so you can brush up on any difficult terms. You'll want to keep this vocabulary list handy once you actually start studying since you may need to add to it along the way.

Time Management

Once you have your set of study concepts, decide how to spread them out over the time you have left before the test. Break your study plan into small, clear goals so you have a manageable task for each day and know exactly what you're doing. Then just focus on one small step at a time. When you manage your time this way, you don't need to spend hours at a time studying. Studying a small block of content for a short period each day helps you retain information better and avoid stressing over how much you have left to do. You can relax knowing that you have a plan to cover everything in time. In order for this strategy to be effective though, you have to start studying early and stick to your schedule. Avoid the exhaustion and futility that comes from last-minute cramming!

Study Environment

The environment you study in has a big impact on your learning. Studying in a coffee shop, while probably more enjoyable, is not likely to be as fruitful as studying in a quiet room. It's important to keep distractions to a minimum. You're only planning to study for a short block of time, so make the most of it. Don't pause to check your phone or get up to find a snack. It's also important to **avoid multitasking**. Research has consistently shown that multitasking will make your studying dramatically less effective. Your study area should also be comfortable and well-lit so you don't have the distraction of straining your eyes or sitting on an uncomfortable chair.

 The time of day you study is also important. You want to be rested and alert. Don't wait until just before bedtime. Study when you'll be most likely to comprehend and remember. Even better, if you know what time of day your test will be, set that time aside for study. That way your brain will be used to working on that subject at that specific time and you'll have a better chance of recalling information.

Finally, it can be helpful to team up with others who are studying for the same test. Your actual studying should be done in as isolated an environment as possible, but the work of organizing the information and setting up the study plan can be divided up. In between study sessions, you can discuss with your teammates the concepts that you're all studying and quiz each other on the details. Just be sure that your teammates are as serious about the test as you are. If you find that your study time is being replaced with social time, you might need to find a new team.

Copyright © Mometrix Media. You have been licensed one copy of this document for personal use only. Any other reproduction or redistribution is strictly prohibited. All rights reserved.
This content is provided for test preparation purposes only and does not imply an endorsement by Mometrix of any particular political, scientific, or religious point of view.

Secret Key #2 – Make Your Studying Count

You're devoting a lot of time and effort to preparing for this test, so you want to be absolutely certain it will pay off. This means doing more than just reading the content and hoping you can remember it on test day. It's important to make every minute of study count. There are two main areas you can focus on to make your studying count.

Retention

It doesn't matter how much time you study if you can't remember the material. You need to make sure you are retaining the concepts. To check your retention of the information you're learning, try recalling it at later times with minimal prompting. Try carrying around flashcards and glance at one or two from time to time or ask a friend who's also studying for the test to quiz you.

To enhance your retention, look for ways to put the information into practice so that you can apply it rather than simply recalling it. If you're using the information in practical ways, it will be much easier to remember. Similarly, it helps to solidify a concept in your mind if you're not only reading it to yourself but also explaining it to someone else. Ask a friend to let you teach them about a concept you're a little shaky on (or speak aloud to an imaginary audience if necessary). As you try to summarize, define, give examples, and answer your friend's questions, you'll understand the concepts better and they will stay with you longer. Finally, step back for a big picture view and ask yourself how each piece of information fits with the whole subject. When you link the different concepts together and see them working together as a whole, it's easier to remember the individual components.

Finally, practice showing your work on any multi-step problems, even if you're just studying. Writing out each step you take to solve a problem will help solidify the process in your mind, and you'll be more likely to remember it during the test.

Modality

Modality simply refers to the means or method by which you study. Choosing a study modality that fits your own individual learning style is crucial. No two people learn best in exactly the same way, so it's important to know your strengths and use them to your advantage.

For example, if you learn best by visualization, focus on visualizing a concept in your mind and draw an image or a diagram. Try color-coding your notes, illustrating them, or creating symbols that will trigger your mind to recall a learned concept. If you learn best by hearing or discussing information, find a study partner who learns the same way or read aloud to yourself. Think about how to put the information in your own words. Imagine that you are giving a lecture on the topic and record yourself so you can listen to it later.

For any learning style, flashcards can be helpful. Organize the information so you can take advantage of spare moments to review. Underline key words or phrases. Use different colors for different categories. Mnemonic devices (such as creating a short list in which every item starts with the same letter) can also help with retention. Find what works best for you and use it to store the information in your mind most effectively and easily.

3

Copyright © Mometrix Media. You have been licensed one copy of this document for personal use only. Any other reproduction or redistribution is strictly prohibited. All rights reserved.
This content is provided for test preparation purposes only and does not imply an endorsement by Mometrix of any particular political, scientific, or religious point of view.

Secret Key #3 – Practice the Right Way

Your success on test day depends not only on how many hours you put into preparing, but also on whether you prepared the right way. It's good to check along the way to see if your studying is paying off. One of the most effective ways to do this is by taking practice tests to evaluate your progress. Practice tests are useful because they show exactly where you need to improve. Every time you take a practice test, pay special attention to these three groups of questions:

- The questions you got wrong
- The questions you had to guess on, even if you guessed right
- The questions you found difficult or slow to work through

This will show you exactly what your weak areas are, and where you need to devote more study time. Ask yourself why each of these questions gave you trouble. Was it because you didn't understand the material? Was it because you didn't remember the vocabulary? Do you need more repetitions on this type of question to build speed and confidence? Dig into those questions and figure out how you can strengthen your weak areas as you go back to review the material.

 Additionally, many practice tests have a section explaining the answer choices. It can be tempting to read the explanation and think that you now have a good understanding of the concept. However, an explanation likely only covers part of the question's broader context. Even if the explanation makes perfect sense, **go back and investigate** every concept related to the question until you're positive you have a thorough understanding.

As you go along, keep in mind that the practice test is just that: practice. Memorizing these questions and answers will not be very helpful on the actual test because it is unlikely to have any of the same exact questions. If you only know the right answers to the sample questions, you won't be prepared for the real thing. **Study the concepts** until you understand them fully, and then you'll be able to answer any question that shows up on the test.

It's important to wait on the practice tests until you're ready. If you take a test on your first day of study, you may be overwhelmed by the amount of material covered and how much you need to learn. Work up to it gradually.

On test day, you'll need to be prepared for answering questions, managing your time, and using the test-taking strategies you've learned. It's a lot to balance, like a mental marathon that will have a big impact on your future. Like training for a marathon, you'll need to start slowly and work your way up. When test day arrives, you'll be ready.

Start with the strategies you've read in the first two Secret Keys—plan your course and study in the way that works best for you. If you have time, consider using multiple study resources to get different approaches to the same concepts. It can be helpful to see difficult concepts from more than one angle. Then find a good source for practice tests. Many times, the test website will suggest potential study resources or provide sample tests.

Copyright © Mometrix Media. You have been licensed one copy of this document for personal use only. Any other reproduction or redistribution is strictly prohibited. All rights reserved.
This content is provided for test preparation purposes only and does not imply an endorsement by Mometrix of any particular political, scientific, or religious point of view.

Practice Test Strategy

If you're able to find at least three practice tests, we recommend this strategy:

UNTIMED AND OPEN-BOOK PRACTICE

Take the first test with no time constraints and with your notes and study guide handy. Take your time and focus on applying the strategies you've learned.

TIMED AND OPEN-BOOK PRACTICE

Take the second practice test open-book as well, but set a timer and practice pacing yourself to finish in time.

TIMED AND CLOSED-BOOK PRACTICE

Take any other practice tests as if it were test day. Set a timer and put away your study materials. Sit at a table or desk in a quiet room, imagine yourself at the testing center, and answer questions as quickly and accurately as possible.

Keep repeating timed and closed-book tests on a regular basis until you run out of practice tests or it's time for the actual test. Your mind will be ready for the schedule and stress of test day, and you'll be able to focus on recalling the material you've learned.

Copyright © Mometrix Media. You have been licensed one copy of this document for personal use only. Any other reproduction or redistribution is strictly prohibited. All rights reserved.
This content is provided for test preparation purposes only and does not imply an endorsement by Mometrix of any particular political, scientific, or religious point of view.

Secret Key #4 – Pace Yourself

Once you're fully prepared for the material on the test, your biggest challenge on test day will be managing your time. Just knowing that the clock is ticking can make you panic even if you have plenty of time left. Work on pacing yourself so you can build confidence against the time constraints of the exam. Pacing is a difficult skill to master, especially in a high-pressure environment, so **practice is vital**.

Set time expectations for your pace based on how much time is available. For example, if a section has 60 questions and the time limit is 30 minutes, you know you have to average 30 seconds or less per question in order to answer them all. Although 30 seconds is the hard limit, set 25 seconds per question as your goal, so you reserve extra time to spend on harder questions. When you budget extra time for the harder questions, you no longer have any reason to stress when those questions take longer to answer.

Don't let this time expectation distract you from working through the test at a calm, steady pace, but keep it in mind so you don't spend too much time on any one question. Recognize that taking extra time on one question you don't understand may keep you from answering two that you do understand later in the test. If your time limit for a question is up and you're still not sure of the answer, mark it and move on, and come back to it later if the time and the test format allow. If the testing format doesn't allow you to return to earlier questions, just make an educated guess; then put it out of your mind and move on.

On the easier questions, be careful not to rush. It may seem wise to hurry through them so you have more time for the challenging ones, but it's not worth missing one if you know the concept and just didn't take the time to read the question fully. Work efficiently but make sure you understand the question and have looked at all of the answer choices, since more than one may seem right at first.

Even if you're paying attention to the time, you may find yourself a little behind at some point. You should speed up to get back on track, but do so wisely. Don't panic; just take a few seconds less on each question until you're caught up. Don't guess without thinking, but do look through the answer choices and eliminate any you know are wrong. If you can get down to two choices, it is often worthwhile to guess from those. Once you've chosen an answer, move on and don't dwell on any that you skipped or had to hurry through. If a question was taking too long, chances are it was one of the harder ones, so you weren't as likely to get it right anyway.

On the other hand, if you find yourself getting ahead of schedule, it may be beneficial to slow down a little. The more quickly you work, the more likely you are to make a careless mistake that will affect your score. You've budgeted time for each question, so don't be afraid to spend that time. Practice an efficient but careful pace to get the most out of the time you have.

Copyright © Mometrix Media. You have been licensed one copy of this document for personal use only. Any other reproduction or redistribution is strictly prohibited. All rights reserved.
This content is provided for test preparation purposes only and does not imply an endorsement by Mometrix of any particular political, scientific, or religious point of view.

Secret Key #5 – Have a Plan for Guessing

When you're taking the test, you may find yourself stuck on a question. Some of the answer choices seem better than others, but you don't see the one answer choice that is obviously correct. What do you do?

The scenario described above is very common, yet most test takers have not effectively prepared for it. Developing and practicing a plan for guessing may be one of the single most effective uses of your time as you get ready for the exam.

In developing your plan for guessing, there are three questions to address:

- When should you start the guessing process?
- How should you narrow down the choices?
- Which answer should you choose?

When to Start the Guessing Process

Unless your plan for guessing is to select C every time (which, despite its merits, is not what we recommend), you need to leave yourself enough time to apply your answer elimination strategies. Since you have a limited amount of time for each question, that means that if you're going to give yourself the best shot at guessing correctly, you have to decide quickly whether or not you will guess.

Of course, the best-case scenario is that you don't have to guess at all, so first, see if you can answer the question based on your knowledge of the subject and basic reasoning skills. Focus on the key words in the question and try to jog your memory of related topics. Give yourself a chance to bring the knowledge to mind, but once you realize that you don't have (or you can't access) the knowledge you need to answer the question, it's time to start the guessing process.

It's almost always better to start the guessing process too early than too late. It only takes a few seconds to remember something and answer the question from knowledge. Carefully eliminating wrong answer choices takes longer. Plus, going through the process of eliminating answer choices can actually help jog your memory.

Summary: Start the guessing process as soon as you decide that you can't answer the question based on your knowledge.

7

Copyright © Mometrix Media. You have been licensed one copy of this document for personal use only. Any other reproduction or redistribution is strictly prohibited. All rights reserved.
This content is provided for test preparation purposes only and does not imply an endorsement by Mometrix of any particular political, scientific, or religious point of view.

How to Narrow Down the Choices

The next chapter in this book (**Test-Taking Strategies**) includes a wide range of strategies for how to approach questions and how to look for answer choices to eliminate. You will definitely want to read those carefully, practice them, and figure out which ones work best for you. Here though, we're going to address a mindset rather than a particular strategy.

Your odds of guessing an answer correctly depend on how many options you are choosing from.

Number of options left	5	4	3	2	1
Odds of guessing correctly	20%	25%	33%	50%	100%

You can see from this chart just how valuable it is to be able to eliminate incorrect answers and make an educated guess, but there are two things that many test takers do that cause them to miss out on the benefits of guessing:

- Accidentally eliminating the correct answer
- Selecting an answer based on an impression

We'll look at the first one here, and the second one in the next section.

To avoid accidentally eliminating the correct answer, we recommend a thought exercise called **the $5 challenge**. In this challenge, you only eliminate an answer choice from contention if you are willing to bet $5 on it being wrong. Why $5? Five dollars is a small but not insignificant amount of money. It's an amount you could afford to lose but wouldn't want to throw away. And while losing

$5 once might not hurt too much, doing it twenty times will set you back $100. In the same way, each small decision you make—eliminating a choice here, guessing on a question there—won't by itself impact your score very much, but when you put them all together, they can make a big difference. By holding each answer choice elimination decision to a higher standard, you can reduce the risk of accidentally eliminating the correct answer.

The $5 challenge can also be applied in a positive sense: If you are willing to bet $5 that an answer choice *is* correct, go ahead and mark it as correct.

Summary: Only eliminate an answer choice if you are willing to bet $5 that it is wrong.

8

Copyright © Mometrix Media. You have been licensed one copy of this document for personal use only. Any other reproduction or redistribution is strictly prohibited. All rights reserved.
This content is provided for test preparation purposes only and does not imply an endorsement by Mometrix of any particular political, scientific, or religious point of view.

Which Answer to Choose

You're taking the test. You've run into a hard question and decided you'll have to guess. You've eliminated all the answer choices you're willing to bet $5 on. Now you have to pick an answer. Why do we even need to talk about this? Why can't you just pick whichever one you feel like when the time comes?

The answer to these questions is that if you don't come into the test with a plan, you'll rely on your impression to select an answer choice, and if you do that, you risk falling into a trap. The test writers know that everyone who takes their test will be guessing on some of the questions, so they intentionally write wrong answer choices to seem plausible. You still have to pick an answer though, and if the wrong answer choices are designed to look right, how can you ever be sure that you're not falling for their trap? The best solution we've found to this dilemma is to take the decision out of your hands entirely. Here is the process we recommend:

Once you've eliminated any choices that you are confident (willing to bet $5) are wrong, select the first remaining choice as your answer.

Whether you choose to select the first remaining choice, the second, or the last, the important thing is that you use some preselected standard. Using this approach guarantees that you will not be enticed into selecting an answer choice that looks right, because you are not basing your decision on how the answer choices look.

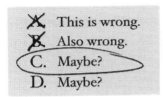

This is not meant to make you question your knowledge. Instead, it is to help you recognize the difference between your knowledge and your impressions. There's a huge difference between thinking an answer is right because of what you know, and thinking an answer is right because it looks or sounds like it should be right.

Summary: To ensure that your selection is appropriately random, make a predetermined selection from among all answer choices you have not eliminated.

Copyright © Mometrix Media. You have been licensed one copy of this document for personal use only. Any other reproduction or redistribution is strictly prohibited. All rights reserved.
This content is provided for test preparation purposes only and does not imply an endorsement by Mometrix of any particular political, scientific, or religious point of view.

Test-Taking Strategies

This section contains a list of test-taking strategies that you may find helpful as you work through the test. By taking what you know and applying logical thought, you can maximize your chances of answering any question correctly!

It is very important to realize that every question is different and every person is different: no single strategy will work on every question, and no single strategy will work for every person. That's why we've included all of them here, so you can try them out and determine which ones work best for different types of questions and which ones work best for you.

Question Strategies

⊘ READ CAREFULLY

Read the question and the answer choices carefully. Don't miss the question because you misread the terms. You have plenty of time to read each question thoroughly and make sure you understand what is being asked. Yet a happy medium must be attained, so don't waste too much time. You must read carefully and efficiently.

⊘ CONTEXTUAL CLUES

Look for contextual clues. If the question includes a word you are not familiar with, look at the immediate context for some indication of what the word might mean. Contextual clues can often give you all the information you need to decipher the meaning of an unfamiliar word. Even if you can't determine the meaning, you may be able to narrow down the possibilities enough to make a solid guess at the answer to the question.

⊘ PREFIXES

If you're having trouble with a word in the question or answer choices, try dissecting it. Take advantage of every clue that the word might include. Prefixes can be a huge help. Usually, they allow you to determine a basic meaning. *Pre-* means before, *post-* means after, *pro-* is positive, *de-* is negative. From prefixes, you can get an idea of the general meaning of the word and try to put it into context.

⊘ HEDGE WORDS

Watch out for critical hedge words, such as *likely, may, can, sometimes, often, almost, mostly, usually, generally, rarely,* and *sometimes.* Question writers insert these hedge phrases to cover every possibility. Often an answer choice will be wrong simply because it leaves no room for exception. Be on guard for answer choices that have definitive words such as *exactly* and *always.*

⊘ SWITCHBACK WORDS

Stay alert for *switchbacks.* These are the words and phrases frequently used to alert you to shifts in thought. The most common switchback words are *but, although,* and *however.* Others include *nevertheless, on the other hand, even though, while, in spite of, despite,* and *regardless of.* Switchback words are important to catch because they can change the direction of the question or an answer choice.

10

Copyright © Mometrix Media. You have been licensed one copy of this document for personal use only. Any other reproduction or redistribution is strictly prohibited. All rights reserved.
This content is provided for test preparation purposes only and does not imply an endorsement by Mometrix of any particular political, scientific, or religious point of view.

⊘ FACE VALUE

When in doubt, use common sense. Accept the situation in the problem at face value. Don't read too much into it. These problems will not require you to make wild assumptions. If you have to go beyond creativity and warp time or space in order to have an answer choice fit the question, then you should move on and consider the other answer choices. These are normal problems rooted in reality. The applicable relationship or explanation may not be readily apparent, but it is there for you to figure out. Use your common sense to interpret anything that isn't clear.

Answer Choice Strategies

⊘ ANSWER SELECTION

The most thorough way to pick an answer choice is to identify and eliminate wrong answers until only one is left, then confirm it is the correct answer. Sometimes an answer choice may immediately seem right, but be careful. The test writers will usually put more than one reasonable answer choice on each question, so take a second to read all of them and make sure that the other choices are not equally obvious. As long as you have time left, it is better to read every answer choice than to pick the first one that looks right without checking the others.

⊘ ANSWER CHOICE FAMILIES

An answer choice family consists of two (in rare cases, three) answer choices that are very similar in construction and cannot all be true at the same time. If you see two answer choices that are direct opposites or parallels, one of them is usually the correct answer. For instance, if one answer choice says that quantity x increases and another either says that quantity x decreases (opposite) or says that quantity y increases (parallel), then those answer choices would fall into the same family. An answer choice that doesn't match the construction of the answer choice family is more likely to be incorrect. Most questions will not have answer choice families, but when they do appear, you should be prepared to recognize them.

⊘ ELIMINATE ANSWERS

Eliminate answer choices as soon as you realize they are wrong, but make sure you consider all possibilities. If you are eliminating answer choices and realize that the last one you are left with is also wrong, don't panic. Start over and consider each choice again. There may be something you missed the first time that you will realize on the second pass.

⊘ AVOID FACT TRAPS

Don't be distracted by an answer choice that is factually true but doesn't answer the question. You are looking for the choice that answers the question. Stay focused on what the question is asking for so you don't accidentally pick an answer that is true but incorrect. Always go back to the question and make sure the answer choice you've selected actually answers the question and is not merely a true statement.

⊘ EXTREME STATEMENTS

In general, you should avoid answers that put forth extreme actions as standard practice or proclaim controversial ideas as established fact. An answer choice that states the "process should be used in certain situations, if..." is much more likely to be correct than one that states the "process should be discontinued completely." The first is a calm rational statement and doesn't even make a definitive, uncompromising stance, using a hedge word *if* to provide wiggle room, whereas the second choice is far more extreme.

Copyright © Mometrix Media. You have been licensed one copy of this document for personal use only. Any other reproduction or redistribution is strictly prohibited. All rights reserved.
This content is provided for test preparation purposes only and does not imply an endorsement by Mometrix of any particular political, scientific, or religious point of view.

⊘ Benchmark

As you read through the answer choices and you come across one that seems to answer the question well, mentally select that answer choice. This is not your final answer, but it's the one that will help you evaluate the other answer choices. The one that you selected is your benchmark or standard for judging each of the other answer choices. Every other answer choice must be compared to your benchmark. That choice is correct until proven otherwise by another answer choice beating it. If you find a better answer, then that one becomes your new benchmark. Once you've decided that no other choice answers the question as well as your benchmark, you have your final answer.

⊘ Predict the Answer

Before you even start looking at the answer choices, it is often best to try to predict the answer. When you come up with the answer on your own, it is easier to avoid distractions and traps because you will know exactly what to look for. The right answer choice is unlikely to be word-for-word what you came up with, but it should be a close match. Even if you are confident that you have the right answer, you should still take the time to read each option before moving on.

General Strategies

⊘ Tough Questions

If you are stumped on a problem or it appears too hard or too difficult, don't waste time. Move on! Remember though, if you can quickly check for obviously incorrect answer choices, your chances of guessing correctly are greatly improved. Before you completely give up, at least try to knock out a couple of possible answers. Eliminate what you can and then guess at the remaining answer choices before moving on.

⊘ Check Your Work

Since you will probably not know every term listed and the answer to every question, it is important that you get credit for the ones that you do know. Don't miss any questions through careless mistakes. If at all possible, try to take a second to look back over your answer selection and make sure you've selected the correct answer choice and haven't made a costly careless mistake (such as marking an answer choice that you didn't mean to mark). This quick double check should more than pay for itself in caught mistakes for the time it costs.

⊘ Pace Yourself

It's easy to be overwhelmed when you're looking at a page full of questions; your mind is confused and full of random thoughts, and the clock is ticking down faster than you would like. Calm down and maintain the pace that you have set for yourself. Especially as you get down to the last few minutes of the test, don't let the small numbers on the clock make you panic. As long as you are on track by monitoring your pace, you are guaranteed to have time for each question.

⊘ Don't Rush

It is very easy to make errors when you are in a hurry. Maintaining a fast pace in answering questions is pointless if it makes you miss questions that you would have gotten right otherwise. Test writers like to include distracting information and wrong answers that seem right. Taking a little extra time to avoid careless mistakes can make all the difference in your test score. Find a pace that allows you to be confident in the answers that you select.

Copyright © Mometrix Media. You have been licensed one copy of this document for personal use only. Any other reproduction or redistribution is strictly prohibited. All rights reserved.
This content is provided for test preparation purposes only and does not imply an endorsement by Mometrix of any particular political, scientific, or religious point of view.

⊘ Keep Moving

Panicking will not help you pass the test, so do your best to stay calm and keep moving. Taking deep breaths and going through the answer elimination steps you practiced can help to break through a stress barrier and keep your pace.

Final Notes

The combination of a solid foundation of content knowledge and the confidence that comes from practicing your plan for applying that knowledge is the key to maximizing your performance on test day. As your foundation of content knowledge is built up and strengthened, you'll find that the strategies included in this chapter become more and more effective in helping you quickly sift through the distractions and traps of the test to isolate the correct answer.

Now that you're preparing to move forward into the test content chapters of this book, be sure to keep your goal in mind. As you read, think about how you will be able to apply this information on the test. If you've already seen sample questions for the test and you have an idea of the question format and style, try to come up with questions of your own that you can answer based on what you're reading. This will give you valuable practice applying your knowledge in the same ways you can expect to on test day.

Good luck and good studying!

Copyright © Mometrix Media. You have been licensed one copy of this document for personal use only. Any other reproduction or redistribution is strictly prohibited. All rights reserved.
This content is provided for test preparation purposes only and does not imply an endorsement by Mometrix of any particular political, scientific, or religious point of view.

Copyright © Mometrix Media. You have been licensed one copy of this document for personal use only. Any other reproduction or redistribution is strictly prohibited. All rights reserved. This content is provided for test preparation purposes only and does not imply an endorsement by Mometrix of any particular political, scientific, or religious point of view.

Basic and Applied Sciences

Anatomy and Exercise Physiology

NERVOUS SYSTEM

The brain and spinal cord make up the **central nervous system**. The brain controls bodily processes consciously (e.g., higher thinking/mental faculties, voluntary muscle action, memory, etc.) and unconsciously (e.g., heart rate, blood pressure, breathing, digesting food, etc.). The spinal cord has nerves that innervate major organs and muscles and initiate muscle movement or organ function at the command of the brain.

NERVOUS SYSTEM FUNCTIONS

The nervous system has three main functions:

1. **Sensing**—perceive internal and external alterations to the body.
2. **Integrating**—compute sensory information to communicate to the body the correct action to take.
3. **Motor**—transmit information to the muscles of the body when it is time to initiate movement and control this movement.

The human body uses sensory inputs to gather information about itself and the surrounding world. This information travels to the central nervous system where the information will be processed and acted upon through a process called **integration**. The brain will make decisions based on the information gathered, or reject the information if necessary. If the brain decides to act on the information gathered, it initiates movement through motor pathways. Because the nervous system controls all human movement, it is important to train it to ingrain correct movement and improve reaction time.

NERVOUS SYSTEM STRUCTURE

The nervous system is composed of the central and peripheral nervous systems. The **central nervous system** includes the main organs of the nervous system: the brain and the spinal column. The **peripheral nervous system** includes all parts of the nervous system that branch off from the central nervous system, such as cranial and spinal nerves.

The nervous system consists of billions of **neurons**—special cells made up of a cell body, axon, and dendrite. Function determines neuron nomenclature:

- **Afferent neurons**—transmit information from muscles and organs to the central nervous system.
- **Interneurons**—transmit information from neuron to neuron.
- **Efferent neurons**—transmit information from the central nervous system to muscles or glands.

MECHANORECEPTORS, MUSCLE SPINDLES, GOLGI TENDON ORGANS, AND JOINT RECEPTORS

Mechanoreceptors reside in the joints and connective tissues of the body (tendons, ligaments, and muscles). They sense changes in the compression or stretching of the muscles or tissues. Muscle spindles, Golgi tendon organs, and joint receptors are types of mechanoreceptors.

15

Copyright © Mometrix Media. You have been licensed one copy of this document for personal use only. Any other reproduction or redistribution is strictly prohibited. All rights reserved.
This content is provided for test preparation purposes only and does not imply an endorsement by Mometrix of any particular political, scientific, or religious point of view.

Muscles contain **muscle spindles**. They sense alteration in the length of the muscle and the rate of alteration. Muscle spindles contract when they are stimulated to protect the muscle from overstretching.

Golgi tendon organs sense alteration in muscle tension and the rate of alteration. Golgi tendon organs operate at the junction of a muscle and a tendon. Golgi tendon organs relax when they are stimulated to protect the muscle from overstressing.

Joint receptors sense changes in speed in the joint. Joint receptors sense overextension of the joint and respond to provide protection for it.

POSSIBLE NERVOUS SYSTEM INJURIES

Cerebrospinal fluid (CSF) surrounds the brain and central nervous system. It helps insulate and protect the brain and central nervous system from hard blows to the head or unanticipated change in speed. The head and neck must be protected during sports play because a hard blow (e.g., tackle in football) could damage the brain and central nervous system by disrupting the CSF.

Afferent neurons pass information to the brain via the spinal cord. **Efferent neurons** transmit information from the brain to effector cells. **Effector cells** initiate action in the muscles or organs. Acute or chronic injury, illness, or inflammation can disrupt afferent and efferent pathways. If this occurs, messages will not travel efficiently to the brain or the body. In extreme cases, the message will not travel at all.

Copyright © Mometrix Media. You have been licensed one copy of this document for personal use only. Any other reproduction or redistribution is strictly prohibited. All rights reserved.
This content is provided for test preparation purposes only and does not imply an endorsement by Mometrix of any particular political, scientific, or religious point of view.

SKELETAL SYSTEM

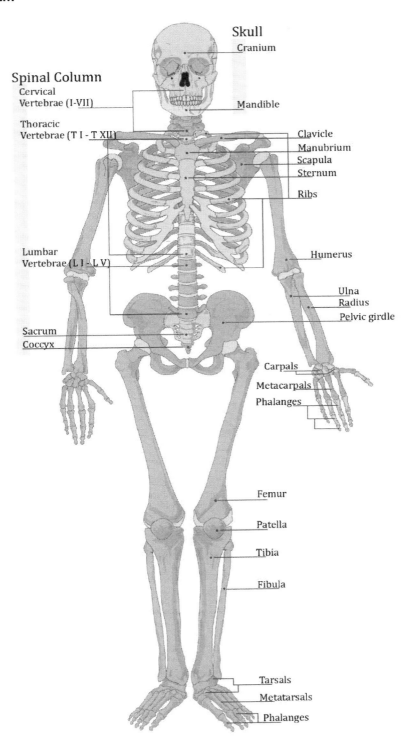

The **skeleton** provides a support system for the muscles and organs of the body and initiates movement. Additionally, the skeletal system protects major organs (heart, brain, etc.) and creates red blood cells (this takes place in the bone marrow). The skeletal system stores minerals (such as

17

Copyright © Mometrix Media. You have been licensed one copy of this document for personal use only. Any other reproduction or redistribution is strictly prohibited. All rights reserved.
This content is provided for test preparation purposes only and does not imply an endorsement by Mometrix of any particular political, scientific, or religious point of view.

calcium and phosphorus) and releases them into the body, which regulates mineral balance and promotes proper body function.

The skeletal system contains into two major sections: the axial skeletal system and the appendicular skeletal system. The **axial skeletal system** has nearly 80 bones and is composed of the head, spine, and rib cage. The **appendicular system** contains the appendages, the shoulders, and the hip complex. It has more than 120 bones.

The two types of tissue that exist within human bones are compact bone and spongy bone. **Compact bone** resides on the outer layer of bones (the surface). Compact bone is very tough and serves a protective function by allowing the bone to bear the entire weight of the body. **Spongy bone** contains more spaces than compact bone and houses bone marrow.

The skeleton is composed of long bones, short bones, flat bones, irregular bones, and sesamoid (round) bones. Examples of **long bones** are the humerus and the femur. The shaft of a long bone, which is called the diaphysis, is made up of compact bone. The ends of a long bone are called the epiphyses, and these are made up of cancellous bone. The epiphyses are the sites of bone growth. **Short bones** are found in groups, and aid in movement. This type of bone is found in the wrist and ankle. Examples of **flat bones** are the ribs, scapula, sternum, and cranial bones. The vertebrae, facial bones, and skull bones are **irregular bones**. Sesamoid bones are located within a tendon. The patella, for example, is a **sesamoid bone**.

Review Video: Skeletal System
Visit mometrix.com/academy and enter code: 256447

BONE MARKINGS

Every bone has **markings** on its exterior that serve various functions. One major function is to provide place for muscles or other connective tissue to attach. There are two major categories of bone markings: processes and depressions.

Processes are bulges that protrude from the bone. Some examples include the rounded ends of the femur or humerus. Listed here are examples of bone processes:

- **Trochanters**—the rounded end of the femur; the hip bone is known as the greater trochanter.
- **Tubercles**—the top of the humerus; there are tubercles in the shoulder complex also.
- **Condyles**—the bottom of the femur, where condyles help form the knee joint.
- **Epicondyles**—the bottom of the humerus, where epicondyles help form the elbow joint.

Depressions are parts of the bone that are smooth or flat. Common depressions are the fossa or sulcus. These are locations where muscle or body tissues can attach or pass between.

SPINE

The human spine contains 33 vertebrae divided into 5 sections: **cervical** (7 bones), **thoracic** (12 bones), **lumbar** (5 bones), **sacral** (5 bones fused into the sacrum), and the **coccygeal** (4 bones fused into the coccyx).The spine can move through all **planes of movement** (frontal, sagittal, midsagittal, and transverse) by bending forward (flexion), bending backward (extension), bnding to the side (side flexion), and twisting (rotation). Some common ailments of the spine include lower back pain, bulging disc (vertebral disc bulges outward), and herniated disc (tear in the wall of the disc). Lower back pain is common among clients and can often be due to increased weight gain in the midsection. If disc problems are present, it is important to have these properly diagnosed by

Copyright © Mometrix Media. You have been licensed one copy of this document for personal use only. Any other reproduction or redistribution is strictly prohibited. All rights reserved. This content is provided for test preparation purposes only and does not imply an endorsement by Mometrix of any particular political, scientific, or religious point of view.

medical personnel and to modify the exercise sessions accordingly. Some twisting movements may need to be avoided, and clients may need to spend most of their time using machine weights where they are properly supported. High-impact activities should be avoided.

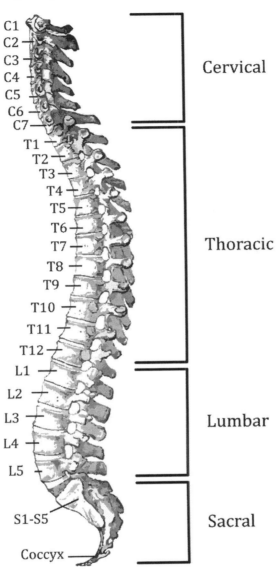

IRREGULAR CURVES

Lordosis is the excessive curvature of the lumbar spine, **kyphosis** is the excessive curvature of the thoracic spine (i.e., hunchback appearance), and **scoliosis** is a lateral S-shaped curve of the spine. If a client displays an abnormal curvature, they should avoid performing movements that put excessive stress on the spine. For example, stable, closed kinetic chain movements are more helpful than open kinetic chain movements. Lordosis can cause discomfort in the lumbar spine and make many high-impact exercises uncomfortable; standing for long periods of time can also be painful. Scoliosis and kyphosis can cause difficulty in completing full range of motion, and certain exercises may need to be off limits for the client. It is not advisable to engage in high impact activities or activities that require excessive torsion (twisting of the spine) if the client has a spinal condition. It is advisable to utilize machine weights to provide proper support for clients with extreme cases of lordosis, kyphosis, and scoliosis. In addition, it may be necessary as to avoid high-impact activities.

Copyright © Mometrix Media. You have been licensed one copy of this document for personal use only. Any other reproduction or redistribution is strictly prohibited. All rights reserved. This content is provided for test preparation purposes only and does not imply an endorsement by Mometrix of any particular political, scientific, or religious point of view.

JOINTS

A **pivot joint** (C1 and C2 of the neck) provides rotation of one bone around another. A **hinge joint** (elbow) provides flexion and extension. A **saddle joint** (between the carpal and metacarpal of the thumb) provides flexion, extension, adduction, abduction, and circumduction. A **gliding joint** (tarsal bones) provides gliding movements between two bones. A **condyloid joint** (between the metacarpals and phalanges) can provide flexion, extension, abduction, adduction, and circumduction. A **ball and socket joint** (e.g., hip) provides flexion, extension, abduction, adduction, internal and external rotation.

Joint type	Example	Movement provided
Pivot	C1, C2 of neck	Rotation about an axis
Hinge	Elbow	Flexion and extension
Saddle	Carpal and metacarpal of the thumb	Flexion, extension, adduction, abduction, and circumduction
Gliding	Tarsal bones	Back and forth or side to side
Condyloid	Metacarpals and phalanges	Flexion, extension, abduction, adduction, and circumduction
Ball and socket	Hip	Flexion, extension, abduction, adduction, internal and external rotation

There are two major types of joints, designated by physiology: synovial and nonsynovial:

- **Synovial joints** are those pulled together by a system of ligaments, which give these types of joints greater range of motion. Some specific types of synovial joints include ball-and-socket joints (such as the hip joints), hinge joints, and pivot joints.
- **Nonsynovial joints** have no system of ligaments and have a limited range of motion. Examples include some of the flat joints of the skull and some of the nonmoving joints in the ankle.
- **Ligaments** are the main connective tissue between the bones of a joint.

HEMATOPOIESIS

Hematopoiesis refers to the formation of new red blood cells within the bone marrow. Red blood cells come from hemocytoblasts that quickly replicate themselves. Red blood cells have a lifecycle of three months, platelets of seven days, and granulocytes of seven hours. Healthy red blood cells are necessary for energy maintenance (among other vital processes) since oxygen must bind to each red blood cell as part of the aerobic energy pathway.

ENDOCRINE SYSTEM

The endocrine system controls and regulates bodily functions through the secretion of **hormones**. The word is derived from Greek and translates to "hormone secreting." The endocrine system consists of glands, hormones, and receptor cells. The primary components of the endocrine system are the pineal gland, hypothalamus, and the pituitary gland in the head, the thyroid and parathyroid glands in the throat, the thymus gland in the chest, the adrenal gland and pancreas in the abdomen, and the reproductive organs (ovaries in females and testes in males). The **pituitary gland** is the command center of the endocrine system and it controls the function of the other endocrine system components. Each hormone controls a specific bodily process.

The endocrine system, specifically the **pancreas**, regulates **glucose** (blood sugar), which plays a vital role in the body's ability to manage blood sugar levels. The pancreas regulates glucose through the production of insulin and glucagon. Glucose levels rise after food is consumed. **Insulin** is

20

Copyright © Mometrix Media. You have been licensed one copy of this document for personal use only. Any other reproduction or redistribution is strictly prohibited. All rights reserved. This content is provided for test preparation purposes only and does not imply an endorsement by Mometrix of any particular political, scientific, or religious point of view.

released to aid in the diffusion of blood glucose, which has the effect of lowering blood glucose levels. The diffusion process allows the liver, muscles, and fat to take in glucose and store it as **glycogen** for future use as an energy source. The pancreas also releases glucagon, but it has the opposite effect (i.e. blood glucose levels rise in response to the liver releasing glycogen stores). Blood sugar levels drop in the hours following consumption of a meal. Lowered blood sugar levels trigger the release of glucagon which raises blood sugar levels by prompting the liver to convert glycogen stores into glucose. **Blood sugar management** is an important function of the endocrine system during exercise, as the body uses more glucose and insulin levels will drop during physical activity. The pancreas secretes more glucagon during exercise allowing the body to maintain a steady supply of blood glucose.

The endocrine system plays a crucial role in preparing the body for physical activity through the **adrenal glands** which produce epinephrine (adrenaline) and norepinephrine. Adrenaline helps the body cope with stress by triggering the "fight or flight" response. The release of adrenaline primes the body for action increasing heart rate and stroke volume, elevating blood glucose levels, redistributing blood to working tissues, and opening up airways.

The endocrine system produces several other hormones that are crucial to aiding the body during physical activity. The body produces **testosterone** in males and females in slightly different way. In males, the testes produce testosterone. The ovaries and adrenal gland perform the task in females. Testosterone helps the body build tissue and repair damaged tissue. **Cortisol** helps the body maintain energy levels as exercise depletes carbohydrates stores. Excess cortisol can contribute to the breakdown of muscle tissue and have other adverse effects on the body. The pituitary gland produces **growth hormone** which controls a variety of bodily functions including bone development, the building of muscle tissue, protein synthesis, fat burning, and immune system function. The thyroid gland controls **metabolism**.

> **Review Video: Endocrine System**
> Visit mometrix.com/academy and enter code: 678939

MUSCULAR SYSTEM

The primary function of muscle is to produce skeletal movement. **Muscle fibers** contain myofibrils consisting of actin (thin) and mysoin (thick) filaments. A repeating section of actin and myosin is called a sacromere (the functional unit of a muscle). **Muscle contraction** is controlled by motor neurons. A motor neuron and the fibers it activates are called a motor unit. According to the sliding-filament theory, when a motor neuron inervates a muscle fiber, the thick and thin filaments shorten by sliding past one another, which produces force. If there is enough action potential, the stimulus is strong enough to contract the muscle fiber. If there is insufficient stimulus, the muscle will not contract. This phenomenon is referred to as the "All or Nothing" law.

Two vital protein structures that affect muscle contraction are troponin and tropomyosin. The actin filament houses troponin and tropomyosin. **Troponin** provides a place for tropomyosin and calcium (which are essential for muscle contraction) to bind. **Tropomyosin** blocks myosin from binding to keep the muscle relaxed.

The three different types of muscle tissue are cardiac, smooth, and skeletal. The heart is composed of **cardiac muscle**. Organs (e.g., the liver or kidneys) contain **smooth muscle**. **Skeletal muscle** attaches to the skeletal system. Examples of skeletal muscle include the deltoid and trapezius muscles. The central nervous system (CNS) controls cardiac and smooth muscle with automatic processes. Skeletal muscle appears striated is voluntary control of the CNS.

Copyright © Mometrix Media. You have been licensed one copy of this document for personal use only. Any other reproduction or redistribution is strictly prohibited. All rights reserved. This content is provided for test preparation purposes only and does not imply an endorsement by Mometrix of any particular political, scientific, or religious point of view.

Type I fibers are considered slow-twitch fibers. They require oxygen and provide power during endurance activities (e.g., running a marathon). **Type II fibers** are fast-twitch fibers. They rely on anaerobic metabolism (glycolysis, and the ATP-PC systems) as their energy source. These fibers are helpful for power- or speed-related activities that require explosiveness in the individual (e.g., sprinting). Type II fibers are subdivided into type IIa and type IIb fibers. *Type IIa* are known as intermediate fast-twitch fibers because they can use aerobic (oxygen) and anaerobic energy pathways. They are a combination of type I and II fibers. *Type IIb fibers* use only the anaerobic energy pathways. The term fast-twitch refers to Type IIb fibers.

The **endomysium** surrounds the muscle fiber (or cell), which separates it from the other muscle fibers. The **fascicle** surrounds a bundle of muscle fibers and is itself wrapped within the perimysium. The **epimysium** (outer covering of the muscle) holds several bundles of muscle fibers. **Blood vessels** are between each fascicle of muscle fibers. The blood vessels act to supply nutrition and energy to the muscle fiber. Each muscle in the body contains the endomysium, fascicle, perimysium, epimysium, and blood vessels.

Review Video: Muscular System
Visit mometrix.com/academy and enter code: 967216

Copyright © Mometrix Media. You have been licensed one copy of this document for personal use only. Any other reproduction or redistribution is strictly prohibited. All rights reserved. This content is provided for test preparation purposes only and does not imply an endorsement by Mometrix of any particular political, scientific, or religious point of view.

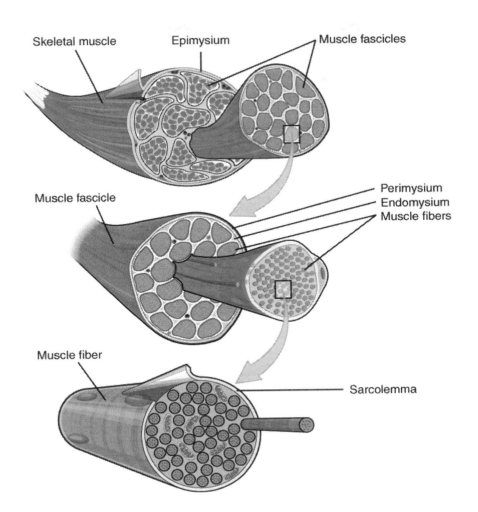

Copyright © Mometrix Media. You have been licensed one copy of this document for personal use only. Any other reproduction or redistribution is strictly prohibited. All rights reserved.
This content is provided for test preparation purposes only and does not imply an endorsement by Mometrix of any particular political, scientific, or religious point of view.

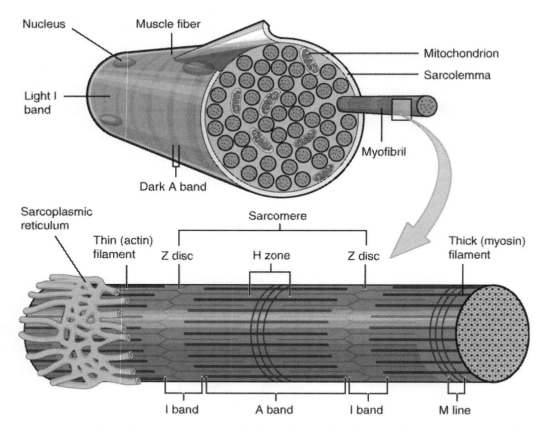

Some common muscular injuries that occur during physical activity include, but are not limited to, sprains, strains, tears, bursitis, and tennis elbow. A **sprain** occurs when a ligament tears or stretches excessively, whereas a **strain** is an injury to the tendon or muscle. **Tearing** of the ligament can lead to a sprain or muscle strain. **Bursitis** affects the bursa between joints (e.g., shoulder, hip) and causes inflammation of the bursa. **Tennis elbow** is a condition occurring when the tendons connecting the forearm to the outside of the elbow become inflamed.

MUSCLE GROUPS

There are four major categories of muscles, differentiated by the primary function of the muscle:

1. **Agonists**—create primary movement. They are called prime movers. The gluteus maximus is an agonist muscle when performing a squatting movement.
2. **Antagonists**—counteract the actions of agonist muscles. The psoas muscle performs the opposite action as the gluteus maximus when performing a squatting movement.
3. **Synergists**—act at the same time as an agonist muscle to assist in the primary movement. The hamstrings are the synergist muscles when performing a squatting movement.
4. **Stabilizers**—stabilize and support agonist muscles while they perform a primary movement. The transversus abdominis stabilize the body during a squatting movement.

Copyright © Mometrix Media. You have been licensed one copy of this document for personal use only. Any other reproduction or redistribution is strictly prohibited. All rights reserved. This content is provided for test preparation purposes only and does not imply an endorsement by Mometrix of any particular political, scientific, or religious point of view.

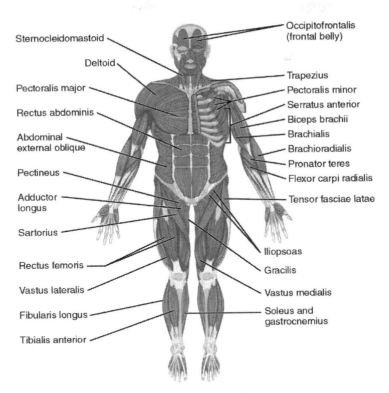

Sternocleidomastoid

Deltoid

Pectoralis major

Rectus abdominis

Abdominal
external oblique

Pectineus

Adductor
longus

Sartorius

Rectus femoris

Vastus lateralis

Fibularis longus

Tibialis anterior

Occipitofrontalis
(frontal belly)

Trapezius

Pectoralis minor

Serratus anterior

Biceps brachii

Brachialis

Brachioradialis

Pronator teres

Flexor carpi radialis

Tensor fasciae latae

Iliopsoas

Gracilis

Vastus medialis

Soleus and
gastrocnemius

Major muscles of the body.
Right side: superficial; left side:
deep (anterior view)

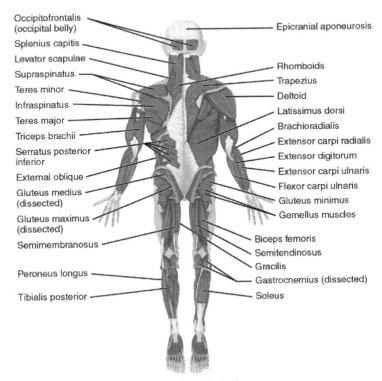

Occipitofrontalis
(occipital belly)

Splenius capitis

Levator scapulae

Supraspinatus

Teres minor

Infraspinatus

Teres major

Triceps brachii

Serratus posterior
inferior

External oblique

Gluteus medius
(dissected)

Gluteus maximus
(dissected)

Semimembranosus

Peroneus longus

Tibialis posterior

Epicranial aponeurosis

Rhomboids

Trapezius

Deltoid

Latissimus dorsi

Brachioradialis

Extensor carpi radialis

Extensor digitorum

Extensor carpi ulnaris

Flexor carpi ulnaris

Gluteus minimus

Gemellus muscles

Biceps femoris

Semitendinosus

Gracilis

Gastrocnemius (dissected)

Soleus

Major muscles of the body.
Right side: superficial; left side:
deep (posterior view)

25

Copyright © Mometrix Media. You have been licensed one copy of this document for personal use only. Any other reproduction or redistribution is strictly prohibited. All rights reserved.
This content is provided for test preparation purposes only and does not imply an endorsement by Mometrix of any particular political, scientific, or religious point of view.

LOWER LEG COMPLEX

Anterior tibialis—runs along the outside of the tibia from under the knee to the ankle. It helps stabilize the foot.

Posterior tibialis—runs along the back of the tibia, under the fibula. It helps control the foot.

Soleus—the fleshy part of the back of the lower leg. It also runs down the sides of the Achilles' tendon. It controls walking motion in the leg and ankle and supports the foot.

Gastrocnemius—on the back of the leg below the knee. It works with the soleus to control walking and stabilize the foot.

Peroneus longus—runs along the tibia on the outer part of the leg. It flexes and everts the foot.

HAMSTRING COMPLEX

Biceps femoris (long head)—emanates from the pelvis and inserts at the top of the fibula. It is essential in knee and hip movement.

Biceps femoris (short head)—runs along the lower part of the back of the femur. It is essential to knee and tibia movement.

Semimembranosus—runs along the back femur, through the center of the leg. It is essential to hip, knee, and tibia movement.

Semitendinosus—runs along the back of the femur toward the inner thigh. It is essential to hip, knee, and tibia movement.

QUADRICEPS COMPLEX

Vastus lateralis—runs along the outside of the front thigh. It stabilizes the knee and controls all movement for that joint.

Vastus medialis—runs along the inner thigh close to the knee. It is essential to all movement for the knee joint.

Vastus intermedius—runs along the vastus lateralis, the length of the front thigh. It is also essential to all movement for the knee joint.

Rectus femoris—runs down the center of the front thigh. It is also essential to knee motion and stability.

HIP MUSCULATURE COMPLEX

Adductor longus, adductor magnus (anterior fibers), **adductor magnus** (posterior fibers), and **adductor brevis**—fall under the pelvis, interwoven at the top of the femur. Together, they control hip adduction, abduction, flexion, and rotation.

Gracilis—runs along the interior of the top of the femur. It is also essential to all elements of hip movement.

Pectineus—runs along the back edge of the upper part of the femur. It is also essential to all elements of hip movement.

Copyright © Mometrix Media. You have been licensed one copy of this document for personal use only. Any other reproduction or redistribution is strictly prohibited. All rights reserved.
This content is provided for test preparation purposes only and does not imply an endorsement by Mometrix of any particular political, scientific, or religious point of view.

Gluteus medius (anterior fibers), ***gluteus medius*** (posterior fibers), ***gluteus minimus***—run along the outer edge of the back of the pelvis. Together, they control hip adduction, abduction, flexion, and rotation.

Tensor fascia lata (TFL)—runs along the top of the outer part of the hip. It is essential to hip flexion, abduction, adduction, and rotation.

Gluteus maximus—the fleshy part of the buttocks. It affects hip rotation and extension as well as stabilizing the lumbo-pelvic-hip (LPH) complex.

Psoas—run along the top of the hips to the base of the lowest vertebrae. These muscles are essential to hip movement and the rotation of the lumbar spine.

Iliacus—runs along the iliac crest. These muscles are essential to hip movement and lumbo-pelvic stability.

Sartorius—runs across the top of the thigh from the outer hip to the inner thigh. This muscle affects hip and knee function.

Piriformis—rests along the front of the sacrum. It affects hip movement stabilizes the hip joint.

ABDOMINAL MUSCULATURE

Rectus abdominis—run along the midline of the abdomen. They affect and control all core motion.

External oblique—run down the sides of the torso. They affect and control all core motion.

Internal oblique—run under the external obliques along the sides of the torso. They affect and control all core motion as well as stabilize the lumbo-pelvic-hip (LPH) complex.

Transversus abdominis—run along the side of the torso up and across under the ribs. They help stabilize the internal organs and the LPH complex.

Diaphragm—runs underneath the rib cage. It pulls open the thoracic cavity to accommodate oxygen intake.

MUSCLES OF THE BACK

Superficial erector spinae—the following muscles run down the length of the spine. Together they control spinal movement and stabilize the spine during activity:

- *Iliocostalis*
- *Longissimus*
- *Spinalis*

Latissimus dorsi—runs across the back under the scapula. It is critical to shoulder movement.

Quadratus lumborum—runs along the lower back and connects to the top of the pelvis. It affects spinal flexion and also stabilizes the lumbo-pelvic-hip (LPH) complex.

Copyright © Mometrix Media. You have been licensed one copy of this document for personal use only. Any other reproduction or redistribution is strictly prohibited. All rights reserved. This content is provided for test preparation purposes only and does not imply an endorsement by Mometrix of any particular political, scientific, or religious point of view.

TRANSVERSOSPINALIS COMPLEX

Semispinalis—the following muscles run from the bottom of the back of the skull to the top of the shoulders and spine. Together they control the movement of the upper spine as well as the head:

- *Iliocostalis*
- *Longissmus*
- *Spinalis*

Multifidus—run along the spine down into the sacrum. They control spinal flexion and lower-hip rotation.

MUSCLES IN THE SHOULDER

Serratus anterior—runs around the rib cage underneath the armpit. They affect the movement of the scapula.

Rhomboids—run across the top middle of the back, just under the neck. They also affect the movement of the scapula.

Lower trapezius, middle trapezius, and upper trapezius—run along the sides of the spine from the base of the neck down. They are also essential to all aspects of movement of the scapula.

Pectoralis major—runs along the front of the chest. It is essential to all movement of the shoulder complex.

Pectoralis minor—connects the front of the shoulder to the top ribs. It pulls the scapula forward.

Deltoid—the fleshy muscle that runs along the top of the arm. It is essential to all shoulder movement.

Teres major—runs along the chest to under the armpit. It is essential to shoulder rotation and movement.

MUSCLES IN THE ARM

Biceps brachii—runs along the top length of the humerus. It is essential to shoulder and elbow movement.

Triceps—runs along the bottom of the humerus (the back of the upper arm). It supports shoulder and elbow movement.

Brachioradialis—runs along the outside of the humerus (the side of the upper arm). It supports elbow movement.

Brachialis—runs along the outside of the humerus (the side of the upper arm). It supports elbow movement.

ROTATOR CUFF MUSCLES

Teres minor—runs along the lateral edge of the scapula. It accelerates and decelerates shoulder rotation.

Infraspinatus—sits under and along the scapula. It accelerates and decelerates shoulder rotation.

Subscapularis—covers the back along the scapula. It accelerates and decelerates shoulder rotation.

Copyright © Mometrix Media. You have been licensed one copy of this document for personal use only. Any other reproduction or redistribution is strictly prohibited. All rights reserved. This content is provided for test preparation purposes only and does not imply an endorsement by Mometrix of any particular political, scientific, or religious point of view.

Supraspinatus—runs along the interior of the top of the shoulder. It helps accelerate abduction and decelerate adduction of the arm.

MUSCLES IN THE NECK

Sternocleidomastoid—runs from the side of the back of the head down to the cervical collar. They help control the movement of the head and cervical spine.

Scalenes—run down the sides of the neck at the shoulders. They help stabilize and control the movement of the cervical spine.

Longus coli—run along the sides of the cervical vertebrae. They help control the movement of the cervical spine.

Longus capitis—runs along the side of the neck. It helps stabilize and move the cervical spine.

Levator scapulae—runs along the side of the neck down to the top of the shoulder. It affects the up/down motion of the scapula.

CARDIOVASCULAR SYSTEM

The elements in the body that create and circulate blood (e.g., the heart, the blood, the veins, and the capillaries) comprise the **cardiovascular system**.

The cardiovascular system has several functions. It removes metabolic waste from and delivers nutrients to the body. White blood cells provide protection from foreign microbes and viruses. Finally, the cardiovascular system helps keep our bodies in a state of homeostasis by controlling body temperature, pH balance, and cellular water retention.

BLOOD AND CHANNELS OF BLOOD DISTRIBUTION

Blood is the liquid that flows throughout the body, carrying out several functions. The average person has about 1.5 gallons of blood circulating at one time, and blood makes up a little less than 10 percent of a person's overall weight on average. Blood:

- carries **oxygen and nutrients** to the body systems.
- acts as a conduit to rid the body of **waste products**.
- **regulates** the body, helping keep body temperature constant and maintaining acid balance.
- is a **defensive mechanism**, clotting when necessary to prevent bleeding and creating and circulating defensive cells to help fight infection.

The cardiovascular system circulates five liters of blood through the body. It takes approximately one minute for a red blood cell to make its way through the entire human body.

Copyright © Mometrix Media. You have been licensed one copy of this document for personal use only. Any other reproduction or redistribution is strictly prohibited. All rights reserved. This content is provided for test preparation purposes only and does not imply an endorsement by Mometrix of any particular political, scientific, or religious point of view.

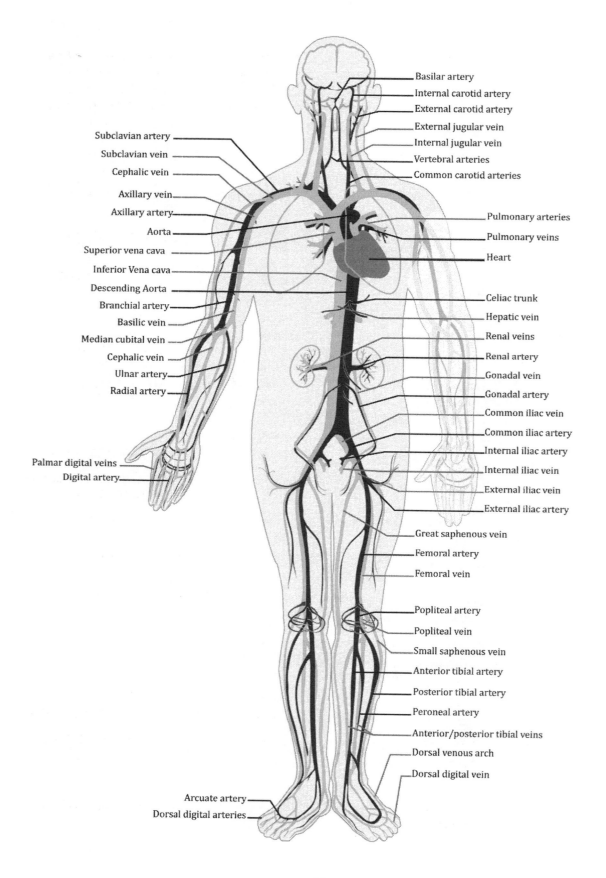

Basilar artery

Internal carotid artery

External carotid artery

External jugular vein

Internal jugular vein

Vertebral arteries

Common carotid arteries

Subclavian artery

Subclavian vein

Cephalic vein

Axillary vein

Axillary artery

Aorta

Superior vena cava

Inferior Vena cava

Descending Aorta

Branchial artery

Basilic vein

Median cubital vein

Cephalic vein

Ulnar artery

Radial artery

Palmar digital veins

Digital artery

Pulmonary arteries

Pulmonary veins

Heart

Celiac trunk

Hepatic vein

Renal veins

Renal artery

Gonadal vein

Gonadal artery

Common iliac vein

Common iliac artery

Internal iliac artery

Internal iliac vein

External iliac vein

External iliac artery

Great saphenous vein

Femoral artery

Femoral vein

Popliteal artery

Popliteal vein

Small saphenous vein

Anterior tibial artery

Posterior tibial artery

Peroneal artery

Anterior/posterior tibial veins

Dorsal venous arch

Dorsal digital vein

Arcuate artery

Dorsal digital arteries

Copyright © Mometrix Media. You have been licensed one copy of this document for personal use only. Any other reproduction or redistribution is strictly prohibited. All rights reserved.
This content is provided for test preparation purposes only and does not imply an endorsement by Mometrix of any particular political, scientific, or religious point of view.

THE HEART

The **superior vena cava** collects blood from the upper half of the body, while the **inferior vena cava** collects blood from the lower half of the body. The superior and inferior vena cava take oxygen-deficient blood to the right atrium. The tricuspid valve pushes blood into the right ventricle. From the right ventricle, it moves through the pulmonary valve and travels through the pulmonary artery to the lungs to become oxygen enriched. Once the blood has become oxygen-rich, it returns to the left atrium via the pulmonary vein. The left atrium contracts and pushes the blood through the mitral valve into the left ventricle. Blood is through the aortic valve into the aorta when the ventricle contracts. Blood travels to the rest of the body from the aorta. Blood flows away from the heart in **arteries**, which branch into arterioles, and then into capillaries. Blood returns to the heart in **veins**.

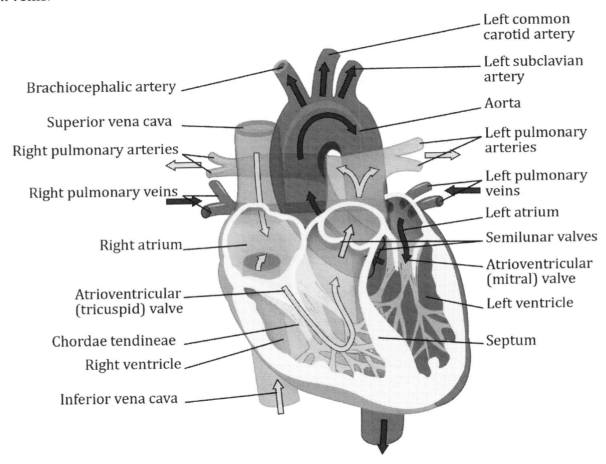

Heart rate is how fast the heart pumps. The resting heart rate is how fast the heart beats when the body is at rest. The average adult has a resting heart rate of between 70 and 80 beats every minute.

Stroke volume refers to much blood the heart pumps out with each beat. The average adult has a stroke volume of between 75 and 80 milliliters per beat. Stroke volume is a more complex measurement than heart rate.

Cardiac output is a measure of the heart's performance. To determine cardiac output, multiply the stroke volume by the heart rate.

Copyright © Mometrix Media. You have been licensed one copy of this document for personal use only. Any other reproduction or redistribution is strictly prohibited. All rights reserved. This content is provided for test preparation purposes only and does not imply an endorsement by Mometrix of any particular political, scientific, or religious point of view.

DIGESTIVE SYSTEM

The food that an individual consumes fulfills the body's energy and nutritional needs. The **digestive system** is responsible for breaking down food so that the body can extract the necessary nutrients and obtain the fuel needed to meet energy demands. The digestive system carries out multiple functions, including ingestion, secretion, digestion, absorption, and excretion. Several organs work in conjunction to perform the digestive functions.

The digestive process begins when food is input through the mouth. Inside the mouth, the **teeth** break the food down to a manageable size and the food is mixed with saliva which moistens the food and begins the breakdown of the food. The **tongue** helps move the food into the pharynx (throat) which transports the food to the esophagus. The **esophagus** connects the upper gastrointestinal (GI) tract to the throat. The esophagus transports food into a storage tank called the **stomach**. Food mixes with hydrochloric acid in the stomach, which further breaks down the food. The **small intestine** is part of the lower GI. The small intestine is approximately 10 feet long. Food absorption occurs in the small intestine for use throughout the body. The **liver** produces bile and secretes it into the small intestine. The **gall bladder** stores and recycles excess bile. The **pancreas** secretes enzymes that aid in digestion into the small intestine. The food then travels to the **large intestine** where water is absorbed. Symbiotic bacteria complete the digestive process in the large intestine. Once food is fully digested, it exits the body through the **anal canal**.

> **Review Video: Gastrointestinal System**
> Visit mometrix.com/academy and enter code: 378740

RESPIRATORY SYSTEM

The respiratory (pulmonary) system brings oxygen to the entire body. **Inhalation** occurs through the nose and mouth. The warm, moist environment of the nose and mouth warms the air. The air then travels to the lungs through the bronchial tubes; while in the lungs, cilia trap foreign particles and germs and remove them through sneezing or coughing. Carbon dioxide exits the body through **exhalation**. The body remains in homeostasis throughout the process.

> **Review Video: Respiratory System**
> Visit mometrix.com/academy and enter code: 783075

Copyright © Mometrix Media. You have been licensed one copy of this document for personal use only. Any other reproduction or redistribution is strictly prohibited. All rights reserved. This content is provided for test preparation purposes only and does not imply an endorsement by Mometrix of any particular political, scientific, or religious point of view.

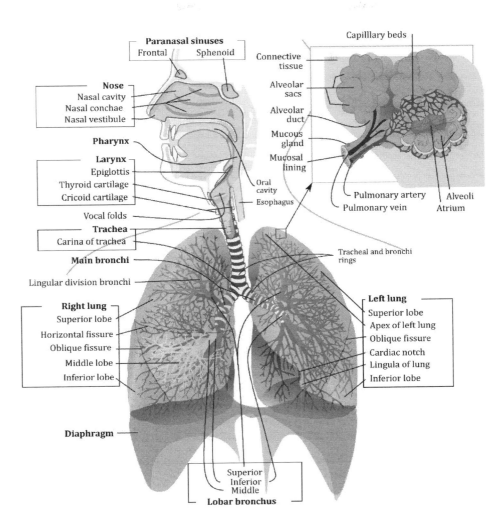

Human respiration is a four-step process involving breathing, external respiration, internal respiration, and cellular respiration. **Breathing** is the process of bringing oxygen into the lungs. **External respiration** occurs when oxygen replaces carbon dioxide within the alveoli. **Internal respiration** removes excess carbon dioxide from the lungs. **Cellular respiration** involves oxygen breaking down sugar within the cells to produce water, ATP, energy, and carbon dioxide.

Breathing is the process of inhaling oxygen (inspiration) and exhaling its waste product, carbon dioxide (exhalation). Inspiration requires the muscles to work while exhalation is an involuntary, reflexive action.

The **respiratory pump** is the entire respiratory physiology, located in the chest and body. It includes hard and soft tissues (bones such as the sternum and ribs) and muscles such as the diaphragm and the sternocleidomastoid.

Copyright © Mometrix Media. You have been licensed one copy of this document for personal use only. Any other reproduction or redistribution is strictly prohibited. All rights reserved.
This content is provided for test preparation purposes only and does not imply an endorsement by Mometrix of any particular political, scientific, or religious point of view.

RESPIRATORY PROCESS

The respiratory process operates in the following order:

1. Oxygen is inhaled through the nose and mouth and down the trachea
2. The oxygen passes into the bronchi
3. The oxygen fills the lungs and alveoli
4. The blood is pumped into the heart
5. The blood is pumped into the lungs
6. The blood is infused with oxygen
7. The oxygenated blood is pumped back into the heart
8. The oxygenated blood is pumped throughout the body

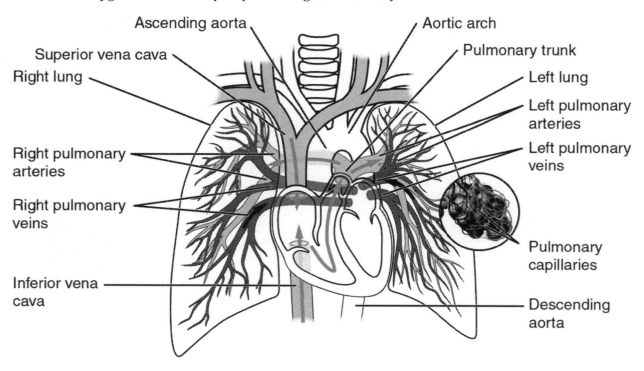

VO₂

The efficient delivery of oxygen depends on the respiratory and cardiovascular systems working in synergy. This process is called **oxygen consumption**, denoted using VO_2. The formula for determining oxygen consumption is:

VO_2 max = cardiac output (which is heart rate × stroke volume) × (C_aO_2 – $C_v O_2$) (which is the difference between the oxygen content of arterial blood and venous blood)

OXYGEN AND ENERGY

Oxygen is necessary for activity lasting longer than 30 seconds. **Aerobic activities** require oxygen. **Anaerobic activities** are short (less than 30 seconds) and sustainable without oxygen. Although only aerobic activity requires oxygen, all activity requires sufficient energy.

Energy is the fuel that powers the body. Bioenergetics is the study of how the body converts fuel (in the form of food and nutrients) into mechanical energy. Converted fuel must travel to a conductor mechanism to a place where muscles can use it. Adenosine triphosphate (ATP) is the most common conductor mechanism.

Copyright © Mometrix Media. You have been licensed one copy of this document for personal use only. Any other reproduction or redistribution is strictly prohibited. All rights reserved. This content is provided for test preparation purposes only and does not imply an endorsement by Mometrix of any particular political, scientific, or religious point of view.

ATP is composed of adenine, ribose, and a series of phosphates. The body can make ATP in three **ways** (referred to as the bioenergetic continuum): without the use of oxygen (anaerobic), with the use of oxygen (aerobic), or through the oxidative pathway.

DYSFUNCTIONAL RESPIRATION

Breathing is the foundation of movement and cardiovascular function. **Disruption** in proper breathing or glitches in the physiology of breathing can affect overall health, act as an impediment to proper training, and disrupt the movement continuum.

Stress and anxiety can affect proper breathing. Altered breathing can result in:

- The **wrong muscles** being used to breathe
- **Overuse** of the muscles needed to support the spine and skull, resulting in tension and headaches
- **Improper oxygen ratio** caused by breathing too much (hyperventilation).

These problems can be precursors to sleep disorders, psychiatric problems such as heightened anxiety, and headaches.

> **Review Video: Human Anatomy**
> Visit mometrix.com/academy and enter code: 229409

EXERCISE
PARASYMPATHETIC AND SYMPATHETIC NERVOUS SYSTEMS EFFECT ON HEART RATE

In the early stage of exercise, the **sympathetic nervous system** activates to increase heart rate and blood pressure, which help handle the stress of exercise. The **parasympathetic nervous system** activates later to help blood pressure and heart rate plateau during the session. During the cool down phase, it allows the heart rate and blood pressure to return to resting levels. Over time, exercise conditions the sympathetic system to become less active during rest, and the parasympathetic system to become more active during rest. Consistent exercise allows blood pressure and heart rate to remain low and keeps them near normal levels during stressful situations.

ACTION POTENTIAL

A neuron is not sending a signal when at rest (resting potential). Potassium ions cross through to the inside of the cell membrane, but chloride and sodium ions do not travel as easily. For every two potassium ions that pass through to the inside of the cell, only three sodium ions pass to the outside. At rest, there will be more potassium inside the cell membrane and more sodium on the outside. An outside stimulus can cause the inside of the cell to move toward positive voltage. Once it moves from -70 mV to -55 mV, an **action potential** begins. Sodium channels open and sodium rushes inside the cell, causing it to become more positive, and it changes polarity. The potassium channels open more slowly than the sodium channels, and when the potassium comes back in the polarity reverses. The cell becomes negatively charged on the inside.

VARIOUS RECEPTORS

Mechanoreceptors respond to mechanical stress, such as lifting a load during resistance training. Mechanoreceptors can be found in the joints and connective tissues of the body (tendons, ligaments, and muscles). They sense changes in the compression or stretching of the muscles or tissues. Muscle spindles, Golgi tendon organs, and joint receptors are forms of mechanoreceptors. **Muscle spindles** are found in the muscles. They sense alteration in the length of the muscle and the

35

Copyright © Mometrix Media. You have been licensed one copy of this document for personal use only. Any other reproduction or redistribution is strictly prohibited. All rights reserved. This content is provided for test preparation purposes only and does not imply an endorsement by Mometrix of any particular political, scientific, or religious point of view.

rapidity of that alteration. When stimulated, they will contract in order to prevent overstretching of the muscle. **Golgi tendon organs** can be found at the junction of a muscle and a tendon. They sense alteration in muscle tension and the rapidity of that alteration. When stimulated, they will relax in order to prevent overstressing the muscle. **Joint receptors** are found around the joints. They sense changes in speed in the joint. Joint receptors also have a protective mechanism; they help sense when a joint is in an overextended position and reflexively respond to protect that joint.

Chemoreceptors, which respond to chemical interactions, convert a stimulus into an action potential. When the sympathetic nervous system activates at the beginning of physical activity, chemoreceptors aid in that process. **Photoreceptors**, which respond to light, include the rods and cones in the eye and provide a picture of the environment around us. Photoreceptors allow someone to see the exercise environment. **Nociceptors**, which respond to pain, identify stimuli that could be dangerous for the body and send a signal to the brain. Nociceptors activate if a client performs a resistance exercise outside the proper range of motion. **Thermoreceptors** identify changes in temperature. During activity in a hot, humid environment, thermoreceptors identify a change in core temperature caused by the environment. **Osmoreceptors** detect a change in osmotic pressure. If one's blood pressure drops drastically during an exercise session, the osmoreceptors identify that issue.

MUSCLE ACTION SPECTRUM

The muscle action spectrum includes concentric, eccentric, isometric, isokinetic, and isotonic force. **Concentric** force is the shortening phase of a movement (e.g., the part of a biceps curl where the biceps is overcoming the load of the weight and gravity to shorten the muscle). **Eccentric** force is the lengthening phase of a movement (e.g., the part of a biceps curl where the biceps muscle is lengthening by not overcoming the load of the weight and gravity). With **isometric** movement, force production is equal to the load. (e.g., maintaining a plank position). With **isokinetic** force, the resistance varies depending on the force exerted (e.g., This movement requires sophisticated machinery that increases the load in proportion to the force exerted on it by the individual.). **Isotonic** movement produces force and tension through a given range of motion.

Muscle Action	Example	Purpose
Concentric	The part of a biceps curl where the biceps is overcoming the load of the weight and gravity to shorten the muscle	The shortening phase of a movement
Eccentric	The part of a biceps curl where the biceps muscle is lengthening by not overcoming the load of the weight and gravity	The lengthening phase of a movement
Isometric	Maintaining a plank position	Force production equals the load
Isokinetic	This movement requires sophisticated machinery that increases the load in proportion to the force exerted on it by the individual.	The resistance varies depending on the force exerted
Isotonic	A client performs a squat.	Produces force and tension through a given range of motion

LACTIC ACID BUILDUP

When the body breaks down carbohydrates into usable energy, **lactic acid** is a byproduct. Lactate serves as fuel during endurance activities. Lactic acid is also used by the liver to generate more

Copyright © Mometrix Media. You have been licensed one copy of this document for personal use only. Any other reproduction or redistribution is strictly prohibited. All rights reserved. This content is provided for test preparation purposes only and does not imply an endorsement by Mometrix of any particular political, scientific, or religious point of view.

glycogen and glucose. Lactic acid splits into lactate and hydrogen ions. The buildup of hydrogen causes muscle soreness and fatigue.

ARTHROKINEMATIC MOVEMENT VS. OSTEOKINEMATIC MOVEMENT

Arthrokinematic movement refers to movements that occur within joints. Rolling, gliding, or sliding motions are examples of arthrokinematic movements. **Osteokinematic movement** refers to motor movement. For example, flexion, extension, internal rotation, external rotation, adduction, and abduction are osteokinematic movements. Kicking a soccer ball is an osteokinematic movement. Twisting movements of the spine are arthrokinematic movements.

PLANES OF MOVEMENT

The skeleton can move through the **coronal** (frontal) plane, **transverse** (horizontal) plane, **sagittal** plane, and **midsagittal** plane. A Warrior II pose in yoga is an example of moving through the coronal plane. Performing twisting or turning movements is an example of moving through the transverse plane. Performing lunges is an example of moving through the sagittal or midsagittal plane.

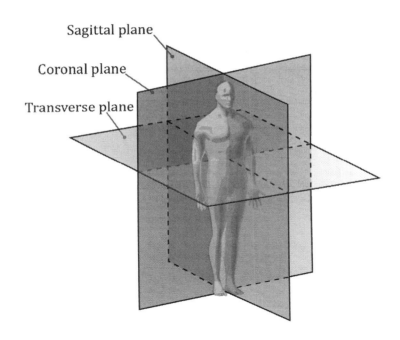

Plane	Bisector	Movement	Example
Coronal (frontal)	Front and back halves	Side to side	Side Lunge
Sagittal	Left and right sides	Front to back	Lunges
Transverse (horizontal)	Top and bottom halves	Rotation (twisting)	Golfing

CATECHOLAMINES

The body releases **epinephrine** and **norepinephrine** rapidly at the beginning of aerobic activity. As the body reaches the exercise threshold, the increase becomes more gradual. The body releases epinephrine and norepinephrine more rapidly during anaerobic activity than during aerobic activity. Epinephrine stimulates an increase in heart rate and blood pressure at the onset of exercise, and norepinephrine causes a plateau in heart rate and blood pressure to maintain

37

Copyright © Mometrix Media. You have been licensed one copy of this document for personal use only. Any other reproduction or redistribution is strictly prohibited. All rights reserved. This content is provided for test preparation purposes only and does not imply an endorsement by Mometrix of any particular political, scientific, or religious point of view.

exercise. The increase in epinephrine and norepinephrine helps stimulate the release of glucagon. The release of glucagon triggers the release of glucose body uses for fuel.

CORTISOL

The body releases **cortisol** from the adrenal glands in response to stress, and to regulate the body's immune system and sleep cycle. The body releases cortisol during exercise. As someone exercises consistently, the body responds by decreasing cortisol levels post-exercise. The effect of consistent training is better control over cortisol release from the adrenal glands.

POSITIVE VS. NEGATIVE FEEDBACK MECHANISMS

A negative feedback mechanism (the most common in the body) is the body's attempt to bring aspects of our system back to their original states. For instance, the release of insulin when sugar level rises in the bloodstream returns the body to normal levels. A **positive feedback mechanism** increases the stimulus acting within the body. For instance, a clot begins to form to repair a damaged blood vessel, and the creation of more platelets increases the size of the clot.

EFFECT OF EXERCISE ON BLOOD PRESSURE AND HEART RATE

Heart rate and blood pressure increase somewhat rapidly at the onset of exercise. This process increases blood flow to the working muscles while keeping the heart nourished with a steady supply of blood. When an individual reaches an exercise plateau, blood pressure and heart rate level off to maintain the flow of blood to the working muscles and the heart. When a client engages in the Valsalva maneuver while exercising, the resulting spike in blood pressure and heart rate can cause the client to lose consciousness.

VENTILATION

The intake of oxygen and expulsion of carbon dioxide requires proper **ventilation**. Oxygen makes its way into the bloodstream and helps create ATP. ATP is broken down into usable energy in the muscles so it can continue to fuel exercise. **Hyperventilation** can prevent the body from replenishing oxygen efficiently, reducing the amount of oxygen that makes it into the bloodstream, which results in less available energy for ATP creation. The client can begin to feel sluggish at this point in the workout.

ANAEROBIC VS. AEROBIC METABOLISM

The primary fuel source for **aerobic metabolism** is oxygen. **Anaerobic metabolism** does not require oxygen. The ATP-PC system and glycolysis create usable energy during anaerobic metabolism. A walk or light jog are examples of light aerobic activity. An example of an anaerobic activity is explosive powerlifting or plyometrics.

ATP FORMATION

ATP stands for **adenosine triphosphate**. The energy found in ATP comes from a process called **hydrolysis**. The enzyme ATP-ase separates a phosphate ion from the ATP, creating usable energy during hydrolysis. ATP becomes ADP (adenosine diphosphate) since it only has two phosphate ions attached. Food is the fuel source consumed during ADP to create more ATP formation.

GLYCOLYSIS

Glycolysis converts glucose into pyruvate, with two net ATP and two NADH as byproducts. The process of glycolysis occurs during aerobic and anaerobic activities. Pyruvate then enters into the Krebs cycle, where it will produce an additional two ATP. The process of glycolysis does not require oxygen (anaerobic) and does not result in substantial energy production.

Copyright © Mometrix Media. You have been licensed one copy of this document for personal use only. Any other reproduction or redistribution is strictly prohibited. All rights reserved. This content is provided for test preparation purposes only and does not imply an endorsement by Mometrix of any particular political, scientific, or religious point of view.

KREBS CYCLE

The Krebs cycle is also called the citric acid cycle or the tricarboxylic acid cycle (TCA). It is a catabolic pathway in which the bonds of glucose and occasionally fats or lipids are broken down and reformed into ATP. It is a respiration process that uses oxygen and produces carbon dioxide, water, and ATP. Cells require energy from ATP to synthesize proteins from amino acids and replicate DNA. One of the products of the Krebs cycle is NADH, which is then used in the electron chain transport system to manufacture ATP. From glycolysis, pyruvate is oxidized in a step linking to the Krebs cycle. After the Krebs cycle, NADH and succinate are oxidized in the electron transport chain.

DIFFERENT TYPES OF LEVERS

There are three classes of levers. The **first class** of lever has the fulcrum positioned between the resistance and output force (e.g., performing conventional sit-ups). The **second class** of levers has the resistance positioned between the fulcrum and the output force (e.g., hitting a baseball with a bat). The **third class** of levers has the output force positioned between the fulcrum and resistance (e.g., performing tire flips).

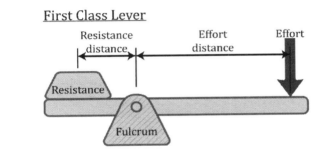

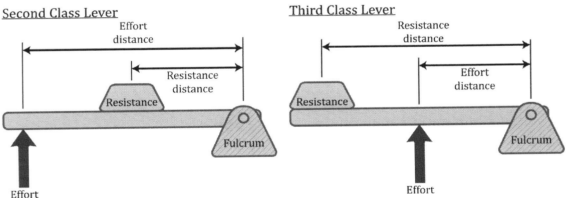

Lever Type	Description	Example
First Class	Fulcrum in the middle	Nodding the head
Second Class	Resistance in the middle	Push-up
Third Class	Effort in the middle	Biceps curl

FORCE AND TORQUE

Force occurs when two objects meet resulting in the acceleration or deceleration of the objects. **Applied force** occurs when a person pushes or pulls on an object. During physical activity, an individual constantly uses applied force. **Normal force** refers to objects exerting force upon each other by resting in a stable position on top of one another (e.g., a stack of weighted plates). **Friction**

39

Copyright © Mometrix Media. You have been licensed one copy of this document for personal use only. Any other reproduction or redistribution is strictly prohibited. All rights reserved.
This content is provided for test preparation purposes only and does not imply an endorsement by Mometrix of any particular political, scientific, or religious point of view.

force occurs when the surface of one object slides across the surface of another object (e.g., tennis shoes sliding across the floor in basketball drills). **Tension force** occurs when a string, wire, or cable exerts a force on an object (e.g., pulley resistance exercises). **Spring force** occurs when there is a compressed or stretched wire or string with an object at the end of it (e.g., weight machines). **Torque** refers to a force that rotates around an axis (e.g., oblique crunches).

Force type	Description	Example
Applied	Person pushes or pulls on an object	Bench press
Normal	Objects resting one on top of the other	Stack of weights
Friction	Two surfaces slide against each other	Shoes sliding on the floor
Tension	String, wire, or cable exerts force on an object	Pulley resistance exercises
Spring	Compressed or stretched wire attached to an object	Weight machines

A **force-couple** refers to two forces acting simultaneously on an object with equal force in the opposite direction; for example, pedaling a bike or working an arm ergometer. Force-couples can also exist inside the body when opposing forces act upon bones. One example would be moving the arm backward in the horizontal plane. The agonist and antagonist muscles are exerting force to pull and push the arm backward.

MUSCLE LENGTH-TENSION RELATIONSHIP

The length of a muscle at rest, and the amount of tension the muscle can produce at rest is referred to as the **length-tension relationship**. The **optimal muscle length** occurs when the actin and myosin have the greatest degree of overlap. Optimal muscle length results in maximal force production. Increasing the length of a muscle reduces force production because actin and myosin overlap is limited. Shortening a muscle causes excessive overlap of actin and myosin which limits force production. When the length-tension relationship is altered, the entire HMS is adversely affected.

RECIPROCAL INHIBITION

Reciprocal inhibition occurs when the muscles on one side of a joint relax while the muscles on the other side of the joint contract. Reciprocal inhibition helps to create coordinated movement during exercise. During a bicep curl, for instance, reciprocal inhibition is the way in which the biceps contract while the triceps lengthen.

SYNERGISTIC DOMINANCE

Synergistic dominance occurs when the secondary mover initiates muscle action in place of the prime mover. Synergistic dominance can occur because of an injured prime mover, an underdeveloped prime mover, or an overdeveloped secondary mover (synergist). An injury is likely once the synergist dominates because it was not designed to handle the load appropriately.

CLOSED VS. OPEN KINETIC CHAIN MOVEMENTS

With closed chain movements, feet or hands are on a surface that is not dynamic. An example of a closed chain movement would be squats. In an **open chain movement**, the feet or hands are free to move and attached to a movable surface. One example of an open chain movement would be a biceps curl.

MOTOR LEARNING

Any movement pattern must be learned and filed in the brain. **Motor learning** allows this to happen by memorizing and understanding a sequence of steps related to a movement pattern. When teaching movement patterns, less complex patterns should be taught first, with more

40

Copyright © Mometrix Media. You have been licensed one copy of this document for personal use only. Any other reproduction or redistribution is strictly prohibited. All rights reserved. This content is provided for test preparation purposes only and does not imply an endorsement by Mometrix of any particular political, scientific, or religious point of view.

complex patterns saved for later in the training process. Repetition should be emphasized to increase memory retention of the pattern.

MOTOR CONTROL

Motor control is the unified activation of the neuromuscular system to initiate and complete a movement. The neuromuscular system can respond to more challenging sequences once movement patterns are established, memorized, and practiced. For example, balance control coupled with open kinetic chain movements challenges the neuromuscular system. As the client masters difficult movements, the foundational movements will become second nature to the individual.

Considerations in Nutrition

Nutrition refers to everything that is consumed or processed by the human body, which nourishes it and provides essential building blocks for growth, repair, energy, and all other necessary body functions. Nutrition can come in the form of food, beverages, vitamins, and topical exposure to such things as sunlight.

It is important for a trainer to be aware of **basic nutrition** because working out is not the only aspect of a healthy life. A client's diet and supplementation routine can directly affect his or her ability to train, and a poor diet can sabotage some of the gains made in training. While a trainer is not a nutritionist, and should refer a client to a nutritionist for specific diet planning, client should be steered away from fad diets and toward a healthful, balanced diet that provides adequate energy for the client's training program.

Body Composition

Food consumption contributes to the shape and makeup of the human body. Modern culture promotes thinness over health, causing many people to seek quick weight loss methods, resulting in many fad diets. Unfortunately, these fad diets are ineffective, provide misinformation and spread myths that may be difficult to deprogram from a new client.

A person must burn more calories than they ingest to **lose weight** (the opposite is true for weight gain). Calories ingested include all food and beverages that are consumed. Calories expended include daily functional activities and fitness activities. In modern society, high-calorie food is readily available, while sedentary work and personal lifestyles are more prevalent than in the past.

Understanding **basic nutritional information** will greatly enhance a trainer's ability to guide the client.

Nutrients for Specific Goals

LOSING WEIGHT

If a person is seeking to lose weight, it is likely that he or she is looking to alter body composition by **losing fat**. To accomplish this, balance micronutrients and include carbohydrates, fat, and protein in each meal. Six smaller meals consumed throughout the day ensure the body is continually processing fuel. Complex carbohydrates and fiber are preferable to simpler sugars. Staying hydrated by drinking up to twelve glasses of water will also help aid digestion and prevent edema, or water retention.

Encourage clients to measure portions to get a realistic sense of **portion control**. They should also be encouraged to avoid junk food and processed foods to avoid nonnutritive calories.

Copyright © Mometrix Media. You have been licensed one copy of this document for personal use only. Any other reproduction or redistribution is strictly prohibited. All rights reserved. This content is provided for test preparation purposes only and does not imply an endorsement by Mometrix of any particular political, scientific, or religious point of view.

BUILDING MUSCLE

Another common fitness goal is to **increase muscle mass**. Certain dietary suggestions should be adhered to, so the body has sufficient materials with which to build lean muscle tissue.

Include a **balance** of micronutrients in the diet and consume carbohydrates, fat, and protein at each meal; protein alone will not suffice. To encourage protein synthesis, the client should eat six times daily.

When food is consumed is important. Ingesting protein and carbohydrates within **two hours of working out** will encourage the body to maximize its muscle-building activities, perhaps due to the increase in blood flow that occurs after a workout. Consider using a liquid supplement product that can be quickly absorbed into the body.

> **Review Video: <u>Nutrition for Personal Trainers</u>**
> Visit mometrix.com/academy and enter code: 293901

PROTEIN

Proteins act as a building block for new or damaged body tissues. Proteins are a viable energy source and are required by the body to synthesize other necessary nutrients.

Proteins are composed of **amino acids**. There are three different categories of amino acids: **essential** (meaning the body cannot create them itself), **semi-essential** (meaning elements can be made by the body, but other parts need an external source), and **nonessential** (meaning the body can create them from other sources).

The essential amino acids have to be ingested from a direct source. The nonessential amino acids can be pieced together by the body from nitrogen and other source material (lipids and carbohydrates).

Essential amino acids	Semi-essential amino acids	Nonessential amino acids
Histidine	Arginine	Alanine
Isoleucine	Cysteine	Asparagine
Leucine	Glutamine	Aspartic acid
Lysine	Glycine	Glutamic acid
Methionine	Proline	Serine
Phenylalanine	Tyrosine	
Threonine		
Tryptophan		
Valine		

Digestion and Use of Proteins

Proteins are made up of chains of **amino acids** held together by peptides. For the body to be able to use these amino acids, the entire protein chain has to be broken down into its individual amino acids. This begins when the proteins come into contact with the hydrochloric acid in the stomach, and it continues as the proteins enter the large and small intestines.

Proteins can then be used in different ways, depending on what the body needs at that time. There are three main things a protein can do once released into the blood via the liver: be used immediately as **energy**, be stored as **fat**, or be used to **build or repair** body tissues.

Copyright © Mometrix Media. You have been licensed one copy of this document for personal use only. Any other reproduction or redistribution is strictly prohibited. All rights reserved. This content is provided for test preparation purposes only and does not imply an endorsement by Mometrix of any particular political, scientific, or religious point of view.

FOODS THAT CONTAIN PROTEINS

A variety of foods contain proteins. Food that comes from animals (e.g., animal meat, eggs, milk, and dairy products) contains substantial amounts of protein. Food that contains all of the essential amino acids is called a **complete protein**. If it only has some of the essential amino acids, it is called an **incomplete protein** (such as peanut butter).

The amino acid that is missing or only present in trace amounts is the limiting factor. A complete protein must be **synthesized**. The missing protein determines (limits) the amount of protein that can be made. Think of a spice recipe that calls for 2 cups of salt, pepper, and garlic. If the chef only has 1 cup of garlic, the spice mix cannot be made, and the garlic is said to be the limiting factor.

Vegetarians eat only certain types of protein, which may be incomplete or have a low limiting factor. Vegetarians should work with a nutritionist who specializes in vegan or vegetarian diets to ensure they eat enough complete protein sources.

COMPLETE PROTEIN PROFILES

Protein is evaluated on how well it functions as a **complete nutrient**, and if it provides all of the essential amino acids in the ratios needed for consumption.

Biologic value (BV) is a popular term used to describe how much a given protein satisfies the needed amino acid values. It is a common catchphrase used in fitness circles and in vitamin supplement advertising. The higher the BV of the protein, the more closely it supplies all the needed amino acids.

Net protein utilization (NPU) and **protein efficiency ratio** (PER) are two terms that mean the same thing: how well a given protein meets the needs of the human body.

AMOUNTS OF PROTEINS

The amount of protein that an individual needs to consume will depend on various factors such as height, weight, activity level, and activity level. For example, if a person does intense aerobic and anaerobic exercises, his or her protein requirements may be higher.

Most of a person's basic energy needs should be met with **carbohydrates and lipids**, with protein used for tissue repair and as a backup energy source, unless the client is a competitive weight lifter.

If a person consumes **high-quality protein sources**, less of it will be needed. If the protein sources are less complete, with a lower BV, more protein will be needed to provide all the essential amino acids.

NEGATIVE ENERGY BALANCE

A negative energy balance (achieved by burning more calories than are consumed) is required if a client wants to lose weight or reduce body fat percentage. When this state is achieved, amino acids are used by the body to generate energy in a process called gluconeogenesis. Protein is required to fuel this process.

Clients who reduce overall calorie intake and increase activity levels will require an increase in **lean protein consumption**. Protein will be used for energy, to repair tissues from exercise, and to help prevent the loss of muscle mass that often accompanies a weight-loss regimen.

43

Copyright © Mometrix Media. You have been licensed one copy of this document for personal use only. Any other reproduction or redistribution is strictly prohibited. All rights reserved. This content is provided for test preparation purposes only and does not imply an endorsement by Mometrix of any particular political, scientific, or religious point of view.

PROTEIN NEEDS

Because protein acts as a building block for body tissues, persons interested in **hypertrophy**, particularly weight-lifting clients seeking maximal hypertrophy for competitive bodybuilding purposes, will need to ingest much more protein than the average healthy adult. This will also help taper body fat down to very low ratios, a necessity during the competition season.

However, this should be used as a temporary diet strictly for use during competition times. Because the body's protein needs will be higher because of the specific training, protein will be upped dramatically while overall calories from other sources will be reduced. Consuming a high-protein diet on a long-term basis is not recommended, and keeping body fat to single-digit percentages is not healthy beyond this purpose.

By cycling back to a **regular diet** when not competing, the bodybuilding client will be able to achieve better muscle mass when competing in the future than he or she would if the high-protein diet was constantly employed.

SATIETY

A feeling of fullness (satiety) after eating is important for several reasons. First, it gives a signal to stop ingesting more calories at that sitting. It also signals to the body that calories have been consumed, something that may not be triggered when a person drinks the same number of calories in a beverage or shake form. Protein also takes longer to process, leading to feeling full for a longer period, with steadier energy levels throughout the day.

Protein is more satisfying than other nutrients, specifically lipids (fats) and carbohydrates. Animal studies have shown that when the animals are given protein, they can go longer until the next feeding than when given fat or carbohydrates alone. This indicates that protein satisfies hunger for a longer period and provides more satiety.

RDA OF PROTEIN

An average healthy person should aim to ingest **0.8 grams** of protein for every kilogram of body weight (approximately 30 percent of daily calorie intake).

Those who are engaged in fitness or training activities should ingest more protein to help with tissue repair and muscle building. For a person who works out regularly, this would include a minimum of **1 gram** of protein for every kilogram of body weight and somewhere around **1.5 grams** of protein for every kilogram of body weight when doing muscle-building activities.

For an endurance athlete, **1.4 grams** of protein for every kilogram of body weight is needed during regular training, bumped up to as much as **2 grams** per kilogram of body weight during competition training.

Competitive weight lifters would need **1 gram** of protein for every kilogram of body weight during noncompetitive periods and jump up to somewhere around **2 grams** per kilogram of body weight during competitive training times.

Normal activity Level	Recommended daily protein intake
Sedentary	0.8 g/kg (0.4 g/lb.)
Strength athlete	1.2–1.7 g/kg (0.5–0.8 g/lb.)
Endurance athlete	1.2–1.4 g/kg (0.5–0.6 g/lb.)

Copyright © Mometrix Media. You have been licensed one copy of this document for personal use only. Any other reproduction or redistribution is strictly prohibited. All rights reserved. This content is provided for test preparation purposes only and does not imply an endorsement by Mometrix of any particular political, scientific, or religious point of view.

PROTEIN-BASED DIET DRAWBACKS

High-protein diets have enjoyed popularity in the last decade, touting weight loss benefits. However, research shows that such diets are not best for people in the long run. High-protein diets tend to include higher levels of bad fats and reduce ingestion of dietary fiber, which can lead to a higher risk of serious diseases.

High-protein diets require much more **water** to digest properly, raising the risk that a person can become dehydrated more easily.

Another serious problem associated with high-protein diets is potential **calcium loss**. When people eat more protein than they need, their bodies lose calcium.

High-protein diets also force the body into **ketosis** (a state where the body uses fat as its main source of energy), which many doctors and nutritionists feel is unsafe on a long-term basis.

EXTRA PROTEIN

There is no scientific evidence to prove that consuming extra protein in the form of **supplements** gives a uniform result to overall fitness gains or muscle hypertrophy. However, when a person is working out, his or her protein needs may go up to supply the body with building blocks to build and repair tissues and as a backup fuel source.

Ingesting protein after a workout has been shown to increase important endocrine activities that may support **muscle building**, rather than straight repair.

Supplements can also be used when a client is trying to **lose body fat** by acting as a replacement, giving needed protein while avoiding excess calories. Supplements can be consumed very quickly and easily in the form of portable shakes or bars, ensuring that a client ingests needed fuel before a workout.

SUPPLEMENTAL PROTEIN

Many supplement manufacturers attempt to create a **perfect protein** that can be used by the body better than actual food sources or other supplements. The perfect protein would assimilate quickly and contain the perfect balance of amino acids.

A popular trend in supplemental protein is **whey protein**, which can be found in a variety of supplements. Whey protein has the best biologic value of all supplemental proteins and has been shown in studies to provide greater benefits than other kinds of protein.

It is debatable if extra protein is necessary, even for active individuals. Whey protein supplements are appropriate for competitive weight lifters in competition mode; these athletes have high protein needs and are seeking to reduce overall calories.

CARBOHYDRATES

Carbohydrates are made up of three basic elements: oxygen, hydrogen, and carbon. Carbohydrates are macronutrients that fall into three categories:

- **Fiber**
- **Simple carbohydrates** (sugar)
- **Complex carbohydrates** (starch)

Copyright © Mometrix Media. You have been licensed one copy of this document for personal use only. Any other reproduction or redistribution is strictly prohibited. All rights reserved. This content is provided for test preparation purposes only and does not imply an endorsement by Mometrix of any particular political, scientific, or religious point of view.

Sugars can further be classified as mono- or disaccharides—having one or two sugar units. Fructose (plant sugar) and glucose (blood sugar) are common monosaccharides. Lactose (milk sugar) and sucrose (table sugar) are common disaccharides.

Carbohydrates are the body's main supply of **energy** and have other wide-ranging functions, including playing a part in the digestion of other micronutrients.

DIGESTION AND USE

Different forms of carbohydrates are digested differently by the body. **Simple sugars** are easily assimilated with little work by the body. These types of sugars are found in various fruits as well as honey.

Starches take more work to break down because of their double bond. Grains, potatoes, rice, and table sugar fall into this category and require more effort for the body to process.

Fiber in the form of cellulose, the fibrous element of many fruits and vegetables, cannot be completely broken down by the body. Roughage (undigested fiber) is extremely important to healthy intestinal function because it helps clean out the digestive tract and regulate bowel movements.

GLYCEMIC INDEX (GI)

The glycemic index (GI) measures how much a given micronutrient affects a person's blood sugar level and the body's insulin response. The test is simple: The measurement is made when a single food is eaten after a fasting period. The blood sugar is measured before and after the food is eaten to gauge the change in blood sugar level.

Eating different foods in combination may change the effect on blood sugar entirely.

Some diets tout the benefits of eating only foods that have a **low GI score**, claiming that foods with high GI scores will lead to negative effects, such as increased weight and fat gain. These diets tend to clump foods into positive and negative categories, ignoring the basic premise of **energy balance** (weight gain is the result of more calories taken in than are expended).

The concept of good versus bad foods is a bit misguided, though foods with a low GI score do tend to be very healthy for the diet.

FOODS ACROSS THE GLYCEMIC INDEX

The highest level on the GI chart is **pure glucose** (commonly known as blood sugar), which is immediately assimilated by the body and causes blood sugar to spike.

The next highest range includes honey, cooked potatoes without skins, and carrots. These are followed (in descending order) by whole wheat bread, cooked potatoes with the skins on, and rice; white bread and bananas; sucrose (table sugar) and corn; pasta, oatmeal, and oranges; dairy

Copyright © Mometrix Media. You have been licensed one copy of this document for personal use only. Any other reproduction or redistribution is strictly prohibited. All rights reserved. This content is provided for test preparation purposes only and does not imply an endorsement by Mometrix of any particular political, scientific, or religious point of view.

products and apples; fruit sugar (fructose) and legumes (such as beans); lowest on the GI scale are soybeans and legumes (such as peanuts).

GI # = Classification
> 70 = High
56–69 = Moderate
< 55 = Low

FIBER

Fiber is an extremely important part of a healthy diet for many reasons. Fiber consists of indigestible cellulose or plant matter that travels through the digestive tract in its original form. Benefits of fiber include:

- Helps keep blood sugar levels even and manageable
- Helps keep a person regular and avoid constipation
- Helps avoid appendicitis
- Helps maintain a healthy bacteria balance
- Helps a person feel more full
- Helps prevent diverticulitis, an infection of the intestines
- Helps lower bad (LDL) cholesterol levels

Diets high in fiber are linked to lower risk factors for diseases such as some **cancers and cardiac-related disorders** (heart disease).

ATHLETIC ABILITY

Carbohydrates are essential for fitness and sports performance because they provide the body with the most accessible source of energy, especially for anaerobic exercises or activities. (These would be categorized as quick, high-impact activities, typical of most sporting activities.) During long-term activities, the body relies on stored glycogen first and then on fat.

The phrase "Fat burns in a carbohydrate flame" has a specific meaning in the context of training. There must be sufficient carbohydrates available to keep the body's **energy cycle** even and continually burning fat, which maximizes fat loss. If there are not enough carbohydrates, muscle glycogen will be depleted, and performance will suffer. This can happen even when sufficient oxygen is circulating in the body.

RECOMMENDED GRAMS OF CARBOHYDRATES

For endurance athletes, carbohydrates are essential. There must be sufficient carbohydrates available to keep the body's energy cycle even without relying on **muscle glycogen stores**, which are finite. If there are not enough carbohydrates, muscle glycogen will be depleted, and performance will suffer. This can happen even when sufficient oxygen is circulating in the body.

Endurance athletes need **high-carbohydrate diets**. Carbohydrates should comprise about two-thirds of calories consumed, or somewhere between 5 and 10 grams of carbohydrate per kilogram of body weight. Complex carbohydrates are the best choice because of the variety of other nutrients and vitamins available in these food sources.

Because a person should not exercise on a full stomach, it is a good idea for him or her to eat several hours before a workout. The meal should include an ample supply of carbohydrates sufficient to build up glycogen stores before exercise. Research has shown that people who eat a solid

Copyright © Mometrix Media. You have been licensed one copy of this document for personal use only. Any other reproduction or redistribution is strictly prohibited. All rights reserved.
This content is provided for test preparation purposes only and does not imply an endorsement by Mometrix of any particular political, scientific, or religious point of view.

carbohydrate source four hours before exercising get a noticeable improvement in performance for that workout, well over ten percent.

Eating before a morning workout is very important because **energy stores** will be depleted after a long sleep. If a full meal is not practical, an energy shake or fitness bar will suffice, so the stomach isn't full, and the body can quickly process the fuel.

CARBOHYDRATE LOADING

Carbo-loading is a system of ingesting large quantities of carbohydrates before an endurance activity that will last more than an hour and a half. This is common for people who run long distances, such as marathoners. This is done because this activity uses a high percentage of the body's stores of **glycogen**. If there is insufficient carbohydrate available and the glycogen stores are used up, a bottoming-out effect can occur. By carbo-loading, the body can reinforce its glycogen stores, doubling its available energy stores.

A carbo-loading diet typically occurs over several days. First comes four days of **lowering glycogen stores** by eating few carbohydrates and engaging in heavy exercise activities. Then, the person **recuperates** for three days and ingests up to 10 grams of carbohydrates for each kilogram of body weight.

Traditional carbo-loading consisted of four days of exhaustive exercise and limited carbohydrates followed by three days of recuperation and maximal carbohydrate intake. This method can be hard on the body by adding extra stressors right before an endurance event, which can lead to increased injury risk and cause blood sugar levels to slip too low, causing fatigue and crankiness.

An **alternate carbo-loading routine**, aimed at increasing the body's stores of glycogen, was formulated in the early 1980s. The client ingests four grams of carbohydrate for every kilogram of body weight on the sixth, fifth, and fourth days before an endurance event. High-intensity exercise is also engaged in for a half hour on the sixth day and for three-quarters of an hour for the fifth and fourth days.

On the third and second days prior, high-intensity exercise is engaged in for only 20 minutes. However, 10 grams of carbohydrates for every kilogram of body weight are ingested. The day before the event entails no workout, but it does include the elevated carbohydrate count.

If a client is going to be doing more than an hour of fairly intense exercise, ingesting carbohydrates **during the training session** may be advisable. This would help keep available energy in a reasonable range, prevent an exhaustion of glycogen stores from muscle tissue, and increase endurance and performance for up to an additional hour.

If the exercise or training requires endurance, **hourly intake** of carbohydrates is a necessity. The best method would be through sports beverages; these not only replace lost fluids, but they also give a balanced stream of carbohydrates to the body without filling the stomach with the bulk that accompanies solid food consumption. NASM recommends drinking from 20 to 40 fluid ounces of liquid with around a 5-percent carbohydrate solution.

Ingesting carbohydrates after working out can have several benefits: It helps the body replenish glycogen stores that were depleted in training; ingesting carbohydrates after exercise also helps the body repair itself after strenuous workouts.

Copyright © Mometrix Media. You have been licensed one copy of this document for personal use only. Any other reproduction or redistribution is strictly prohibited. All rights reserved.
This content is provided for test preparation purposes only and does not imply an endorsement by Mometrix of any particular political, scientific, or religious point of view.

It is important that carbohydrates be ingested fairly **quickly after exercising** to maximize benefits. It is advisable to consume between 1 to 2 grams of carbohydrates for every kilogram of body weight within 30 minutes of completing a workout.

Research has shown that waiting two hours to ingest carbohydrates can have a serious negative impact on **glycogen replenishment**. This could be because the body is more receptive after the rigors of working out, due to its systems working at a higher performance level and the blood rapidly circulating.

PERCENTAGE OF DIET

If a person is looking to lose fat and gain lean muscle, **carbohydrates** should be the most plentiful aspect of the diet, comprising at least half to three-quarters of all calories consumed. The person can further maximize the benefits of that carbohydrate intake by ingesting a good deal of **dietary fiber** in that 50 to 75 percent.

This advice is contrary to many popular fad diets, which continue to assert that carbohydrates are a dieter's enemy and contribute significantly to fat gain or the body's inability to lose fat. This is based on junk science. The more reasoned and accepted point of view is that a diet must consist of a higher percentage of carbohydrates to prevent the body from sapping **muscle glycogen stores** for energy, which then strips **lean muscle**. Water loss associated with this process can account for apparent weight loss, but it does little in the way of altering body composition.

WEIGHT GAIN

There is an ongoing claim that carbohydrates contribute to the increase in **obesity** in the United States. Because the fitness industry and the diet and supplements industry are so powerful, a substantial amount of time and scientific research has been devoted to proving that carbohydrate consumption leads to weight gain.

Research indicates that even though Americans ate a higher percentage of carbohydrates and less fat at the turn of the twentieth century, obesity was far less widespread than it is today. This is due to two simple factors: Modern people are **less active** and ingest **far more overall calories** than did their ancestors.

This supports the basic theory that body composition, weight gain, and obesity are not related to high carbohydrate intake as much as to **energy imbalance** (more calories consumed than burned).

LIPIDS

A **lipid** is a macronutrient that can be used by the body for various functions and includes oils, fatty substances, sterols, and phospholipids. Lipids in foods are almost always either oil or fat, which are also called triglycerides. This is also the form that lipids are stored in the human body.

Lipids, or **fatty acids**, are further classified as unsaturated or saturated, sometimes labeled good and bad fats respectively. **Unsaturated fats** have a double-bond structure and cannot only lower bad cholesterol (LDL) but also can also raise good cholesterol (HDL). These kinds of fats come from plant sources, such as olive oil and avocados.

Saturated fats, on the other hand, do not have this double bond and raise LDL levels, which can lead to atherosclerosis (plaque collecting in the arteries and narrowing them). Saturated fats come from animal sources, such as meat, milk, and eggs and fried foods.

Copyright © Mometrix Media. You have been licensed one copy of this document for personal use only. Any other reproduction or redistribution is strictly prohibited. All rights reserved.
This content is provided for test preparation purposes only and does not imply an endorsement by Mometrix of any particular political, scientific, or religious point of view.

MONOUNSATURATED AND POLYUNSATURATED FATTY ACIDS

Monounsaturated and polyunsaturated fatty acids are two different categories of unsaturated fats, one of two categories of fatty acids. (The other category is saturated fats.) These terms derive from the way the atoms are formed. If there is one double bond of carbon holding the fatty acid together, it is monounsaturated. If there are two or more double bonds of carbon holding the fatty acid together, it is polyunsaturated.

Monounsaturated fats are usually liquid when at room temperature. They include a host of natural oils: olive, grapeseed, flaxseed, and peanut, to name just a few. Monounsaturated fats lower so-called bad cholesterol (LDL).

Polyunsaturated fats come from a variety of sources, such as grains and oily fish. They provide benefits against cardiovascular disease and cancer.

Both fats provide needed elements that help the body run properly and are a necessary part of a balanced diet.

PURPOSE OF LIPIDS

Although low-fat diets have been in vogue at various times, based on the misguided belief that fat is harmful, **lipids** serve a vital role in a healthy diet. Lipids have the most **energy per gram** when compared to other macronutrients, with nine calories per gram. Lipids are essential for carrying some vitamins, such as vitamin D, and are needed for calcium to be absorbed in the body.

Lipids are important for many other reasons:

- Body fat is used as a thermal layer and as an energy source for a nursing mother
- Fats are needed for proper cell growth and regeneration
- Fats digest more slowly and help a person feel full longer
- Fat plays a role in endocrine function

DIGESTION AND USE OF LIPIDS

Fat is digested along the entirety of the digestive tract. The process begins when it comes into contact with saliva. Body acids from the stomach and the intestines continue to break the fats down into components that can be used by the body. From the intestines, these components enter the bloodstream. The process goes like this:

- Lipids are broken down through the digestive tract
- Triglycerides are formed in the intestines
- Chylomicrons are formed in the lymphatic system
- Chylomicrons are distributed from the lymphatic system into the bloodstream

Triglycerides are broken down by the lipoprotein lipase (LPL) enzyme and used by body tissues, and the fat content can then be stored in muscle, organs, and fat cells.

Fat can be used as an immediate **fuel source** if the body has no available carbohydrate energy. However, if a person eats too much fat, it is far easier for the body to convert this into stored fat than it is for the body to alter excess carbohydrates chemically and store them as fat.

SATIETY

Lipids have a very distinct effect on **satiety**, beginning with a hormonal response triggered in the mouth and stomach. Fats begin to trigger hormones that tell the brain the body is full. Fats also take

Copyright © Mometrix Media. You have been licensed one copy of this document for personal use only. Any other reproduction or redistribution is strictly prohibited. All rights reserved. This content is provided for test preparation purposes only and does not imply an endorsement by Mometrix of any particular political, scientific, or religious point of view.

longer to digest, giving the body a steady supply of fuel to process, leading to a full feeling for a longer period.

Many factors contribute to satiety beyond caloric intake (which is why people rarely feel full after drinking a high-calorie protein shake). Food volume and some of the actions of eating (such as crunching, ingesting mass, and getting a full stomach) are also important and cannot be satisfied by lipids alone.

A diet containing **30 percent fat or less** will gain the benefits of containing fats while providing enough other foods and nutrients to satisfy a person's sensations of hunger.

INGESTING EXTRA FAT

There has been research in recent years regarding different types of lipids and how they might be used to the advantage of athletes and others who are engaged in fitness training. As a general rule, fats take a long time to **digest** and are not necessarily the ideal supplement for sports or fitness activities.

However, some lipids can be more quickly digested for use in the body, namely **medium-chain triglycerides**. Unlike long-chain triglycerides, which are the most-common types of lipids people ingest, medium-chain triglycerides do not go through such a long digestive process and can be used by the body more quickly.

While there is a theory that this energy could be a viable backup source for athletes, sparing glycogen sources, there is not enough current research to support this claim. Therefore, supplementation with fat should not be a top priority.

Metabolic syndrome is an umbrella term for a host of problems associated with digestive and endocrine problems such as diabetes, insulin resistance, obesity, and high blood pressure. People who tout protein-rich diets point to high carbohydrate consumption as being the underlying cause of metabolic syndrome, also known as syndrome X.

However, it seems more likely that the common denominator for these conditions is not carbohydrates, but rather an excess of **free fatty acids**. When free fatty acids are available, the body will use them first instead of more-optimal fuel sources, which in turn leads to problems processing glucose. This will lead to elevated insulin levels, which can then lead to insulin resistance and a host of other problems.

Therefore, it is more likely that higher fat content in the diet is the actual culprit, not high-carbohydrate diets.

WATER

Water is composed of two hydrogen molecules and one oxygen molecule (H_2O). Water is one of the most abundant compounds on the planet and makes up almost two-thirds of the human body. Because it is used for many purposes (e.g., cooling the body off and removing waste from the body) and excreted, it must be regularly replaced to avoid **dehydration**. While nutritional deficiencies can take a long time to become a problem, humans cannot live for very long without ingesting clean water, or they will suffer serious, and potentially fatal effects. Basic body functions are impacted if a person loses as little as 2 percent of his or her total weight in water.

Benefits of adequate **hydration** include adequate blood levels, consistent body temperature, optimally functioning hormonal systems, and preventing edema, or water retention.

Copyright © Mometrix Media. You have been licensed one copy of this document for personal use only. Any other reproduction or redistribution is strictly prohibited. All rights reserved. This content is provided for test preparation purposes only and does not imply an endorsement by Mometrix of any particular political, scientific, or religious point of view.

TRAINING AND SPORTS ACTIVITIES

Water and fluids are essential to fitness training. The body is composed largely of water and needs a continual replenishment to function properly. Exercise and fitness activities hasten the loss of fluids, primarily through perspiration, and require a person to replace lost fluid to maintain performance capabilities.

Dehydration is associated with lower blood volume, lower blood pressure, heightened heart rate, and sodium retention, which in turn lead to fluid retention.

A person's **weight** can be used as a starting point to determine how much liquid is needed. An individual's weight upon waking in the morning can be considered 0. Before exercising or beginning any strenuous fitness activity; a person should ingest enough liquids to put his or her weight back to the 0 mark.

GUIDELINES FOR HYDRATION

NASM has developed guidelines for how an athlete should **rehydrate** to make up for fluids lost through sweat and elimination. A few hours before any exercise, the client should drink 16 ounces of fluids and consume up to twice that amount if it is hot out. During exercise, the client should replenish each hour with 20 to 40 ounces of fluids. After exercising, the client should weigh him- or herself and assess how many pounds off the 0 mark he or she is; the client should then drink 20 ounces per pound lost, especially if he or she is in heavy training or is an endurance athlete.

If the client is having a regular training session and the exercising will last approximately an hour, **water** will be the best choice for rehydration. If the client plans to train for more than an hour, **Gatorade** or a similar drink will be most beneficial. To stimulate faster stomach emptying, encourage the drinking of cold beverages.

VITAMINS AND SUPPLEMENTS

DISCOVERY AND INITIAL USE

The importance of **vitamins** was not completely understood until early in the twentieth century. Augmenting diet through the use of supplements then became popular.

Early **supplements** were a one-size-fits-all variety; a one-a-day pill which included all of the essential vitamins and minerals was the most-common. While this is still popular today, there are thousands of varieties of supplements now, with individual vitamins or minerals in a plethora of dosages and special blends touting specific health benefits.

In 1990, it was estimated that there were over $3 billion in vitamin-supplement sales in the United States. This figure skyrocketed to almost $18 billion by the year 2002.

In 1994, the federal government passed the **Dietary Supplement Health and Education Act** (DSHEA) to supply guidelines for the manufacture and sale of vitamins and supplements. These are different than the guidelines used by the Food and Drug Administration (FDA).

SUPPLEMENTS

DSHEA specifically states what can be classified as a **supplement**. This definition includes:

- The item must be intended to be ingested as a liquid, powder, or pill/caplet/capsule
- It is not marketed as food
- It clearly marked as a dietary supplement
- It is intended to increase the regular intake of a particular vitamin or mineral

Copyright © Mometrix Media. You have been licensed one copy of this document for personal use only. Any other reproduction or redistribution is strictly prohibited. All rights reserved. This content is provided for test preparation purposes only and does not imply an endorsement by Mometrix of any particular political, scientific, or religious point of view.

- It is a concentrated version of the vitamin or mineral, a metabolized version, a part of a vitamin or mineral, an extract of a vitamin or mineral, or a mixture of these components
- It is a nontobacco product with at least one of the following: a mineral, a vitamin, some plant product, or an amino acid compound

Supplements are used to augment a diet in which some component is missing or lacking.

REASONS FOR TAKING DIETARY SUPPLEMENTS

Supplements can be used for a variety of reasons: to augment a diet that may be missing some nutrients, to prevent particular health problems, or to encourage better fitness performance. Some use supplements for better mental clarity, for help sleeping, and for possible weight-loss benefits.

There are many reasons why a diet may be **deficient** in some nutrients. This can include not eating a healthy number of calories, not eating healthy foods, eating a restricted diet (such as vegetarian or vegan), overuse of fad diets, and even financial barriers to purchasing nutrient-rich foods.

Seniors can often use supplementation to make sure they are receiving the proper amount of vitamins and minerals needed for healthy body function. Pregnant and nursing women can also greatly benefit from supplementation, but they must do so under a doctor or nutritionist's supervision.

GENERAL PARAMETERS

As with any substance that can be introduced to the body, supplements, while usually helpful and beneficial, can be **overused** or used **incorrectly**. Therefore, it is necessary to determine appropriate supplemental quantities.

The best reference guides available are the **dietary reference intakes** (DRIs), a series of reviews performed by the Food and Nutrition Board of the Institute of Medicine. These give not only the recommended healthy dosage but also the dosage considered excessive and potentially harmful. DRIs also account for different gender, age, and special-needs groups (such as pregnant women and nursing mothers).

The goal of DRIs is to give a person an adequate amount of a given vitamin or mineral without overdoing it.

SUPPLEMENTATION TERMS

When discussing supplements, there are many terms to describe the ideal dosages and the point at which doses are too high for safe or recommended consumption. These terms include:

- **Recommended dietary allowance** (RDA)—the total amount that persons of a given age range, gender, and possibly special population group (such as pregnant women) should ingest in one day to get all the needed vitamins and nutrients. From this amount, percentage values can be calculated to show how much of the RDA is met with one serving.
- **Estimated average requirement** (EAR)—how much of a nutrient will satisfy the dietary needs of half the population.
- **Adequate intake** (AI)—an estimated figure used when an RDA cannot be calculated; it indicates how much should be enough of a given nutrient to satisfy the body's needs.
- **Tolerable upper intake level** (UL)—the high end of what should be ingested in a day: the point at which further intake could be harmful.
- **Safe upper limit** (SUL)—the maximum amount a person should take on a daily basis.

Copyright © Mometrix Media. You have been licensed one copy of this document for personal use only. Any other reproduction or redistribution is strictly prohibited. All rights reserved.
This content is provided for test preparation purposes only and does not imply an endorsement by Mometrix of any particular political, scientific, or religious point of view.

TOXICITY

Vitamins and minerals are necessary for proper body function, but can be **toxic** or cause adverse health effects when taken in excessive amounts. For example, too much vitamin B6 can affect the nerves, while too much vitamin D can cause kidney damage.

For this reason, **tolerable upper intake levels** (ULs) are set when possible to give individuals guidance on just how much should be ingested. ULs are set using a normal, healthy individual as the basis for the measurement. This means that these values may not apply to members of special populations, people on special diets, or those who are taking certain medications.

The absence of a UL value does not mean that a possible toxic level does not exist. Rather, this could indicate that there is not enough information to make a determination.

RECOMMENDED VALUES

VITAMIN A

The RDA, or adequate intake (AI) amount, for vitamin A is 700 for women and 900 for men. The DV for vitamin A is 5,000 international units (IU), or 1,500 mg. The UL is 3,000 IU; this value is based on a person who is approximately 130 lbs. The SUL is 5,000 IU or 1,500 mg.

There are potentially serious side effects associated with ingesting too much Vitamin A, including vomiting, headaches, pain in the joints, dry hair and skin, and damage to the liver.

BETA CAROTENE

The RDA, (AI amount), DV and the UL, values are not defined for beta carotene. Although these values have not yet been defined, there are still potential risks. The values are undefined because there is insufficient information to make a determination. The SUL is 11,655 IU or 7 mg.

There are potentially serious side effects associated with ingesting too much beta carotene, which include a higher risk of developing cancer of the lungs for those who are in high-risk groups (those chronically exposed to asbestos as well as smokers).

VITAMIN D

The RDA, or adequate intake (AI) amount, for vitamin D is 5 mg for women and men. The DV for vitamin D is 400 international units (IUs), or 10 mgs. The UL is 50 mg; this value is based on a person who is approximately 130 lbs. The SUL is 1,000 IU or 25 mg.

There are potentially serious side effects associated with ingesting too much Vitamin D, which include nausea and an increase of calcium in the blood, which can lead to calcification of brain and artery tissue.

VITAMIN E

The RDA, or AI amount, for vitamin E is 15 mg for women and men. The DV for vitamin E is 30 IU or 20 mg. The UL is 1,000 IU; this value is based on a person who is approximately 130 lbs. The SUL is 800 IU or 400 mg.

There are potentially serious side effects associated with ingesting too much Vitamin E, which include a lowered ability for the body to clot blood, leading to bleeding problems.

VITAMIN K

The RDA, or AI amount, for vitamin K is 90 for women and 120 for men. The DV for vitamin K is 80 mg. There is no defined UL, although there is a SUL of 1,000 mg.

Copyright © Mometrix Media. You have been licensed one copy of this document for personal use only. Any other reproduction or redistribution is strictly prohibited. All rights reserved. This content is provided for test preparation purposes only and does not imply an endorsement by Mometrix of any particular political, scientific, or religious point of view.

There are potentially serious side effects associated with ingesting too much Vitamin K, including damage to the liver, blood problems such as anemia (not enough iron), and red blood cell disorders

THIAMINE (VITAMIN B1)

The recommended daily allowance (RDA), or adequate intake (AI) amount, for thiamine, or vitamin B1, is 1.1 for women and 1.2 for men. The daily value (DV) for thiamine is 1.5 mg. The tolerable upper level intake (UL) has not been defined, although this does not mean there is not a safe upper level, only that not enough information is available to set a value. The safe upper level (SUL) is 100 mg.

There are potentially serious side effects associated with ingesting too much Vitamin B1, which include nausea, headaches, crankiness, and an inability to sleep properly. An elevated heart rate and dizziness can occur at doses above 7,000 mg.

RIBOFLAVIN (VITAMIN B2)

The RDA, or AI, for riboflavin (vitamin B2) is 1.1 for women and 1.3 for men. The DV for riboflavin is 1.7 mg. The UL has not been defined, although this does not mean there is not a safe upper level, only that not enough information is available to set a value. The SUL is 40 mg.

Ingesting too much riboflavin is considered fairly harmless, although it may cause a slight discoloration of urine.

NIACIN

The RDA, or AI amount, for niacin is 14 for women and 16 for men. The DV for niacin is 20 mg. The UL is 35 mg; this value is based on a person who is approximately 130 lbs. The SUL is 500 IU.

There are potentially serious side effects associated with ingesting too much niacin, including redness in the face, nausea, damage to the liver and digestive problems.

VITAMIN B6

The RDA, or adequate intake (AI) amount, for vitamin B6 is 1.3 for women and men. The daily value for vitamin B6 is 2 mg. The UL is 100 mg; this value is based on a person who is approximately 130 lbs. The SUL is 10 international units (IU).

There are potentially serious side effects associated with ingesting too much Vitamin B6, which may cause discomfort and a loss of feeling in the limbs.

VITAMIN B12

The RDA, or AI amount, for vitamin B12 is 2.4 mg for women and men. The DV for vitamin B12 is 6 mg. The UL has not been defined, although this value has not yet been defined, there are still potential risks. The value is undefined because there is insufficient information to make a determination. The SUL is 2,000 IU.

There have been no recorded cases of toxic reactions to excessive doses of vitamin B12 when taken orally.

FOLIC ACID

The RDA, or AI amount, for folic acid is 400 for women and men. The DV for folic acid is 400 mg. The UL is 1,000 mg; this value is based on a person who is approximately 130 lbs. The SUL is 1,000 mg.

Copyright © Mometrix Media. You have been licensed one copy of this document for personal use only. Any other reproduction or redistribution is strictly prohibited. All rights reserved. This content is provided for test preparation purposes only and does not imply an endorsement by Mometrix of any particular political, scientific, or religious point of view.

There are potentially serious side effects associated with ingesting too much folic acid, which include hiding a deficiency of the vitamin B12, which in turn can result in nervous-system problems involving brain function.

PANTOTHENIC ACID

The RDA, or AI amount, for pantothenic acid is 5 mg for women and men. The DV for pantothenic acid is 10 mg. Although the UL has not yet been defined, there are still potential risks. The value is undefined because there is insufficient information to make a determination. The SUL is 200 IU.

Ingesting too much pantothenic acid can cause adverse effects, which include digestive-tract problems, general stomach upset, and diarrhea.

BIOTIN

The recommended daily allowance (RDA), or adequate intake (AI) amount, for biotin is 30 mg for women and men. The daily value (DV) for biotin is 300 mg. The tolerable upper level intake (UL) has not been defined, although this does not mean there is no upper limit, rather there may is insufficient information to determine a value. The safe upper level (SUL) is 900 mg.

There have been no noted cases of toxic reactions to excessive doses of biotin taken orally.

VITAMIN C

The RDA, or AI amount, for vitamin C is 75 mg for women and 90 for men. The DV for vitamin C is 60 mg. The UL is 2,000 international units (IU); this value is based on a person who is approximately 130 lbs. The SUL is 1,000 mg.

There are potentially serious side effects associated with ingesting too much Vitamin C, including kidney stones, nausea, gastrointestinal upset, and diarrhea.

BORON

The RDA, (AI amount), DV and the UL, values are not defined for boron. Although these values have not yet been defined, there are still potential risks. The values are undefined because there is insufficient information to make a determination.

The UL is 20 IU; this value is based on a person who is approximately 130 lbs. The SUL is 9.6 mg.

There are potentially serious side effects associated with ingesting too much boron, which include problems with the reproductive systems of men and women.

CALCIUM

The RDA, or AI amount, for calcium is 1,000 mg for women and men. The DV for calcium is 1,000 mg. The UL is 2,500 mg; this value is based on a person who is approximately 130 lbs. The SUL is 1,500 mg.

There are potentially serious side effects associated with ingesting too much calcium, including kidney stones, nausea, and constipation.

CHROMIUM

The RDA, or adequate intake (AI) amount, for chromium is 35 international units (IU) for women and men. The DV for chromium is 120 IU. The UL has not been defined, but this does not mean there is no UL value; rather, there may not be enough information to make this determination at present. The SUL is 10,000 IU.

Copyright © Mometrix Media. You have been licensed one copy of this document for personal use only. Any other reproduction or redistribution is strictly prohibited. All rights reserved. This content is provided for test preparation purposes only and does not imply an endorsement by Mometrix of any particular political, scientific, or religious point of view.

There are potentially serious side effects associated with ingesting too much chromium, including damage or malfunction of the kidneys or liver. It is also possible that chromium picolinate may cause cell mutations.

COBALT

The RDA, or AI amount, DV, and UL for cobalt have not been defined for women or men. This is not to suggest there are no upper limits or daily recommendations; rather, there may not be enough information from which to make these determinations. The SUL is 1.4 mg.

There are potentially serious side effects associated with ingesting too much cobalt, which include toxicity in heart function. It is understood that cobalt should not be used as a supplement unless it is in the form of vitamin B12.

COPPER

The RDA, or AI amount, for copper is 900 IU for women and men. The DV for copper is 2,000 IU. The UL is 10,000 IU; this value is based on a person who is approximately 130 lbs. The SUL is 10,000 IU.

There are potentially serious side effects associated with ingesting too much copper, including problems with digestive function, upset stomach, and damage to the liver.

FLUORIDE

The recommended daily allowance (RDA), or adequate intake (AI) amount, for fluoride is 3 mg for women and 4 mg for men. The daily value (DV) for fluoride has not been defined, although this should not be taken to mean that a daily value does not exist; rather, there may not be sufficient information to determine this value.

The tolerable upper level intake (UL) is 10 mg; this value is based on a person who is approximately 130 lbs. The safe upper level (SUL) has not been defined yet.

There are potentially serious side effects associated with ingesting too much fluoride, including damage to body tissues, such as bones, muscles, and nerves. Fluoride should only be added to the diet with the advice and supervision of a medical professional.

GERMANIUM

The RDA, AI amount, DV, and UL values for the micronutrient germanium are undefined. The SUL value has been determined to be none, or zero.

Ingesting too much germanium can cause serious adverse effects, given that this is a known toxic substance for the liver. Because of this, germanium should not be used as a supplement or be included in any other supplemental mixture.

This trace mineral is not considered necessary for proper body function and has been deemed by the Food and Drug Administration (FDA) to be potentially hazardous to human health.

IODINE

The RDA, or AI amount, for iodine is 150 international units (IU) for women and men. The DV for iodine is 150 IU. The UL is 1,100 IU; this value is based on a person who is approximately 130 lbs. The SUL is 500 IU.

There are potentially serious side effects associated with ingesting too much iodine, which include endocrine irregularities—specifically higher thyroid hormone levels.

Copyright © Mometrix Media. You have been licensed one copy of this document for personal use only. Any other reproduction or redistribution is strictly prohibited. All rights reserved.
This content is provided for test preparation purposes only and does not imply an endorsement by Mometrix of any particular political, scientific, or religious point of view.

IRON

The RDA, or AI amount, for iron is 8 mg for women and 18 mg for men. The DV for iron is 18 mg. The UL is 45 mg; this value is based on a person who is approximately 130 lb. The SUL is 17 mg.

There are potentially serious side effects associated with ingesting too much iron, which include a higher risk for cardiovascular problems and digestive-system problems including upset stomach.

MAGNESIUM

The RDA, or adequate intake (AI) amount, for magnesium is 320 for women and 420 for men. The daily value for magnesium is 400 mg. The UL is 350 mg; this value is based on a person who is approximately 130 lbs. The SUL is 400 mg.

There are potentially serious side effects associated with ingesting too much magnesium, which include gastrointestinal distress in the form of stomachache and diarrhea.

MANGANESE

The RDA, or AI amount, for manganese is 1.8 mg for women and 2.3 mg for men. The DV for manganese is 2 mg. The UL is 11 mg; this value is based on a person who is approximately 130 lb. The SUL is 4 mg.

There are potentially serious side effects associated with ingesting too much manganese, which include damage to the brain and nervous-system tissue and functioning, with toxicity more common in children than adults. High levels of manganese exposure occur more often as an occupational or environmental hazard, such as with miners or welders. Manganese exposure is regulated by the Occupational Safety and Health Administration (OSHA).

MOLYBDENUM

The RDA, or AI amount, for molybdenum is 45 mg for women and men. The DV for molybdenum is 75 mg. The UL is 2,000 mg; this value is based on a person who is approximately 130 lbs. The SUL is none, or zero.

Ingesting too much molybdenum can cause serious adverse effects, which include body toxicity, pain in the connective tissue areas, and side effects similar to those associated with the disease gout.

NICKEL

The RDA, or adequate intake (AI) amount, DV, and UL for nickel have not been defined for women or men. This does not mean there are no daily values or upper levels; rather, there may be insufficient information to determine these values at this time. The SUL is 260 international units (IU).

Ingesting too much nickel can cause serious adverse effects, which include the skin becoming more sensitive to surface touch of nickel, leading to dermatitis or contact allergies.

PHOSPHORUS

The RDA, or AI amount, for phosphorus is 700 mg for women and men. The DV for phosphorous is 1,000 mg. The UL is 4,000 mg; this value is based on a person who is approximately 130 lbs. The SUL is 250 mg.

Ingesting too much phosphorus can cause serious adverse effects, which include a decline in the density of bone tissue (a precursor to osteopenia and osteoporosis) and changes in endocrine function.

Copyright © Mometrix Media. You have been licensed one copy of this document for personal use only. Any other reproduction or redistribution is strictly prohibited. All rights reserved. This content is provided for test preparation purposes only and does not imply an endorsement by Mometrix of any particular political, scientific, or religious point of view.

POTASSIUM

The RDA, or AI amount, for potassium is 700 mg for women and men. The DV for potassium is 1,000 mg. The UL is 4,000 mg; this value is based on a person who is approximately 130 lbs. The SUL is 250 mg.

Ingesting too much potassium can cause serious adverse effects, which include a decline in the density of bone tissue (a precursor to osteopenia and osteoporosis) and changes in endocrine function.

SELENIUM

The RDA, or AI amount, for selenium is 55 IU for women and men. The DV for selenium is 70 international units (IU), or 1,500 mg. The UL is 400 IU; this value is based on a person who is approximately 130 lbs. The SUL is 450 IU.

Ingesting too much selenium can cause serious adverse effects, which include gastrointestinal upset such as feeling queasy or loose bowel movements, an overall feeling of tiredness, and damage to the nails and hair.

SILICON

The RDA, or AI amount, the DV, and the UL for silicon have not yet been established. This does not mean an upper level does not exist; rather, the information is insufficient at this time to make a full determination. The SUL is 700 mg.

Ingesting too much silicon has not been shown to cause too many serious side effects due to its very low level of toxicity, though there is some evidence that high intake can contribute to kidney stones.

VANADIUM

The RDA, or AI amount, and the DV for vanadium have not yet been established. This does not mean an upper level does not exist; rather, the information is insufficient at this time to make a full determination. The UL is 1.8 mg; this value is based on a person who is approximately 130 lbs. There is no SUL.

Ingesting too much vanadium can cause serious adverse effects, which include stomach irritation and an overall feeling of tiredness.

ZINC

The RDA, or AI amount, for zinc is 8 mg for women and 11 mg for men. The DV for zinc is 15 mg. The ULI is 40 mg; this value is based on a person who is approximately 130 lbs. The SUL is 25 mg.

Ingesting too much zinc can cause serious adverse effects, which include a low count of good cholesterol (HDL) and a dampening of the effectiveness of the immune system.

PERCENTAGE NEEDED

A person should take the 100% **recommended daily allowance** of a vitamin or mineral by ingesting a one-a-day type multivitamin.

There are some **exceptions** to this general rule. For example, if one pill held all the calcium a person needed for the day, it would likely be too large to swallow. Calcium should not be taken all at once, but over the course of the day because of its large size.

59

Copyright © Mometrix Media. You have been licensed one copy of this document for personal use only. Any other reproduction or redistribution is strictly prohibited. All rights reserved. This content is provided for test preparation purposes only and does not imply an endorsement by Mometrix of any particular political, scientific, or religious point of view.

Vitamin A intake also differs from the one-a-day formula. If a person is taking vitamin A in the form of retinol, less than 100 percent of the daily dose should be taken, because studies have shown an increase in the risk of hip fracture. Vitamin A in carotene form could be used instead.

There are also mixed results with studies of high use of beta carotene, with some showing higher lung cancer rates, but others showing lower prostate cancer rates. Clients should speak with their physicians about beta carotene supplementation.

SUPPLEMENT FACTS PANELS

A supplemental facts panel is the small panel of information that is on all food products, which indicates the nutritional facts about a single serving of that product. This will include what size a serving is, how many calories a single serving contains, and what nutrients are provided by that serving.

Percent daily value (%DV) refers to how much of the recommended daily value of a given micronutrient is satisfied by ingesting one serving. If the %DV indicates 100%, one serving satisfies all of a person's requirements for that micronutrient for one day. This value is based on what was recommended for an adult in 1968, with the higher value for a man or woman taken as the 100% value. While these have been revised from time to time since then, the values are due for revision because they do not necessarily reflect accurate values. For example, the iron value is calculated for a woman who has her menstrual period and is thus too high for most of the population at any given time.

SUPPLEMENT CONSIDERATIONS

First and foremost, a person should discuss his or her nutritional and dietary needs with a **licensed dietitian or physician** before beginning any course of supplementation. Tests can be performed to check for deficiencies, and patient/physician can engage in a dialogue about what is needed and how to go about obtaining that. Results can vary, and are dependent on the person's physical and mental state and the quality of the supplement. A good multivitamin should be looked into to ensure that all daily nutritional needs are met. A calcium supplement is also a good idea.

A person should research the **brand and company** that is producing the supplement. Because supplements are not regulated in the same manner as drugs and the FDA does not check the accuracy of the claims made, it is essential that a person uses a trusted brand with safe products.

Copyright © Mometrix Media. You have been licensed one copy of this document for personal use only. Any other reproduction or redistribution is strictly prohibited. All rights reserved. This content is provided for test preparation purposes only and does not imply an endorsement by Mometrix of any particular political, scientific, or religious point of view.

Assessment

The **fitness assessment** is a tool for gathering information that provides insight into a client's past, present, and future. After determining a person's health issues and fitness level, the **Certified Personal Trainer** (CPT) can set goals for the client and progress through an integrated training program (as well as modify acute variables— which are important aspects of exercise training that ensure progression through adequate challenge).

By design, the fitness assessment does not replace a medical exam or diagnose medical conditions. A health and fitness professional should refer clients to qualified healthcare providers whenever necessary. A CPT should not attempt to provide:

- Medical rehabilitation
- Exercises intended to serve as medical treatments
- Specific diets or nutritional supplements
- Treatment for chronic diseases or injuries
- Personal counseling

> **Review Video: 4 Skills Every Personal Trainer Should Have**
> Visit mometrix.com/academy and enter code: 588982

PAR-Q

PAR-Q stands for **Physical Activity Readiness Questionnaire**.

The PAR-Q is used to gather information about a client's **general history**. It is a yes-or-no questionnaire designed to determine if a client can safely begin a fitness regimen. The PAR-Q identifies risk factors that may require clearance from a medical professional before beginning an exercise program. It also allows the fitness professional to determine the client's appropriate fitness level using a low-medium-high scale.

Questions on the PAR-Q are intended to determine whether a potential client:

- Feels chest pain (at any time)
- Loses balance or consciousness
- Experiences bone or joint problems
- Takes medication for high blood pressure or a heart condition
- Knows of any other reason that he or she should not perform physical activity

Copyright © Mometrix Media. You have been licensed one copy of this document for personal use only. Any other reproduction or redistribution is strictly prohibited. All rights reserved.
This content is provided for test preparation purposes only and does not imply an endorsement by Mometrix of any particular political, scientific, or religious point of view.

Subjective Assessment

INFORMATION AND CONCLUSIONS

Understanding the broad details of a client's personal life can provide details about the way they move throughout their daily life. **Subjective information** about a person's general history may include his or her occupation, recreational activities, and hobbies.

Knowledge of a client's **daily patterns** provides the CPT with a better understanding of the client's lifestyle and may provide clues to potential imbalances. The CPT can use this information to determine the client's capacity for movement. For instance, those who enjoy relatively sedentary activities are not likely to start training at the same level as those who regularly play recreational sports. A woman who spends most of her day sitting in front of a computer is likely to have tight hip flexors.

MEDICAL BACKGROUND

Injury or surgery alters the kinetic chain's function. The CPT must discuss a potential client's medical history to determine dysfunctions that contraindicate physical fitness activities.

Ask about:

- Injuries and pain, including:
    - Sprains of the ankle, groin, or hamstrings
    - Tendinitis of the shoulders, knee (patellar), shins (posterior tibialis), or arch of the foot (plantar fasciitis)
    - Chronic headaches
- **Surgeries**, especially those that:
    - Are performed on the joints (shoulder, back, knee, ankle, or foot)
    - Involve cutting of the abdominal wall (Cesarean section or appendectomy)
- Chronic conditions or diseases, such as:
    - Coronary heart/artery disease or congestive heart failure
    - Cardiovascular disease or hypertension
    - High cholesterol
    - Lung or breathing problems
    - Diabetes mellitus
- Any medications

MEDICAL RISK FACTORS

Evidence supports the hypothesis that **muscular and skeletal ailments** are more prevalent in modern society than they were a generation ago. Many factors contribute to this decline in the health of the average American. An increase in automation and a decrease in physical activity have altered the overall health and physical fitness level of Americans over the last century. Extensively researched ailments include:

- **Low back pain**—This problem is estimated to affect four out of five American adults and is common among those who work in offices and remain seated for long periods of time.
- **Knee injuries**—There are approximately 100,000 injuries to the anterior cruciate ligament (ACL) each year, with the vast majority resulting from non–sport-related incidents. Most of these injuries occur to young people between the ages of 15 and 25 and may be a result of a less-active population.

Copyright © Mometrix Media. You have been licensed one copy of this document for personal use only. Any other reproduction or redistribution is strictly prohibited. All rights reserved. This content is provided for test preparation purposes only and does not imply an endorsement by Mometrix of any particular political, scientific, or religious point of view.

- **Chronic disease**—A decrease in activity can lead to or exacerbate chronic problems such as obesity, diabetes, hypertension, and other heart conditions.
- **Kinetic chain injuries**—Kinetic chain injuries are a leading cause of doctor visits. Repetitive sitting and sedentary lifestyles weaken muscle support and contribute to kinetic chain injuries.

PHARMACOLOGICAL INFORMATION

While it is never appropriate for a CPT to suggest or administer **medications** to clients, it is important to know what medications a client is taking and the general effects of those medicines. A summary of common medications and the general physiological effects each might have on the body includes:

- **Beta blockers**—treat high blood pressure (hypertension) or irregular heart rate (arrhythmia).
- **Calcium-channel blockers**—treat high blood pressure or angina, which is chest pain caused by inadequate blood flow to the heart.
- **Nitrates**— treat high blood pressure or congestive heart failure, which results from the heart's inability to pump blood to the body's organs adequately.
- **Diuretics**—help purge excess water from the body and are used to treat edema, congestive heart failure, or high blood pressure.
- **Bronchodilators**—alleviate constriction in the bronchi and bronchioles of the lungs and are often used to treat pulmonary disorders such as asthma.
- **Vasodilators**—relax blood vessels and are often used to treat high blood pressure.
- **Antidepressants**—mood elevators and stabilizers often used to help alleviate symptoms of depression and other psychiatric disorders.

Copyright © Mometrix Media. You have been licensed one copy of this document for personal use only. Any other reproduction or redistribution is strictly prohibited. All rights reserved.
This content is provided for test preparation purposes only and does not imply an endorsement by Mometrix of any particular political, scientific, or religious point of view.

Special Population Risk Factors

A special population is a group of people that have a common health problem, impairment, or a particular affliction that makes it necessary to alter the general rules of training to accommodate his or her needs.

The basic concepts that NASM teaches apply to adults who are healthy and can cope with the basic rigors of a workout regimen. Some special populations may require a **modified program**. Examples of special populations requiring additional considerations include:

- Young persons or those who have not finished growing physically
- The elderly or those older than age 65
- Those with osteoporosis or low bone density
- Pregnant women
- Overweight clients whose body mass index (BMI) exceeds the normal healthy range but does not exceed 30
- Obese clients whose BMI is 30 or more
- Diabetic clients
- Arthritic clients
- Persons with hypertension
- Individuals suffering from coronary heart disease (CHD)

For example, **children or adolescents** have not completed their growing cycles. They often have superior cardiorespiratory capabilities, but should be monitored in their strength-training routines.

Likewise, those with **osteoporosis**, a disease characterized by low bone density, need to engage in weight-bearing exercise to help increase their bone density, but the condition necessitates special consideration. It is important to perform weight-bearing exercises in a manner that keeps physical limitations in mind to promote client safety.

Pregnant women can also work out effectively, but a trainer needs to be aware of several important physiological changes that take place during gestation. These include a much higher volume of blood as well as a general loosening of the body's ligaments, which may affect stability and limit ability to maintain certain positions.

YOUNG PEOPLE

Health and fitness professionals often work with **younger clients** in varying contexts. This population ranges from grade-school age (from 5 or 6 to 12), through adolescence (12 to 18), and up to young adulthood (approximately 21).

Younger clients differ from the adult population, and a well-designed **training regimen** should accommodate their unique needs. Many training guidelines for young people deal with physical-education–type training or youth sports. **Childhood obesity** is a much more widespread problem today than it was in previous generations, and the result has been a dramatic increase in the demand for regular training designed for young people. Younger people need at least 20 minutes of activity that increases the heart rate at least three times each week, with an hour being ideal.

OXYGEN CONSUMPTION

With proper calibration for height and weight, adults and young clients have similar **oxygen consumption rates** (VO2). Similar VO2 rates suggest that young people and adults have a similar

Copyright © Mometrix Media. You have been licensed one copy of this document for personal use only. Any other reproduction or redistribution is strictly prohibited. All rights reserved. This content is provided for test preparation purposes only and does not imply an endorsement by Mometrix of any particular political, scientific, or religious point of view.

capacity for performing cardiorespiratory training activities that require endurance. Younger children (6 to 12) should be able to tolerate vigorous activity for 30 to 60 minutes daily.

Increases in training volume should not go beyond **10 percent of the previous week's activity**. For example, if a young person engages in 30 minutes of exercise three times per week, or 90 minutes total for the week, the following week should only increase by nine additional minutes (three minutes per session), to progress safely.

SUBMAXIMAL OXYGEN

A young person's submaximal oxygen consumption exceeds that of the average adult for activities such as walking, jogging, and sprinting. Reduced VO2 capacity means that younger people have a higher risk of tiring and overheating during vigorous exercises.

Trainers should make sure that youth clients **hydrate** adequately. Trainers must take care to ensure that clients do not **overexert** themselves during high-intensity exercise, particularly when the weather is hot and humid. Exercise that increases the heart rate can safely be enjoyed at least three times a week for at least 20 minutes. An anaerobic activity lasting more than ten seconds is not advisable.

GLYCOLIC ENZYME LEVELS

A young person has lower levels of glycolic enzymes than the average adult, which means that he or she would have a lower tolerance for very intense activities that are anaerobic in nature (lasting more than 10 seconds and up to 90 seconds).

A weight-training regimen should include the following:

Choose between 8 and 10 different exercises. Have the client perform one or two sets of each exercise. Each set should consist of 8 to 12 repetitions. Sets of twenty repetitions promote endurance and sets of six repetitions are ideal when strength is the goal. The trainer should make sure that the client is using proper form and is completely controlling the movements when performing these exercises, so as not to put excessive strain on the joints.

RATE OF SWEATING

A young person cannot handle extreme environments and require extra caution to exercise safely in hot and humid conditions. Schedule a **warm-up** and **cool-down** to give the young person's body enough time to adjust to environmental factors.

Increasing the number of repetitions before adding weight builds tolerance. Add weight only after the repetitions have increased.

Be sure the youth client hydrates properly, watch for diminishing performance, and identify visual cues that might signal distress or overheating. Younger clients may lack the ability to identify abnormalities and may not communicate physical distress as well as adults.

WEIGHT TRAINING

There is a common misconception that weight training is not appropriate for youth clients. Research has shown that it is not harmful and can have positive benefits. Research has demonstrated that weight training has a lower risk of causing a serious injury participation in organized youth sports.

Copyright © Mometrix Media. You have been licensed one copy of this document for personal use only. Any other reproduction or redistribution is strictly prohibited. All rights reserved. This content is provided for test preparation purposes only and does not imply an endorsement by Mometrix of any particular political, scientific, or religious point of view.

There are some risks involved with resistance training, primarily of **pulls and tears**. Proper training and effective monitoring can mitigate risk. It is also important to perform a movement assessment much like the one given to an adult client to determine a youth client's capabilities before beginning a systematic, progressive weight-training regimen.

MOVEMENT ASSESSMENT

A youth client can perform 10 squats and 10 push-ups for a **modified weight-training assessment** (these can be modified for a female client or lower-strength client). Gauge all the of the appropriate kinetic-chain checkpoints, as you would with any NASM fitness assessment. The results will help the trainer determine which exercises will be the best for the particular client and also identify specific areas that require careful monitoring during training sessions.

Weight training for youth clients can increase strength, bone density, and general coordination.

OPTIMUM PERFORMANCE TRAINING (OPT) MODEL

The health and fitness professional should take into account the fitness assessment of the youth client and other general background information when designing an appropriate **resistance-training program**. Taking a client from the stabilization level into the higher phases will depend on physical ability, the client's overall ability to handle the regimen, and the recommendation of his or her doctor.

Another important factor is that training for the youth client should be engaging and fun. To maintain motivation and interest and encourage a lifelong interest in fitness, keeping the routines fun is vitally important.

BASIC GUIDELINES

Youth clients should have a **fun training experience** with **safe activities** that are **adequately supervised** by an adult. Games, sports, walking, running, water sports, and even weight training are good types of exercise for youth clients. Training can be engaged in from three to five times per week for at least 20 minutes, with an hour being ideal. A movement assessment should observe kinetic-chain checkpoints while the youth client performs 10 push-ups and 10 squats. Follow NASM's flexibility continuum and resistance training guidelines as outlined in the OPT model. High-level training requires physical ability and enough maturity to understand and duplicate instructions safely.

SENIORS

A senior citizen is an individual aged 65 years and older. The senior population is growing exponentially now that the baby boomer generation is maturing. There is a need for health and fitness professionals who understand how to work with members of this population safely and effectively.

Keeping fit can dramatically improve a senior client's quality of life. Training can help increase bone density, maintain coordination, and improve overall muscle tone. Many primary functions of the body decline with age, including:

- Elasticity of tissues
- Muscle mass
- Bone density
- Blood volume output

Copyright © Mometrix Media. You have been licensed one copy of this document for personal use only. Any other reproduction or redistribution is strictly prohibited. All rights reserved. This content is provided for test preparation purposes only and does not imply an endorsement by Mometrix of any particular political, scientific, or religious point of view.

- Neuromuscular coordination
- Maximum heart rate

DISEASES OR CHRONIC CONDITIONS

Common chronic conditions associated with older age include lower bone density (osteoporosis), arthritis, weight gain or obesity, and back problems. The CPT should treat any problem that fits into a special population according to NASM guidelines for the relevant condition.

However, just because a senior has a different body condition than a younger adult does not mean there is a problem. An older adult may have a higher resting blood pressure measurement, but this may not indicate that something is wrong or require compensation during training. As with all clients, a senior client should have a thorough medical examination before beginning a training regimen.

CARDIOVASCULAR SYSTEM

A senior's body is different from that of a younger adult. The cardiovascular output, lung capacity, and maximum heart rate that a senior client can achieve during exercise decrease as they age.

Decreased cardiorespiratory capability means that a trainer should ease into exercise routines with an older client, use lower weight, prescribe light workloads, and increase gradually. Training sessions should last from 20 to 45 minutes. Three to five sessions per week is ideal. Training intensity should be in the middle range, from 40 to 80 percent.

BODY COMPOSITION

A senior's body composition changes with age, with lean muscle mass and bone density decreasing, and fat stores increasing. Weight training counteracts these changes because it builds muscle and decreases fat. Weight-bearing exercise also helps build **bone density**.

The health and fitness professional should start the client with lower weights and add more weight gradually. Select 8 to 10 exercises. The client can perform three sets of 20 repetitions to achieve this goal. Training lessons should run for about a half an hour.

NEUROMUSCULAR EFFICIENCY

An older adult will have differences in his or her **neuromuscular system** that can significantly alter balance, and a trainer needs to be aware of this possibility to train the senior safely. Coordination and gait can suffer as well. Observe carefully and identify impairments when performing standard assessments.

The health and fitness professional chooses modes of exercise that account for a client's **limitations**. Walking on a treadmill with two handrails might be a good option. Training on stationary equipment such as an exercise bike, or performing cardiorespiratory training in an aquatic environment may also benefit seniors.

CARDIAC CONDITION

Older clients have an increased risk of suffering from **heart problems**, and the condition is often undiagnosed. It is important for an older client to have a full medical exam and to be aware of potential heart complications before beginning a workout regimen.

During the health and fitness professional's assessments, it is important to pay attention to the **pulse assessments** and note anything unusual. It is important to determine a baseline heart rate for each client, which will help the trainer identify issues during training.

Copyright © Mometrix Media. You have been licensed one copy of this document for personal use only. Any other reproduction or redistribution is strictly prohibited. All rights reserved. This content is provided for test preparation purposes only and does not imply an endorsement by Mometrix of any particular political, scientific, or religious point of view.

OPT MODEL

The **degeneration** that occurs with age, and **decreased maximum workout capacity**, can make working with the elderly challenging for health and fitness professionals. The goal of a training program should be to counteract these processes.

Walking can be challenging for seniors because of changes to bones, muscles, coordination, and, cardiorespiratory capacity. Physiological changes can cause seniors to become more sedentary, which increases the danger of degenerating. Over time, they can lose their ability to live independently.

The **OPT model** is an excellent way to work with senior clients because it uses thorough assessments to spot potential existing body concerns, and then takes the client through a systematic workout approach.

Assessment process and intensity level: To implement the OPT model with a senior client, a health and fitness professional must begin with a series of **assessments** that will help gauge the client's current exercise capability, physical condition, and overall fitness goals. Begin this process with NASM's **Physical Activity Readiness Questionnaire** (PAR-Q).

Introduce **cardiorespiratory training** gradually. Account for prescribed **medications** and **diseases or chronic conditions**. Phases 1 and 2 of training are ideal for the senior client. Explore phase 1 thoroughly to build core stability and improve nervous system communication. The result is improved balance and coordination.

COMMUNICATION

When a health and fitness professional works with a senior client, he or she must be aware of potential **psychological aspects** that may impact the working relationship and approach these with sensitivity and tact.

Senior clients may have **reservations** about engaging in physical activity. Be sure the client has a thorough physical examination before beginning any new workout routine and speaks with his or her doctor about concerns of legitimate physical limitations.

A senior client might be resistant to incorporating **weight training** into their workout routine because he or she is afraid of injury. Treat this concern with respect, and offer some insight into research showing that resistance training is highly beneficial for seniors.

FLEXIBILITY TRAINING

Flexibility training is important to warm up and cool down muscles, improve range of motion, and add elasticity to connective tissue. Flexibility training reduces the risk of injury. Flexibility training is especially important for senior clients who may experience reduced muscle tone, lower body tissue elasticity, and poor coordination as they age. Increased flexibility is a good foundation for better training results and ultimately increases the ability to perform daily activities necessary for independence.

The senior population can benefit from **static stretches** and **self-myofascial release**. **Dynamic stretching** is an excellent tool to prepare the body for a workout and to preserve the body after physical activity.

Copyright © Mometrix Media. You have been licensed one copy of this document for personal use only. Any other reproduction or redistribution is strictly prohibited. All rights reserved. This content is provided for test preparation purposes only and does not imply an endorsement by Mometrix of any particular political, scientific, or religious point of view.

TRAINING MODES

Seniors can engage in **cardiorespiratory** and **weight-training activities**, though the trainer should use extra caution for those seniors with balance or coordination problems. For those seniors, equipment with handrails or exercise bikes may be a good choice. **Aquatic activities** are also effective for seniors. Seniors should work out two to five times each week for up to an hour each day, depending on their ability. The standard set of movement assessments will help the trainer understand these capabilities before beginning a workout regimen. All forms of stretching are appropriate, depending on the client's ability.

Prescribe three sets of 8 to 10 different exercises, beginning with 20 repetitions per set. Explore the first two phases of the OPT model before moving on. Ensure the client demonstrates adequate stabilization of the core muscles, balance, before advancing.

OBESITY

Obesity is a clinical term defined as the class of people who have a body mass index (BMI) of 30 or greater. BMI is calculated by taking a person's metric weight (in kilograms) and dividing it by their metric height (in meters) squared. **Morbid obesity** is considered to be a BMI greater than 40.

An individual with a BMI reading less than 18.5 is considered **underweight**. A BMI reading between 18.5 and 24.9 falls within the **healthy range**. Clients with BMI readings between 25 and 30 have an **overweight** designation.

BMI = Classification
$< 18.5 =$ Underweight
$18.6-21.99 =$ Acceptable
$22.0-24.99 =$ Acceptable
$25.0-29.99 =$ Overweight
$30-34.99 =$ Obese
$35.0-39.99 =$ Obesity II
$\geq 40 =$ Obesity III

Obese usually seek health and fitness training for weight loss and because their overall health status dictates a more healthful lifestyle. Obesity can cause a long list of physical problems that exercise and a healthy diet can address.

CAUSES OF OBESITY

Individual factors or a combination of two or more compounding factors can lead to obesity. **Improper energy balance** is a significant problem in the United States. An energy imbalance is a calorie surplus caused by ingesting more calories than the body burns. The body stores excess calories as fat, which results in weight gain.

Inactivity and consumption of **excessive amounts of calories** contribute to energy imbalance. Given the fast-food culture of the United States and the prevalence of office jobs, in which sitting all day is the norm, it is not surprising that weight gain and obesity have been steadily on the rise over the past few generations. Recreational activity is often sedentary. Watching television and playing video games are more common than is playing outside.

AGING

Age can contribute to obesity. As a person ages, the body's lean muscle mass (which burns calories) decreases. Body fat may increase at the same time. Additionally, cardiorespiratory capability and bone density may decrease.

Copyright © Mometrix Media. You have been licensed one copy of this document for personal use only. Any other reproduction or redistribution is strictly prohibited. All rights reserved. This content is provided for test preparation purposes only and does not imply an endorsement by Mometrix of any particular political, scientific, or religious point of view.

A senior may be less likely to work out regularly because of limitations arising from **degenerative conditions**, which potentially leads to weight gain. While obesity and age do not correlate directly, the physical problems associated with aging can result in a reduction in physical activity, which leads to the overweight condition.

A health and fitness trainer must take age, weight, and chronic diseases associated with old into account when designing a training regimen. Reducing fat and increasing lean muscle mass are important goals for obese clients.

CLIENT'S GAIT

When working with an obese client, the health and fitness professional should be aware that the person's **gait**, or how the core musculature coordinates the lower part of the body when walking, can be significantly different than a person in the healthy BMI range. Changes in gait can have a serious impact on balance and coordination.

Research has shown that obese individuals take shorter strides and have lower balance, even when they have superior strength. Shorter strides and poor balance mean that an obese client should improve coordination by fully exploring **phase 1 of the OPT model**. Additionally, obesity has been linked with neuropathy, which can further destabilize a person's gait. Stabilization exercises can help maximize core stability and improve communication between the brain and nervous system, improving overall coordination.

WEIGHT LOSS

A two-pronged approach is the most effective path to help an obese client lose weight. Modify the client's **diet** and prescribe a systematic **exercise** regime to promote weight loss.

The client should discuss his or her diet issues with a licensed dietitian. The dietitian will design a healthy plan for the individual, taking overall activity level and constraints from work or family obligations into account. It is important to support the client's efforts, which will likely include reducing his or her caloric intake by a few hundred calories per day.

Give the client a combination of cardiorespiratory training and weight training to help spur weight loss. Cardiorespiratory training helps improve the body's energy-burning capabilities. Adding lean muscle mass helps burn calories as well.

OPT MODEL

When working with an obese client, it may be more comfortable for the client, and more effective for the overall workout regimen, for him or her to perform exercises in an **upright or recumbent** (standing or sitting) position. Machines with cables, as well as isometric exercises that use body weight, may be ideal for a beginning client in this population.

Modification of certain fitness assessments may be advisable. Keep all assessments on a manageable gradient to get a good idea of fitness capability, but also keep the client safe. For example, modify a squat to a simple balance exercise, and pay attention to kinetic-chain compensations that occur while the client is standing on one leg.

Upright stretching may be more comfortable for obese clients. Performing a floor stretch from a modified standing or sitting position is beneficial for obese clients.

Copyright © Mometrix Media. You have been licensed one copy of this document for personal use only. Any other reproduction or redistribution is strictly prohibited. All rights reserved. This content is provided for test preparation purposes only and does not imply an endorsement by Mometrix of any particular political, scientific, or religious point of view.

CORE TRAINING AND STABILIZATION EXERCISES

Because obese individuals often have issues with gait and coordination, **stabilization exercises**, particularly those that focus on the **core musculature**, are an excellent starting point for the health and fitness professional. Given that stabilization exercises tie in directly with Phase 1 of OPT, the trainer has a great jumping-off point to create a systematic, integrated program that follows the OPT model.

When working with an obese client, it may be advisable to avoid positions in which the client is reclining or positioned on his or her **back** due to the higher risk of hypertension found in this population. It may also be more comfortable for an obese client to begin working from standing or seated positions. For example, abdominal work might be easier to begin on a reclining bench rather than on the floor, or by using cables in an upright position.

PSYCHOLOGICAL ASPECTS

When working with someone who is overweight or obese, it is important for the health and fitness professional to be aware of, and sensitive to, the fact that this condition can often cause intense **emotional issues** for the client. These issues are real and require professionalism and tact to help the client achieve their ultimate goals.

A trainer must do his or her best to motivate all clients and help them feel as though they are in a **safe environment**. A feeling of safety is important for physical health and emotional well-being. Creating a safe environment is essential to creating a professional relationship founded on trust and cooperation.

When dealing with an obese client, use language that is **neutral** regarding weight and make thoughtful, encouraging statements. Choose your words carefully to establish rapport, motivate, and keep the client interested in the training routine. Avoid making comments that can make the client feel, self-conscious or distracted.

COMORBIDITIES

Obese clients are much more likely to have serious **health problems** that require special considerations when training than individuals within the healthy BMI range. These problems can lead to obesity, or they can result from obesity, but the CPT must consider them when designing a program.

Some common problems obese individuals may experience include:

- Diabetes
- Arthritis
- Hypertension
- Asthma

Having the client get a full **physical examination** before beginning a new training routine is essential. A medical examination will help identify physical problems and allow the client to begin necessary medical treatment for those problems. Fitness assessments allow the CPT to tailor the program to the client's capabilities by providing insight into kinetic-chain problems, gait problems, and musculature compensations.

CARDIOVASCULAR ABILITIES

An obese client may have different **cardiovascular and cardiorespiratory capabilities** than a person in the healthy BMI range. The maximum amount of oxygen that can be taken in during

Copyright © Mometrix Media. You have been licensed one copy of this document for personal use only. Any other reproduction or redistribution is strictly prohibited. All rights reserved. This content is provided for test preparation purposes only and does not imply an endorsement by Mometrix of any particular political, scientific, or religious point of view.

exercise may not be adequate to support his or her body for vigorous activities, and the ability to perform extended, anaerobic workout activities may be limited.

When beginning a workout regimen, include modalities that account for these factors. Beginning in an **aquatic environment** is very helpful. Submersion in water has many benefits. Water immersion can improve overall conditioning while reducing stress on the body and joints. As the client's capabilities improve, they can progress to walking on flat terrain or on a treadmill to improve cardiovascular endurance and lung capacity.

DIET PROGRAM

Obese clients are likely to have spent a good deal of their adult lives **dieting**. A lifetime of unsuccessful dieting can lead to many hang-ups or misconceptions about diet and exercise that the health and fitness professional must navigate to help the client achieve his or her goals.

Be sure the obese client meets with a registered **dietitian or nutritionist** to create a healthy eating plan that reduces daily caloric intake. Low-impact exercise should be the starting point, with a goal of increasing the client's daily activity level. Lengthen each training session to an hour before increasing the impact level. Initially, the client should burn approximately 1,200 calories per week. Progress the client until they are consistently burning 2000 calories a week through exercise.

BODY COMPOSITION

When working with an obese client, it is best to use BMI as the method of measuring **body fat composition**. Circumference measurements may also work well. Other methods of body composition measurement may not be accurate for a person who is clinically obese, and taking measurements with skinfold calipers may not appeal to an obese client who is already self-conscious about his or her weight.

The exact measurement of body fat is not important when working with an obese client. BMI measurement is not 100 percent accurate. However, it gives an excellent starting point for the client to use. It is valuable for setting goals for the client because it is a concrete number that serves as a baseline for future comparison.

MODES OF TRAINING

Low-intensity activities are ideal when beginning a training program with an obese client. Low-intensity activities include walking, using a stationary bike, or training in an aquatic environment. **Frequency and duration** of exercise are more important when beginning than is intensity level. The client should train as many as five times a week. Initially, workouts should be 20 minutes, and should last increasingly longer as the client's fitness level improves. Increase intensity after the client can perform exercises at low-intensity for an hour. It is important to note that uninterrupted workouts are unnecessary. Two 20-minute walks are as productive as one 40-minute walk if the client reaches the proper heart rate for both sessions.

Movement assessments designed to determine client capability are important, but simple balance exercises can replace squatting exercises if necessary. Observe the kinetic-chain checkpoints for postural distortions.

Select up to ten exercises for the client and have them perform three sets of 15 repetitions.

OTHER ISSUES

Obesity is a significant problem in modern American society, with record numbers of obese children and adults in the United States. At present, 66% of Americans over 20 are classified as

Copyright © Mometrix Media. You have been licensed one copy of this document for personal use only. Any other reproduction or redistribution is strictly prohibited. All rights reserved. This content is provided for test preparation purposes only and does not imply an endorsement by Mometrix of any particular political, scientific, or religious point of view.

overweight. Approximately 34% (72 million) of those individuals are considered obese. Further, 9 million children between the ages of 2 and 19 are overweight or obese. Many obese people want to begin a training regimen to lose weight and to alleviate other physical problems that obesity exacerbates. Many obese individuals start an exercise program with a goal of improving their overall health and quality of life.

By understanding the common problems associated with this special population, a health and fitness professional can offer superior services to its members. It is important for a trainer to understand not only the additional **physical considerations** but also the **emotional concerns** an obese person may have in dealing with a training regimen so the trainer can help guide the client with professionalism and sensitivity.

Reducing calorie intake, increasing activity, and building muscle are the cornerstones of working with an obese client.

DIABETIC INDIVIDUALS

Diabetes describes two related endocrine, or hormonal, disorders. One stems from the inability of the pancreas to produce insulin, a necessary hormone, while the other makes it difficult for the body to convert simple carbohydrates.

More than five percent of the American population has diabetes, with hundreds of thousands of new diagnoses every year. Diabetes affects the young and the elderly, and it is a leading cause of death.

A trainer must be aware that a client with diabetes has **limitations** on his or her body's ability to process, convert, and utilize glucose (blood sugar). While exercise can be very beneficial for a diabetic client, careful monitoring is required to ensure that exercise regimens are safe. The CPT must protect a diabetic's **feet**, which are easily injured and slow to heal.

TYPE 1 DIABETES

The pancreas of a Type 1 diabetic does not produce the hormone **insulin**. Because insulin is not circulating in the bloodstream, the cells of the body are not able to convert blood sugar into energy. An insulin deficiency creates too much blood sugar (hyperglycemia) and not enough available energy. Type 1 diabetics need to introduce insulin manually into their bodies, usually by injecting synthetic insulin.

Synthetic insulin is important because exercise can use blood sugar, so if a diabetic is not mindful of his or her blood sugar levels when engaging in exercise, he or she can use up too much blood sugar, resulting in levels that are too low (hypoglycemia).

Low blood sugar can cause a person to faint or feel lightheaded. Discuss this potential problem with your client, and ascertain what recommendations his or her doctor has made for managing blood sugar during exercise. A common solution is for the client to keep a high-sugar snack or drink on hand for low-blood-sugar incidents.

TYPE 2 DIABETES

Type 2 diabetes is referred to as **adult-onset diabetes**. People who are overweight and eat a diet high in refined foods (especially sugars) can be at a higher risk of developing Type 2 diabetes. Young people are at risk of developing Type 2 diabetes because of poor diet and a higher incidence of obesity.

Copyright © Mometrix Media. You have been licensed one copy of this document for personal use only. Any other reproduction or redistribution is strictly prohibited. All rights reserved. This content is provided for test preparation purposes only and does not imply an endorsement by Mometrix of any particular political, scientific, or religious point of view.

Type 2 diabetics do not usually have trouble making insulin, which is the primary problem of type I diabetics. Rather, the body cannot properly recognize the insulin and allow it to perform its function of converting blood sugar into a form of energy that cells can readily use.

The body's inability to recognize insulin means that the **blood sugar levels** remain high (hyperglycemia). If the blood sugar remains high over a long period, damage to other parts of the body can occur.

Exercise can help use blood sugar and alleviate some of the stress placed on the body by extra weight.

EXERCISE SELECTION

When working with someone with diabetes, it is important for the health and fitness professional to be aware of the method the client uses to control glucose levels. **Exercise** is a very effective method of controlling blood sugar because it reduces the level of glucose in the bloodstream.

The trainer must have an **action plan** to manage the client's blood sugar levels. It is important for the trainer to monitor the client, recognize the signs of hyperglycemia and hypoglycemia, and to take appropriate actions based on these observations. In extreme cases, skipping a workout may be necessary to protect the client's health. The action plan should consider all recommendations from the client's physician.

It is also important to help the client avoid damage to the feet (e.g., blisters, infections, cuts), as the feet are a sensitive area of the body for diabetics.

COMORBIDITIES

People with diabetes are highly likely to have **other conditions** that place them in other special populations. Diabetics may be overweight or obese, have hypertension (high blood pressure), or a host of other medical issues. It is very important to make sure the diabetic client has a full physical examination before beginning training, so the client's physician can properly diagnose and treat any problems.

Because obesity can be a cause of diabetes, or can be an effect of diabetes, it is advisable to put a diabetic client on a training regimen that encourages weight loss and the building of lean muscle tissue. Set the routine to burn at least 1,000 calories each week, and build to 2,000 calories.

GLUCOSE CONTROL MECHANISMS

A person with diabetes does not have the same **glucose control mechanisms** that a nondiabetic has. Introducing exercise, which uses blood sugar, into a diabetic's routine requires caution. Though exercise is very beneficial to a diabetic in the larger scheme, each training session runs the risk of causing hypoglycemia, or low blood sugar.

Because of this, it is important for the trainer to notice when a client's **blood sugar drops**. Symptoms of low blood sugar include fatigue, dizziness, and disorientation. Set up an action plan with the client in case this happens.

A client should be aware that their blood sugar may drop many hours after a training session. A person who has had diabetes for some time will likely know how to regulate his or her blood sugar, but a person with a recent diagnosis may want to take more frequent blood sugar readings when starting a training regimen.

Copyright © Mometrix Media. You have been licensed one copy of this document for personal use only. Any other reproduction or redistribution is strictly prohibited. All rights reserved. This content is provided for test preparation purposes only and does not imply an endorsement by Mometrix of any particular political, scientific, or religious point of view.

BETA BLOCKER MEDICATION USE

Clients in the diabetic population often have comorbidities. A common comorbidity is **high blood pressure** (hypertension). Beta blockers are commonly used to treat this hypertension.

Beta blockers can mask the symptoms of low blood sugar that may occur during a workout. If the client is not aware of a dip in blood sugar, hypoglycemia (low blood sugar) may occur during the training session.

It is advisable for the client to take **less insulin** before working out to compensate for the effects of exercise. The client should have simple carbohydrates (e.g., juice, snack bar) on hand that can be ingested before or during the workout, to assist in regulating blood sugar levels. If a diabetic client also takes beta blockers, encourage them to have a discussion with a physician.

TOLERANCE TO HEAT

It is more difficult to recognize the symptoms of low blood sugar (hypoglycemia) when diabetic individuals exercise in **hot environments**, or when they become overheated. These symptoms include fatigue, dizziness, and disorientation.

Training should begin with low-impact activities and progress to longer training sessions (up to an hour at a time). It is helpful to conduct frequent training sessions (as often as daily). **Frequent exercise** will help control glucose levels. Initially, intensity should be moderate, giving the client time to acclimate to the workouts and learn to recognize symptoms of hypoglycemia that may occur during training sessions.

TRAINING MODES

The guidelines for working with a diabetic client are similar to those for working with an obese individual. The primary difference is the recommended **modality** of exercise. While obese clients can greatly benefit from walking as the primary starting point for workouts, this may not be advisable for diabetic clients, whose feet can be susceptible to injuries that do not heal properly. Thus, other exercises, such as aquatic workouts, might be a good starting point.

Use the basic flexibility continuum with modifications for self-myofascial release if the client has nervous-system concerns with their feet. Check with the client's physician before recommending self-myofascial release.

The first two phases of the **OPT model** are ideal for diabetic clients.

TRAINING LENGTH AND INTENSITY

Diabetic clients often have the goals of controlling glucose levels and losing weight. Employ **low-intensity activities** (such as riding a stationary bike or performing aquatic exercises) gradually to accomplish these goals safely. Start with short sessions, work up to hour-long sessions, exercise frequently (as often as seven days a week).

Use the **standard assessments** unless there is comorbidity that limits the client's ability to perform the test. The flexibility continuum as outlined by NASM is appropriate.

The first two phases of the OPT model are ideal, and two or three resistance-training sessions per week are beneficial. High-level power training is usually not advisable.

Copyright © Mometrix Media. You have been licensed one copy of this document for personal use only. Any other reproduction or redistribution is strictly prohibited. All rights reserved. This content is provided for test preparation purposes only and does not imply an endorsement by Mometrix of any particular political, scientific, or religious point of view.

Keep all physician recommendations in mind when working with a diabetic client, know the symptoms of hypoglycemia, have a simple carbohydrate source on hand and be sure the client wears appropriate protective footwear.

HYPERTENSIVE INDIVIDUALS

A client has hypertension (high blood pressure) if the **systolic** (top number) is greater than 140, and the **diastolic** (bottom number) is more than 90. To be diagnosed hypertensive, a client's systolic and diastolic readings must exceed the normal range. The reading taken when the individual is not taking any medication is the relevant reading.

People who smoke, are overweight, or eat an unhealthy diet are at a higher risk for hypertension. Many individuals diagnosed as hypertensive will be on medication to help control the problem, and they may seek exercise as another way to control hypertension and alleviate some of the underlying causes.

It is important for the health and fitness professional to encourage hypertensive individuals to take the **medication** prescribed by their doctors. Often, people in this population avoid consistently taking their medications because they do not feel sick.

BODY POSITIONING

Proper body positioning is important when working with hypertensive clients because improper body positioning can affect **blood pressure**. Positions that place the head below the heart can cause the blood pressure to rise. Lying on the back or the stomach are examples of positions that can cause the blood pressure to rise.

Try to keep the hypertensive client in **seated** or **upright** positions for all exercises. To perform abdominal work, the health and fitness professional should consider using cable machines or putting the client on an inclined weight bench.

The trainer should advise the client not to overstrain or grip equipment too tightly, as this can increase blood pressure.

It is acceptable to prescribe the first two phases of the Optimum Performance Training (OPT) model for this population. Monitor high-intensity power training carefully.

BLOOD PRESSURE CHANGE DURING EXERCISE

Clients without hypertension tend to have predictable **blood pressure responses**. A client with high blood pressure may not have a predictable blood pressure response. It may spike, rise slightly, or vary from session to session. It is important to create a low-impact training routine that gradually increases in frequency, intensity, and duration to avoid aggravating this condition.

Begin with three twenty-minute sessions per week, and build to five to seven one-hour sessions per week, which will help stabilize the body's blood pressure response. Add more exercise to facilitate additional weight loss goals.

BLOOD PRESSURE MEDICATION CONSIDERATIONS

Even with medication, a client with high blood pressure may not have his or her condition completely under control before arriving for an exercise session. To compensate, the health and

Copyright © Mometrix Media. You have been licensed one copy of this document for personal use only. Any other reproduction or redistribution is strictly prohibited. All rights reserved. This content is provided for test preparation purposes only and does not imply an endorsement by Mometrix of any particular political, scientific, or religious point of view.

fitness professional can use program design to support the client's specific needs. Some types of medication to be aware of are:

- **Beta-blockers** – Used for high blood pressure or arrhythmia.
- **Calcium-channel blockers** – Used for hypertension and angina.
- **Nitrates** – Used for hypertension and congestive heart failure
- **Diuretics** – Used for hypertension, congestive heart failure, and peripheral edema
- **Bronchodilators** – Used for asthma and other pulmonary diseases
- **Vasodilators** – Used for hypertension and congestive heart failure
- **Antidepressants** – Used for psychiatric and emotional disorders

For example, **circuit training** two or three times a week can be a very effective tool for hypertensive clients. The trainer should select eight to ten exercises and have the client perform up to three sets of twelve to twenty repetitions.

The client should not over-grip equipment and should avoid performing the Valsalva maneuver (forcing expiration when the airway is closed). It is also important for the client to breathe evenly throughout the training session.

COMORBIDITIES

Hypertension frequently occurs in **conjunction** with other health problems, such as diabetes and obesity. It is important for the client to have a thorough physical examination before beginning any training regimen and to discuss potential limitations with the physician.

When creating a training regimen for anyone who belongs to more than one special population, the health and fitness professional should take into account all of the special guidelines for **each** of the special populations.

A **hypertensive routine** should aim to burn 1,500 calories each week and build to burning 2,000 calories weekly. Burning calories in this range will facilitate weight loss and keep cardiovascular gains on target for supporting the hypertensive condition.

BETA BLOCKER USE

When a hypertensive client utilizes beta blocker medication, this can alter the way the **heart** responds to training. NASM's formula to determine maximum heart was not designed for clients on beta blockers so the health and fitness professional should use the **talk test** (which tests the client's ability to maintain a conversation while exercising) as an alternative.

If the client's blood pressure exceeds 200 over 115, he or she should not engage in exercise. A trainer should be aware of the policies at their fitness training facility.

TRAINING LENGTH AND INTENSITY

Use training modalities that keep the client **upright** (walking and the stationary bicycle are excellent) to avoid body positions in which the head is even with or lower than the heart. Start with three training sessions per week, and progress to daily workouts. Initially, workouts can last for half an hour, and can increase to an hour in duration. Administer the standard assessments and prescribe stretching according to the flexibility continuum, using upright or seated positioning.

The first two phases of the Optimum Performance Training (OPT) model and circuit training are ideal for this special population.

Copyright © Mometrix Media. You have been licensed one copy of this document for personal use only. Any other reproduction or redistribution is strictly prohibited. All rights reserved. This content is provided for test preparation purposes only and does not imply an endorsement by Mometrix of any particular political, scientific, or religious point of view.

CORONARY ARTERY DISEASE (CAD)

Heart disease is one of the leading causes of death in the United States. Up to 18 million Americans have received a diagnosis for CAD or another heart issue. CAD is a condition characterized by a narrowing of the arteries caused by a build-up of plaque, resulting in less oxygenated blood traveling to the heart. Eventually, CAD can lead to damage of the heart muscle and, ultimately, heart attack.

Stress, use of tobacco products, and diets high in LDL (bad) cholesterol contribute to **plaque accumulation**. It is important to determine if the client has heart-related health concerns and to understand the treatment the client's physician has recommended.

> **Review Video: Coronary Artery Disease**
> Visit mometrix.com/academy and enter code: 950720

RESPONSE TO EXERCISE

Because the client with CAD has special heart-related limitations, it is important to keep an accurate measure of the **upper levels of capability**, to ensure client safety. The health and fitness professional should not use the traditional methods of estimating heart rate maximum. The client's physician should determine the maximum heart rate.

Determining the proper **heart rate maximum** is important because a client with CAD may not have the usual symptoms of impending heart trouble, such as sharp chest pains If the client experiences chest pain frequently, they misinterpret serious chest pains and ignore them. Medication that reduces chest pains may mask these symptoms during exercise. Therefore, self-monitoring of heart rate is vital.

COMORBIDITIES

Clients with CAD often have other **related health problems**. These can include being overweight or obese, being diabetic, and having high blood pressure. It is important for the client to undergo a thorough physical examination and to discuss potential limitations with a physician before beginning any training regimen. CAD is related to a diet high in saturated fats and cholesterol. Refer the client to a **dietitian or licensed nutritionist** who can create a healthful and realistic diet plan to help support the training benefits he or she will derive from fitness training.

When creating a training regimen for anyone who belongs to more than one special population, the health and fitness professional should take into account all of the special **guidelines** for each of the special populations.

PEAK OXYGEN CAPACITY

When an individual suffers from CAD, the heart muscle is not functioning at capacity, which limits the maximum amount of available **oxygen**. The health and fitness professional should begin with low-impact workloads under the guidance of the client's physician or heart specialist. Cardiovascular work should stay below the maximum guidelines suggested by the physician.

Opt for short (approximately 20 minutes) workouts three times a week initially, and gradually work up to sixty-minute workouts five times a week. Closely observe how the client is tolerating the workload, and follow the client's capabilities. The goal is to build the client's heart muscle and overall cardiorespiratory conditioning while proceeding with care due to the client's condition and any medications he or she may be using.

Copyright © Mometrix Media. You have been licensed one copy of this document for personal use only. Any other reproduction or redistribution is strictly prohibited. All rights reserved. This content is provided for test preparation purposes only and does not imply an endorsement by Mometrix of any particular political, scientific, or religious point of view.

CHANGES WITH IMPROVEMENT

A client with **CAD** should set a goal of burning 1500 calories from exercise per week initially and work toward burning 2000 calories weekly. Given the client's condition and potential limitations, progress gradually and under the advisement of the client's physician to reach these levels.

After the client has trained steadily and tolerated the regimen without cardiac symptoms for three months, it is safe to introduce **weight training** to the workout routine. Select up to ten exercises based on the client's goals and capabilities, and have the client perform up to three sets of each exercise. NASM recommends prescribing between 10 and 20 repetitions. **Circuit training** is advisable to maximize the cardiovascular benefits of the routine.

PERCEIVED EXERTION SCALE

Clients with CAD will not be able to use age-related guidelines to determine maximum heart rate because their heart capacity and heart function are **lower** than the average client's, which means that their heart rate reading will likely also be lower in a given situation. Since this is an unpredictable measure, use other methods.

One way to make sure the client does not exceed the heart rate maximum recommended by his or her physician is by using the **perceived exertion scale**, a subjective test that allows the client to gauge his or her exertion level based on physical cues. The original scale ranged from 6 to 20. A 6 signified light exertion and a 20 indicated strenuous exertion. The old version was modified, and the new one runs from 0 (no exertion at all) through 11 (absolute top-level exertion).

Old version		New version	
6		0.0	No intensity
7	Very, very light	0.3	
8		0.5	Just noticeable
9	Very light	0.7	
10		1.0	
11	Fairly light	1.5	
12		2.0	Light
13	Somewhat hard	2.5	
14		3.0	
15	Hard	4.0	
16		5.0	Heavy
17	Very hard	6.0	
18		7.0	
19	Very, very hard	8.0	
20		9.0	
		10.0	Strongest intensity
		11.0	
			Highest possible

TRAINING LENGTH AND INTENSITY

NASM recommends beginning work on **large muscle areas** when commencing training with a person with CAD, including exercises that work the legs and the gluteals, such as walking, rowing, or riding a stationary bike.

Start slowly, and progress to longer and more frequent workouts. Three 20-minute workouts are ideal as a starting point. Gradually increase to hour-long workouts five times weekly, to accomplish

79

Copyright © Mometrix Media. You have been licensed one copy of this document for personal use only. Any other reproduction or redistribution is strictly prohibited. All rights reserved.
This content is provided for test preparation purposes only and does not imply an endorsement by Mometrix of any particular political, scientific, or religious point of view.

the client's overall goals. NASM recommends the talk test and the perceived exertion scale for measuring intensity; use a doctor's guidelines to dictate maximum heart rate.

Include warm-up and cool-down periods for these clients to help the heart prepare for exercise and to relax afterward. Flexibility exercises can follow NASM's flexibility continuum.

OSTEOPOROSIS

Osteoporosis is the name of a disease typified by a lower level of **bone density**, leading to brittle bones that are susceptible to breaking. Osteoporosis is an ailment more common in postmenopausal women. When the body of a postmenopausal woman reabsorbs bone cells instead of creating new bone cells, bone density decreases. Decreased bone density leaves extra space between bone cells, making the bones themselves more porous.

There is a precursor to osteoporosis called **osteopenia**, marked by a decrease in overall bone density that can ultimately develop into osteoporosis.

Osteoporosis can be very dangerous for **older women** who can suffer irreversible injury if a bone breaks in a fall. Commonly broken bones include the hip and the collarbone; many persons never fully recover from such an injury.

PREVENTING OSTEOPOROSIS

Many factors increase the risk of developing osteoporosis. Although men can develop osteoporosis, **postmenopausal females** are at greatest risk of developing the disease.

Increased bone density is a benefit of exercise (especially weight-bearing exercise). **Weight-bearing exercise** places stress on the body, causing the bones to remodel (add more cells) to compensate, resulting in denser bone tissue. Osteoporosis is associated with lower levels of activity because the bones of inactive individuals do not reap the benefits associated with weight-bearing exercise. Other lifestyle choices that can increase the risk of developing osteoporosis include smoking, drinking alcohol, and poor diet.

A health and fitness regimen can address risk factors by increasing physical activity and promote healthier lifestyle choices.

OSTEOPOROSIS VS. OSTEOPENIA

It is important for the health and fitness professional to know whether the client has osteopenia or osteoporosis to determine how intense his or her **weight training** can and should be.

A client with **osteopenia** can train at a higher intensity level than a client with **osteoporosis** can. Increased bone density is a benefit of high-intensity weight training, which can reverse the effects of osteopenia. The risk is that high-intensity exercise places strain on already weakened bones, which can lead to injury. The certified personal trainer must weigh the risks versus the rewards when prescribing high-intensity weight training to a client with osteopenia.

When working with older clients, training novices, or individuals who have had low levels of activity throughout life, it may be preferable to develop balance and coordination to avoid falls altogether, rather than focusing on increasing bone density through high-intensity weight training.

Copyright © Mometrix Media. You have been licensed one copy of this document for personal use only. Any other reproduction or redistribution is strictly prohibited. All rights reserved. This content is provided for test preparation purposes only and does not imply an endorsement by Mometrix of any particular political, scientific, or religious point of view.

TRAINING LENGTH AND INTENSITY

Since **falls** are a very dangerous possibility for people with osteoporosis, cardiorespiratory training that prevents falls is vital. Aquatic activities and supported cardiorespiratory training (recumbent bike or a treadmill with railing) are ideal.

Begin slowly, and gradually increase frequency and duration. Twice-weekly workouts of 20 minutes are a good starting point. Progress the client to complete 60-minute workouts five times weekly. More than one daily session may be useful, so consider breaking the session into shorter chunks of time.

For people with osteoporosis, weakened bones affect **core musculature**. The first two phases of the OPT model are very important to build muscle strength, coordination, and balance—all of which will help the client to avoid falling and suffering from injuries. Focus on hinging areas, such as the hips and thighs, and monitor for proper alignment and posture.

ARTHRITIC INDIVIDUALS

Arthritis is a condition that causes chronic pain and inflammation of the joints. There are many different types of arthritis; each causes pain in various joints that can seriously affect a person's ability to function on a daily basis, exercise, and engage in physical activity.

Osteoarthritis is a condition characterized by worn down cartilage, which causes the bones to wear on each other. **Rheumatoid arthritis** is a condition in which the body attacks its soft tissues, causing pain and stiffness in the joints, especially in the hands and feet. Rheumatoid arthritis is a chronic degenerative disease of the immune system.

It is important for the trainer to monitor how the training regimen affects the client's arthritic condition. The trainer should adjust intensity and frequency to avoid aggravating the condition.

OXYGEN CAPACITY

The chronic pain and loss of mobility associated with arthritic conditions can lead to decreased physical activity levels, which can lower the client's **oxygen capacity**.

Workouts can be broken into **shorter segments** performed throughout the day to avoid aggravating the condition. Separate sessions on different equipment can help provide adequate daily cardiorespiratory training while avoiding overstressing any one joint area. Separate sessions are preferable to single high-impact sessions.

Ideally, the client will train for a total of thirty minutes a day, five times each week.

ABILITY TO EXERCISE

Acute episodes may prevent clients with arthritic conditions from exercising as long or as frequently as desired. The trainer should not force the issue—if a client is having excessive pain and does not feel up to exercising, his or her condition should take precedence. Over time, the client may build up stamina and endurance and be able to exercise more frequently for longer stretches of time.

Consider **avoiding morning workouts** with clients that suffer from rheumatoid arthritis, because these individuals often have early morning pain and stiff joints. Clients may take medication to manage their arthritis pain; be sure that the client follows doctor recommendations for medication use, especially before training.

Copyright © Mometrix Media. You have been licensed one copy of this document for personal use only. Any other reproduction or redistribution is strictly prohibited. All rights reserved. This content is provided for test preparation purposes only and does not imply an endorsement by Mometrix of any particular political, scientific, or religious point of view.

COMORBIDITIES

An individual with arthritis often suffers from **other health problems**, such as having osteopenia or osteoporosis. It is extremely important for the client to have a thorough physical examination before beginning a training regimen and for him or her to discuss potential limitations with the physician.

When creating a training regimen for anyone who belongs to more than one special population, the health and fitness professional should take into account the special **guidelines** for each of the special populations.

Weight training is beneficial for clients with arthritis. The client should progress as much as their condition allows. Select as many as 10 exercises, and work through them up to three times a week. With arthritic clients, the health and fitness professional will want to use a minimal number of repetitions and work up to 12 or more repetitions.

TRAINING LENGTH AND INTENSITY

Select **low impact exercise modalities** for arthritic clients. These might include aquatic exercise activities or walking on a treadmill with handrails. The health and fitness professional should progress as the client's condition allows, working from three sessions a week up to five. Sessions should be shorter in length, up to a half an hour, and can be broken up into shorter sessions throughout the day. When beginning, five-minute sessions may be required; use the client's pain threshold as a guide.

Administer NASM's regular assessments, and use the flexibility continuum if the client can tolerate it.

During resistance training, prescribe six to twelve repetitions. Avoid having the client lift heavy weights, and make sure the client does not grip equipment too tightly.

CANCER

Cancer is the umbrella term for a variety of disorders characterized by mutated body cells that attack and damage the body. Even with aggressive treatment, cancer can be fatal. It is one of the top causes of death in the United States.

Improved treatments have dramatically improved the long-term prognosis of cancer patients. Research has shown that **exercise** can help maximize the benefits of treatment and keep a person healthy after treatment is over.

It is important for the health and fitness professional to understand that many of the **medications** used to treat cancer can have side effects that may affect the ability of the client to train. Clients may feel ill, be anemic, and have cardiac problems caused by cancer medicines. Cancer treatments fall along a wide spectrum and can have a broad range of effects.

FATIGUE

Cancer wreaks havoc on the body by attacking vital cells, organs, and body systems. The medications designed to treat it are also harsh. The cycle of medication **exhausts** patients physically and emotionally. It can be difficult to rally for a training session even when the session is part of the treatment routine.

Cardiovascular training should be **low impact** and at 76%-85% of the client's maximal heart rate, in Zone 2, 14-16 on the perceived exertion scale, three to five times a week. Breaking up the

82

Copyright © Mometrix Media. You have been licensed one copy of this document for personal use only. Any other reproduction or redistribution is strictly prohibited. All rights reserved. This content is provided for test preparation purposes only and does not imply an endorsement by Mometrix of any particular political, scientific, or religious point of view.

training cycle throughout the day, with a target of 30 minutes of exercise in aggregate might be the best option for a client with cancer. Walking, rowing, and using a stationary bicycle are all good options for clients in this population.

IMMUNE FUNCTION AND MUSCLE TISSUE

Cancer and its various treatments can affect the body in a multitude of ways. **Immune system function** will be lower due to the onslaught of medications used to kill cancer cells. Exercise can help increase immune function and improve the client's overall condition, adding an emotional boost.

Weight training is especially effective. Select up to 10 appropriate exercises for the client, and have them perform just one set (of around twelve repetitions) a few times per week, as their body allows. Weight training will help combat the atrophy of lean muscle that can result from cancer and its various treatments. Pay special attention to coordination and balance deficiencies that may occur because of the loss of muscle mass.

TRAINING LENGTH AND INTENSITY

Clients with cancer face physical challenges unique to their special population, including physical **weakness** and acute **fatigue** that may vary depending on the day or the stage of their treatment. It is best for the client to do several short cardiorespiratory sessions for a total of 30 minutes to avoid overtaxing the body. As the client's fitness level improves, build to training three to five times per week.

Walking and pedaling on a stationary bicycle are good exercise modalities. Administer the standard NASM assessments, and use the flexibility continuum if the client can tolerate it.

To introduce weight training, select 10 exercise and have the client can perform a low repetition set for each exercise.

PREGNANCY

A pregnant woman is carrying a fetus through a 40-week gestational period. The body of a pregnant woman is undergoing dramatic changes to support the growing baby and prepare for birth. Pregnancy causes **physiological changes** including hormonal shifts, loosening of ligaments and connective tissue, increased blood volume, and changes in gait and balance.

Exercise is beneficial to pregnant women. Exercise helps prepare a woman's body for the rigors of **childbirth**, and it promotes **recovery** once the baby is born. It is very important that the health and fitness professional understand the physical changes that women go through to keep mother and child safe.

EXERCISE LIMITATIONS

Although exercise is beneficial for a pregnant woman, there are **risk factors** for the trainer to consider. There are instances that necessitate restricting or suspending a pregnant woman's exercise program. Constant diligence is required to avoid potentially dangerous situations.

A physician should examine a pregnant woman if she experiences **bleeding** in the second or third trimesters. She should not resume exercising without clearance from a physician. Heavy vaginal bleeding during pregnancy is a serious warning sign.

A physician must address cervical issues such as **early dilation** (incompetent cervix) or **improper placenta placement**, and clear the client before she can continue a training program.

Copyright © Mometrix Media. You have been licensed one copy of this document for personal use only. Any other reproduction or redistribution is strictly prohibited. All rights reserved. This content is provided for test preparation purposes only and does not imply an endorsement by Mometrix of any particular political, scientific, or religious point of view.

High blood pressure during pregnancy and **gestational diabetes** (pregnancy hormones interfere with the body's ability to process and use glucose properly) are serious issues that require caution. While exercise can help with these conditions, it is essential that the pregnant woman consults with her physician first.

BLOOD VOLUME

When a woman is pregnant, her body produces up to a third more **blood** than it normally does. This is a protective mechanism that helps support the demands of the growing fetus while ensuring the woman has an extra blood supply should she bleed during delivery.

Despite having more blood volume, a pregnant woman may have a **lower oxygen capacity** for training sessions. She may also experience shortness of breath if the fetus presses upward on her lungs.

NASM advises prescribing **low-impact exercises** to compensate for these factors. Aquatic exercises or machine-based cardiorespiratory training work well. Avoid having the client lift heavy weights. The trainer should begin with three sessions per week and work up to five.

NUTRITIONAL NEEDS

A pregnant woman has **increased nutritional demands** because she is supporting another life. A pregnant woman needs an extra 300 calories each day to support the fetus and to build fat stores required for breast feeding once the child is born.

When a woman adds exercise to her activities, she must compensate for this added **caloric expenditure**. It is not advisable for pregnant women to engage in a calorie restricted diet in an attempt to lose weight during pregnancy. A pregnant woman should consume the proper amount of calories and focus on nutritionally sound food sources rich in calcium and other vitamins and minerals to support fetal growth.

The client should discuss her training routine with her physician and a dietitian to determine a positive **nutritional balance** that is appropriate for her particular gestational stage and fitness activity level.

RISK CATEGORIES

Some women have a higher risk of developing serious **complications** during pregnancy. Major risk factors include:

- Age (women older than 35 are at higher risk for complications and for having a baby with certain birth defects)
- History of pregnancy-related problems, such as miscarrying
- Endocrine problems (thyroid or insulin-related)
- Being obese or overweight

These risk factors potentially add more **stress** onto the already hardworking pregnant body. If the client has risk factors, be sure that she has discussed her training routine with a physician. It is not advisable to engage in weight training without a doctor's endorsement. Closely observe how the client tolerates training and track notable changes.

LOOSENING OF THE LIGAMENTS

During pregnancy, a woman's body releases hormones to help prepare for childbirth. These include hormones that **loosen ligaments**. Although the hormones help the pelvis accommodate the baby's

Copyright © Mometrix Media. You have been licensed one copy of this document for personal use only. Any other reproduction or redistribution is strictly prohibited. All rights reserved. This content is provided for test preparation purposes only and does not imply an endorsement by Mometrix of any particular political, scientific, or religious point of view.

head during birth, the hormones do not discriminate among ligaments, and there can be a loosening of all connective tissues throughout the body.

A pregnant woman with loosened ligaments may have impaired **balance** and less control of her **core musculature**. She may have dull or sharp pain in the groin and pelvic area from the loosened ligaments. Consider using supported cardiorespiratory training, such as aquatic activities and walking on a treadmill with handrails. Use extra caution with weight-bearing exercises.

TRAINING LENGTH AND INTENSITY

There are several important things to keep in mind when working with a pregnant client. Due to the added pressure that the fetus places on the circulatory system, avoid exercises that require the client to lie on her **back**. Core body temperature tends to run higher for pregnant women, so they are at increased risk of **overheating**, especially if they overexert.

Lower-intensity activities are ideal for pregnant women. The trainer should avoid **supine** exercises because the weight of the baby can tax the circulatory system by pressing on the vena cava, which can result in dizziness or fainting. Sessions should range from three to five per week, with weight training incorporated once or twice per week. As the pregnancy progresses, use only phase one of the Optimum Performance Training (OPT) model.

POSTPARTUM CONSIDERATIONS

Exercise and fitness training are excellent ways for a postpartum mother to combat **fatigue** and help her body return to its **pre-pregnancy shape**. However, the health and fitness trainer must be aware of certain aspects of postpartum training before commencing with someone who has recently given birth.

Physicians discourage women from entering into exercise routines for the first **six weeks** after childbirth. Giving birth is a strenuous task that requires downtime for the body to heal. The period immediately following birth is one of great transition as a woman adapts to caring for a baby, while her hormone levels shift dramatically, and she begins breastfeeding (if she chooses to). Complications during the birth, or a surgical delivery, can lengthen recovery time.

Many women are so keen on returning to their pre-pregnancy weight that they rush to work out before it is advisable. When beginning a training routine with a woman who has just had a baby, be sure her **doctor** has sanctioned the activity.

LUNG DISORDERS

Lung disease is an umbrella term for any chronic disorder of the pulmonary system. In many instances, it is caused by **smoking** cigarettes or having been exposed to **second-hand smoke**.

There are two types of lung disorders: obstructive disorders and restrictive disorders. **Obstructive lung disease** is characterized by lower lung function caused by an obstruction (often the body's fluids) of the free flow of gasses. Obstructive lung diseases include emphysema and asthma. In **restrictive lung disease** (e.g., pulmonary fibrosis), the lung tissue is damaged and does not function properly. Restrictive and obstructive disorders impair oxygen levels, reducing stamina and increasing feelings of fatigue and dizziness at low-impact levels.

PHYSICAL CHARACTERISTIC

People who have chronic lung disorders may show the **physical signs** of the wear the disease places on the body. Those with obstructive lung disease may be underweight and have lower

Copyright © Mometrix Media. You have been licensed one copy of this document for personal use only. Any other reproduction or redistribution is strictly prohibited. All rights reserved.
This content is provided for test preparation purposes only and does not imply an endorsement by Mometrix of any particular political, scientific, or religious point of view.

muscle tone. Those with restrictive lung disease may be overweight and have oversized rib cages, which are side effects of constantly working against their bodies to breathe.

Working with a person who has lung disease is similar to working with a regular adult. The health and fitness professional should anticipate **lower energy levels** and adjust accordingly. Additionally, the trainer should focus on **lower-body activities** to avoid stressing upper-body muscles that may be compensating for pulmonary issues. Incorporate adequate rest times into the workout to help the person recover from heightened activity.

COMORBIDITIES

Individuals with lung disease often have **comorbidities** that can affect a health and fitness training regimen. People with lung disease are often long-term smokers and may have heart issues as a result (over time, lack of oxygen to the heart muscle can enlarge the heart and cause vascular problems).

It is extremely important for a client with a history of lung disease to undergo a thorough **examination** with a physician before commencing physical training, which will help establish parameters for safely working around the lung disease issues. The physician may diagnose and treat concurrent health problems at this time.

OXYGEN CONVERSION

Lung disease lowers the level of **oxygen** converted for the body's use at any given time. Reduced oxygen stresses the cardiovascular system. Exercise, even low-impact activities, further taxes the pulmonary system.

The lower oxygen levels can cause shortness of breath even when the client is engaged in low-impact activities. A health and fitness professional should be aware of how to use a **pulse oximeter** to obtain oxygen levels during exercise to ensure they do not dip below acceptable levels. Record results to use as a point of comparison for future readings, to ascertain whether the client is tolerating certain activities, and to determine if there have been improvements in oxygen levels

PHYSICAL SHAPE

A person with lung disease is likely to be out of shape. Lung disease may limit activities and necessitate a sedentary lifestyle, lowering the client's **cardiovascular health level** and promoting **muscle atrophy**.

Regular exercise helps to reverse these limitations. Under the guidance and supervision of the client's physician, begin working out five times a week for twenty minutes, and build to 45-minute workouts five times a week. Observe how well the client tolerates the routine, and progress based on the client's comfort level. Consider breaking up training sessions throughout the day, to avoid overtaxing the pulmonary system with one long session. Schedule more rest time to allow recuperation between exercises or sets.

UPPER BODY TRAINING REGIMEN

Training a client with **pulmonary considerations** impacts exercise selection. A health and fitness professional should choose exercises that target lower-body muscle groups or lower-body activity, such as using a stationary bike, and avoid exercises that tax the upper-body muscles.

Because clients with lung disorders struggle to receive adequate supplies of oxygen, there is a tendency to overuse **secondary respiratory muscles** to compensate. These secondary breathing

Copyright © Mometrix Media. You have been licensed one copy of this document for personal use only. Any other reproduction or redistribution is strictly prohibited. All rights reserved. This content is provided for test preparation purposes only and does not imply an endorsement by Mometrix of any particular political, scientific, or religious point of view.

muscles stabilize the upper body during certain movements. Stressing the secondary muscles can lead to shortness of breath and fatigue.

MUSCLE MASS

When a person has a serious pulmonary disorder, it can result in **muscle loss** from lack of exercise. In extreme cases, severe atrophy occurs, resulting in the client dipping below the healthy BMI range (less than 18).

If the client is dangerously **underweight**, refer them to a nutritionist or dietitian. The dietitian should place the client on a healthy eating plan designed to return them to a healthy weight. Incorporate weight training into the routine to build muscle mass and to help the client put on weight.

OXYGEN TANK CONSIDERATION

Clients with lung disorders may need an **oxygen tank** to maintain their oxygen levels during exercise (and possibly in daily life). The use of an oxygen tank can present a unique challenge in health and fitness training activities.

It is vitally important for health and fitness professionals to understand that they may not interfere with or adjust the **levels of oxygen** that a client is taking. The use of an oxygen tank is a medical treatment that only a physician can administer and control. Use a pulse oximeter to keep track of oxygen saturation levels during exercise and record results for all of the client's sessions to track of notable patterns. Consult the physician if there is an issue with the client's oxygen levels.

TRAINING LENGTH AND INTENSITY

Low-impact activities are the best for those with impaired lung function, especially those that work the lower extremities and avoid taxing the upper body. Training sessions should be short, starting with 20 minutes and working up to 45 minutes, depending on the client's tolerance. Several shorter sessions in a day may be more attainable than one long session.

Only employ phase 1 of the Optimum Performance Training (OPT) model. Limit weight training intensity: two or three sessions of one set of repetitions per exercise a couple of times per week.

Have the client perform all of the NASM assessments, and employ the full spectrum of stretching activities.

Give the client adequate rest time between sets or exercises; they might require longer rest than the average client.

PERIPHERAL ARTERY DISEASE (PAD)/INTERMITTENT CLAUDICATION

Peripheral artery disease (PAD) is a disorder in which a person's arteries do not function properly due to a narrowing of the arteries or a failure of the artery closure flaps. PAD results in poor **lower-body circulation** that can affect training. **Intermittent claudication** is the umbrella term for the effects of PAD.

One of the main symptoms of PAD is **leg pain**, which can limit a client's ability to train. The health and fitness professional will have to proceed cautiously to determine if the pain is due to PAD or if it is associated with beginning a training regimen. It is important for the client to have a full physical examination before beginning the training regimen. The client should follow the doctor's recommendations as prescribed.

Copyright © Mometrix Media. You have been licensed one copy of this document for personal use only. Any other reproduction or redistribution is strictly prohibited. All rights reserved. This content is provided for test preparation purposes only and does not imply an endorsement by Mometrix of any particular political, scientific, or religious point of view.

Training sessions should proceed according to the client's tolerance for pain or discomfort. If pain continues during training sessions, have the client discuss the problem with a physician before continuing.

COMORBIDITIES

Clients with PAD are often prone to having other health problems, or **comorbidities**. Coronary artery disease and insulin-related disorders (e.g., type 1 and type 2 diabetes) are common comorbidities.

If a client has **coronary artery disease** in addition to PAD, the health and fitness professional should make sure the client stays within a set heart rate maximum. (This upper limit can be determined using a test in which the client walks to the extent his or her pain will permit.)

Acknowledge the client's pain and stop if necessary. Avoid encouraging the client to continue or ignore the pain. Leg pain acts as a good barometer, and it can help prevent overworking the heart.

Walking is ideal for those with PAD, and the client should walk for at least 10-minute sessions.

SMOKING

If a client with PAD **smokes**, they should be encouraged to quit. Encourage the client to discuss methods of quitting with his or her physician. Advise the client that smoking affects circulation and is very dangerous when combined with PAD. Smoking also lessens the client's ability to perform the exercise routine.

There are many options for quitting smoking to explore, including medications. Tread lightly when discussing this topic because many smokers have indulged for years and may be resistant to any perceived negative judgments of this habit.

If the client cannot or will not quit, try to get him or her to agree not to smoke for a period preceding health and fitness workouts. Ideally, the client will not smoke for 60 minutes before a session.

STAMINA

Clients with PAD are more likely to be significantly **out of shape** when compared to the average healthy adult due to leg pain, which limits their fitness activities. PAD itself can affect a person's ability to circulate oxygenated blood, leading to fatigue more quickly than with the average healthy adult.

NASM recommends **walking** for people with peripheral artery disease. Walking is tolerable for clients with PAD. If the client can handle increased intensity, increase the speed or change the incline of the treadmill.

If the client is having difficulty with pain, consider breaking up the workout into shorter chunks of time, aiming to have at least 10-minute segments at a time.

WEIGHT TRAINING

Although weight training has many benefits, it does not specifically improve the issues associated with PAD. The focus of the training program should be on **cardiorespiratory exercises**. Add a few supplementary weight-training sessions if the client is capable. Incorporate up to 10 exercises and include as many as three moderate repetition sets (around 10). Working in a circuit method maximizes the cardiorespiratory training.

Copyright © Mometrix Media. You have been licensed one copy of this document for personal use only. Any other reproduction or redistribution is strictly prohibited. All rights reserved. This content is provided for test preparation purposes only and does not imply an endorsement by Mometrix of any particular political, scientific, or religious point of view.

Allow adequate rest time and to progress to the extent that the client's pain will allow.

TRAINING LENGTH AND INTENSITY

Prescribe **aerobic exercises**, such as walking and using a stationary bicycle, for clients who have pulmonary issues. Start with three sessions per week and progress to five, as the client can tolerate. Sessions should be relatively short, beginning with 20 minutes and not exceeding 60 minutes. Consider breaking the session up over the day, aiming for shorter sessions of more than 10 minutes each.

NASM's normal range of assessments and the flexibility continuum are acceptable for use with this special population. Avoid SMR with this population.

Weight training is acceptable but focus primarily on aerobic exercise. These sessions should incorporate up to 10 exercises and can include up to three sets of a moderate number of repetitions (around 10). Working in a circuit method maximizes the cardiorespiratory training.

ABNORMAL CURVATURES OF THE SPINE

Lordosis is the excessive curvature of the lumbar spine, **kyphosis** is the excessive curvature of the thoracic spine (i.e., hunchback appearance), and **scoliosis** is a lateral S-shaped curve of the spine. If a client displays an abnormal curvature, they should avoid performing movements that put excessive stress on the spine. For example, stable, closed kinetic chain movements are more helpful than open kinetic chain movements.

> **Review Video: Exercise and Special Cases**
> Visit mometrix.com/academy and enter code: 690677

Copyright © Mometrix Media. You have been licensed one copy of this document for personal use only. Any other reproduction or redistribution is strictly prohibited. All rights reserved. This content is provided for test preparation purposes only and does not imply an endorsement by Mometrix of any particular political, scientific, or religious point of view.

Objective Assessment

FIVE TYPES OF OBJECTIVE INFORMATION

There are five types of objective information a CPT should gather about a client's general history during the fitness assessment:

1. Heart/lung (cardiorespiratory) efficiency
2. Dynamic movement (posture)
3. Physiology, including heart rate and blood pressure
4. Fat and muscle composition, which may include body mass index (BMI) and waist-to-hip ratios
5. Athletic ability or performance, which may include a bench press assessment and a squat assessment

Objective information is essential to a trainer because it establishes a client's **fitness capabilities** and a **starting point**. Objective information also provides a baseline to serve as a comparison for future results which can be used to determine client progress and program efficacy.

HEART RATE

To find the **radial pulse**, place two fingers on the inside of the wrist in line with (and just above) the thumb and count the number of beats. Place two fingers on the neck, just to the side of the larynx, right underneath the jawline to find the carotid pulse. When measuring the carotid pulse, apply minimal pressure to decrease the risk of reduced blood flow to the brain.

Although resting heart rates vary, men average 70 beats per minute, and women average about 75.

To find an estimated **maximum heart rate**, subtract the client's age from the number 220.

BLOOD PRESSURE

Blood pressure is a measurement of the force exerted by the blood on the interior walls of the arteries. Blood pressure emanates from the heart, which pumps the blood throughout the body.

A **stethoscope** (to listen to the pulse at the brachial artery) and a **sphygmomanometer** (cuffed around the arm, above the elbow) measure blood pressure.

To take a blood pressure reading, rapidly inflate the cuff to 20–30 mm Hg above the point at which the pulse at the wrist is undetectable. Release the pressure at 2 mm Hg per second.

The **systolic reading** is the top number of a blood pressure measurement. The systolic reading registers when the pressure releases and the sound of the pulse is audible. It reflects the maximum force produced by the cardiac cycle. The **diastolic reading** records when the sound of the pulse fades away. It appears on the bottom of the reading and reflects the lowest amount of pressure produced during the cardiac cycle.

A normal reading for an adult is between 120 to 130 mm Hg for the systolic number and from 80 to 85 mm Hg for the diastolic number.

Copyright © Mometrix Media. You have been licensed one copy of this document for personal use only. Any other reproduction or redistribution is strictly prohibited. All rights reserved. This content is provided for test preparation purposes only and does not imply an endorsement by Mometrix of any particular political, scientific, or religious point of view.

BODY FAT PERCENTAGE

USE OF SKIN CALIPERS

The **Durnin-Womersly formula** requires caliper measurements (in millimeters) at four sites on the body. To promote consistency when measuring skin folds, take all measurements on the right side of the body. The four measurement locations are:

1. A vertical fold of skin on the **anterior side of the biceps**, halfway between the elbow and shoulder
2. A vertical fold of skin on the **posterior side of the triceps**, halfway between the elbow and shoulder
3. An angled fold of skin (about 45 degrees) at the **subscapula**, about two centimeters below the inner angle of the scapula
4. An angled fold of skin (of about 45 degrees) just above the **iliac crest** and in line with the apex of the armpit

The Durnin-Womersly chart or formula provides the client's body fat percentage based on the sum of the four caliper measurements, the client's age, and the client's gender.

BMI AND WAIST-TO-HIP RATIO

To find a person's waist-to-hip ratio, measure the smallest part of his or her waist and largest part of his or her hips. Divide the waist measurement by the hip measurement. Women whose ratio exceeds 0.80 are at risk of having obesity-related health problems. The same is true for men with ratios greater than 0.95.

To reveal whether a person's weight is appropriate for his/her height, simply divide weight (in kilograms) by height (in meters squared). The likelihood of obesity-related health problems increases when BMI exceeds 25.

BMI is an acronym that stands for **body mass index**. BMI is inexact. It is a simple method to determine if a client's weight is proportional to their height. BMI indicates general health risks but is not a reliable indicator of fitness level. A muscular individual will have a high BMI without the health risks associated with a high BMI. A lean marathon runner may have a low BMI but is still fit. The Quetelet index is another name for BMI.

BMI does not measure body fat, but it is a useful assessment tool to determine whether a person's weight **correlates** in a healthy manner to his or her height. Use the following formula to determine BMI:

$$BMI = \frac{\text{Weight (in kilograms)}}{\text{Height}^2 \text{ (in meters}^2)}$$

Copyright © Mometrix Media. You have been licensed one copy of this document for personal use only. Any other reproduction or redistribution is strictly prohibited. All rights reserved. This content is provided for test preparation purposes only and does not imply an endorsement by Mometrix of any particular political, scientific, or religious point of view.

BMI = Classification
< 18.5 = Underweight
18.6– 21.99 = Acceptable
22.0– 24.99 = Acceptable
25.0– 29.99 = Overweight
30– 34.99 = Obese
35.0– 39.99 = Obesity II
≥ 40 = Obesity III

CARDIORESPIRATORY ASSESSMENTS

The three-minute step test and Rockport walk test are **cardiorespiratory assessments** that estimate a cardiovascular starting point (the trainer should modify the assessments according to the person's ability level).

The **three-minute step test** requires a client to step onto a 12-inch step 24 times per minute, for a total of three minutes (72 steps total). After a one-minute rest, measure the client's recovery pulse for 30 seconds. To determine the client's cardiovascular (CV) efficiency level, locate the client's heart rate in the table below.

Three-Minute Step Test Chart								
	Age	Very Poor	Poor	Below Average	Average	Above Average	Good	Excellent
Male	18-25	124-157	111-119	102-107	95-100	88-93	79-84	50-76
	26-36	126-161	114-121	104-110	96-102	88-94	79-85	51-76
	36-45	130-163	116-124	108-113	100-105	92-98	80-88	49-76
	46-55	131-159	121-126	113-119	103-111	95-101	87-93	56-82
	56-65	131-154	119-128	111-117	103-109	97-100	86-94	60-77
	65+	130-151	121-126	114-118	104-110	94-102	97-92	59-81
Female	18-25	135-169	122-131	113-120	104-110	96-102	85-93	52-81
	26-36	134-171	122-129	113-119	104-110	95-101	85-92	58-80
	36-45	137-169	124-132	115-120	107-112	100-104	89-96	51-84
	46-55	137-171	126-132	120-124	113-118	104-110	95-101	63-91
	56-65	141-174	129-135	119-127	113-118	106-111	97-103	60-92
	65+	135-155	128-133	123-126	116-121	104-111	96-101	70-92

Copyright © Mometrix Media. You have been licensed one copy of this document for personal use only. Any other reproduction or redistribution is strictly prohibited. All rights reserved. This content is provided for test preparation purposes only and does not imply an endorsement by Mometrix of any particular political, scientific, or religious point of view.

To perform the **Rockport walk test**, have a client walk for one mile on a treadmill as fast as possible without losing control. At the one-mile mark, quickly record the time and the client's heart rate. Determine the client's VO2 (maximal oxygen uptake) score, and locate it in the Rockport Chart.

Male: $V0_2max \left[\frac{ml}{kg \times min}\right] = 11.33 - (0.42 \times heart\ rate\ in\ beats\ per\ minute)$

Female: $V0_2max \left[\frac{ml}{kg \times min}\right] = 65.81 - (0.1847 \times heart\ rate\ in\ beats\ per\ minute)$

Rockport Walk Test Chart							
	Age	Very Poor	Poor	Fair	Average	Good	Very Good	Excellent
Male	18-20	<33	38-33	45-39	50-46	56-51	62-57	>63
	21-25	<32	37-32	44-38	50-45	55-51	62-56	>62
	26-30	<30	35-30	41-36	47-42	54-48	59-55	>59
Female	18-20	<28	32-28	37-33	42-38	47-43	53-48	>53
	21-25	<27	31-27	35-32	41-36	45-42	50-46	>50
	26-30	<26	30-26	34-31	39-35	43-40	48-44	>48

FUNCTIONAL BIOMECHANICS

Biomechanics is the study of the kinetic chain, including the movements it makes and the forces that act internally and externally upon it. Important elements of biomechanics include joint motion, muscle movement, force, and leverage.

Human movement is an interrelated cycle that encompasses the nervous system, the skeletal system, and the muscular system:

- The central nervous system (CNS) collects information from the internal and external environments
- The CNS processes this information
- Nerve impulses are passed to the muscles
- The muscles move the skeletal system

KINETIC CHAIN

The kinetic chain refers to the system of bones, joints, and muscles connected through the nervous system that allows the human body to move. The health and stability of the kinetic chain directly correlate to how well a person can move and how comfortable (or uncomfortable) the movement is.

Because the kinetic chain integrates several different body systems, each must be fully functional for **optimal movement**. If any component of the kinetic chain is impaired, the entire chain will function at a suboptimal level. The CPT should understand each aspect of the kinetic chain and address each particular client's needs in his or her training.

Copyright © Mometrix Media. You have been licensed one copy of this document for personal use only. Any other reproduction or redistribution is strictly prohibited. All rights reserved. This content is provided for test preparation purposes only and does not imply an endorsement by Mometrix of any particular political, scientific, or religious point of view.

PLANES OF MOTION

Optimal training techniques use exercises that span all three **planes of motion**. While many movements occur on a primary plane of motion, the movement does not occur solely in one plane. The best way to visualize these planes is by picturing a pane of clear glass passing through the body:

- **Frontal plane**—The pane of glass passes through the body from the head to the toes, bisecting the body into front and back halves.
- **Transverse plane**—The pane of glass passes through the center of the body at the abdomen, bisecting the body into top and bottom halves.
- **Sagittal plane**—The pane of glass passes through the body from the head to the toes, bisecting the body into right and left halves.

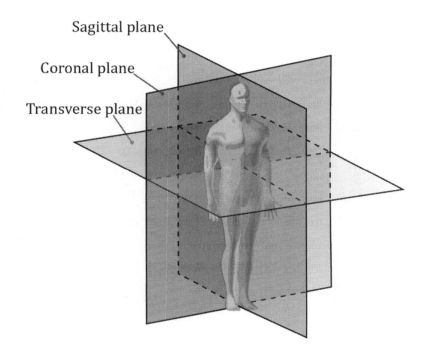

Plane	Bisector	Movement	Example
Coronal (frontal)	Front and back halves	Side to side	Side Lunge
Sagittal	Left and right sides	Front to back	Lunges
Transverse (horizontal)	Top and bottom halves	Rotation (twisting)	Golfing

TYPES OF MOTION

The body can make many different types of motion. Knowing the terminology can help define these movements quickly and efficiently.

- **Adduction**—movement in toward the center of the body.
- **Abduction**—movement away from the center of the body.
- **External rotation**—movement of a joint away from the center of the body.
- **Internal rotation**—movement of a joint in toward the center of the body.

94

Copyright © Mometrix Media. You have been licensed one copy of this document for personal use only. Any other reproduction or redistribution is strictly prohibited. All rights reserved.
This content is provided for test preparation purposes only and does not imply an endorsement by Mometrix of any particular political, scientific, or religious point of view.

- **Pronation**—rotation in of either the radioulnar joint or subtalar joint.
- **Supination**—rotation out of either the radioulnar joint or subtalar joint.
- **Extension**—the straightening out of a joint to increase its angle.
- **Flexion**—the bending of a joint to decrease its angle.

MUSCLE ACTIONS

There are three main muscle actions:

1. **Concentric muscle action**—A concentric contraction results in the shortening of the muscle—when the muscle exerts sufficient force to overcome the force acting on it.
2. **Eccentric muscle action**—An eccentric contraction results in the lengthening of the muscle—when the force acting on the muscle exceeds the force the muscle is exerting. Eccentric contractions are negative forces because the weight exerts a force on the muscle. The negative occurs when a muscle is returning to its original position or decelerating.
3. **Isometric muscle action**—The muscle is exerting a force equal to the force acting on it—when the muscle is stabilizing and balancing.

MUSCULAR FORCE

These terms help define the interrelation of the kinetic chain and musculoskeletal system and how force and energy come into play regarding human movement. Understanding these terms improves the health and fitness professional's ability to recognize and describe movement and impairments and improve the client's training regimen.

- **Muscular force**—describes the interplay between two objects that creates an acceleration or deceleration of one or both objects. Force has magnitude and direction.
- **Length-tension relationships**—the optimum length for a muscle at which it can achieve its top force. Hyperextension and underextension do not allow the muscle fibers to work at their peak capacity.
- **Force-velocity curve**—the ability of muscles to produce more force at a higher rate of speed.
- **Force-couple relationships**—the synergistic relationship between certain muscles and muscle groups that result in the movement of an entire joint. Force-couple relationships often involve a pushing and pulling action on the joint.

MOTOR CONTROL

Motor control is the body's ability to control the elements of the kinetic chain based on the information it collects from internal and external sources. It is important to train each element individually and in an integrated manner to manipulate motor behavior. Increased motor behavior improves motor control (the body's response to internal and external stimuli).

Muscle synergies (the way muscles interact and work together), **proprioception** (how the body interprets incoming sense information), and **sensorimotor integration** (the ability of the nervous system to process sense information and translate it into motion) affect motor control. Each of these components features the interaction of more than one body system. Increased efficiency of individual components positively affects overall motor control.

INTEGRATING MOTOR BEHAVIOR AND CONTROL

Motor learning hones motor behavior and motor control. **Motor learning** refers to the body's ability to hardwire movement into the body's neuromuscular pathways through repetition and practice.

Copyright © Mometrix Media. You have been licensed one copy of this document for personal use only. Any other reproduction or redistribution is strictly prohibited. All rights reserved. This content is provided for test preparation purposes only and does not imply an endorsement by Mometrix of any particular political, scientific, or religious point of view.

The body receives sensory feedback from internal and external sources. **Internal feedback** facilitates motor learning and refers to information that comes from the body via internal sensors. **External feedback** is information that comes from an outside source, such as watching oneself in the mirror or working with a trainer. Incorporating external feedback benefits motor learning.

Results and performance are components of external feedback. Knowledge of results focuses on the outcome of a given movement (e.g., a trainer indicating that the client completed the target number of repetitions). Knowledge of performance sheds light on the quality of the movement (e.g., a trainer observing that the client broke form during the set).

FLEXIBILITY CONCERNS

Postural distortions caused by muscle imbalances can lead to poor movement coordination and ultimately to injury. The human movement system responds to poor flexibility by seeking the path of least resistance, a process called **relative flexibility**. Relative flexibility causes the body to learn to improper movement patterns, and the inefficient movement becomes ingrained (think a shortcut cutting the corner of a ninety-degree angle).

A client's toes pointing out during a squat are an excellent illustration of relative flexibility. When an individual performs a squat correctly, the back is straight, the knees are in line with the toes, and the toes point straight ahead (or point out slightly). If a person has overactive calf muscles, he or she must compensate for a lack of flexion in the ankles by spacing the feet further apart and rotating them out. Poor flexibility (tight calves and poor dorsiflexion of the ankle) causes the body to move in an inefficient manner (toes turn out during a squat), over time the pattern becomes ingrained, and injury can occur.

BIOMECHANICAL ASSESSMENTS

Movement assessments provide information on postural distortions caused by overactive or underactive muscles. The following contains descriptions of assessments, including which muscles are causing the problems:

OVERHEAD SQUAT ASSESSMENT

The overhead squat assessment is an excellent tool to determine a client's balance, flexibility, core strength, and proprioceptive ability. It will provide evidence of postural distortions or abnormal movement patterns. To administer the test, have the client stand with feet shoulder width apart. With arms raised overhead and elbows fully extended, the client will perform a squat movement. The client will repeat this movement 5 times in a slow, controlled manner. Observe and record any postural distortions.

	Overactive muscles	Underactive muscles
Knees that buckle inward are evidence of:	Adductor complex Biceps femoris Tensor fascia lata (TFL) Vastus lateralis	Gluteus medius Gluteus maximus Vastus medialis oblique

Copyright © Mometrix Media. You have been licensed one copy of this document for personal use only. Any other reproduction or redistribution is strictly prohibited. All rights reserved. This content is provided for test preparation purposes only and does not imply an endorsement by Mometrix of any particular political, scientific, or religious point of view.

	Overactive muscles	Underactive muscles
An arch in the lower back at the lumbo-pelvic hip (LPH) complex is evidence of:	Hip flexor complex Erector spinae	Gluteus maximus Hamstrings All intrinsic core stabilizers (such as the transverse abdominus, multifidus, transversospinalis, internal obliques, and pelvic-floor muscles)

The overhead squat assessment is used by CPTs to determine a client's total body strength and dynamic flexibility.

SINGLE-LEG SQUAT ASSESSMENT

The single-leg squat assessment is an excellent tool to determine a client's balance, flexibility, core strength, and proprioceptive ability. It will provide evidence of postural distortions or abnormal movement patterns. To administer the test, have the client stand on one leg with hands on hips. Have the client perform a squat, but do not require them to go lower than their comfort level allows. For each leg, the client will repeat this movement 5 times in a slow, controlled manner. Observe and record any postural distortions.

	Overactive muscles	Underactive muscles
Knee moving inward is evidence of:	Adductor complex Biceps femoris Tensor fascia lata (TFL) Vastus lateralis	Gluteus medius Gluteus maximus Vastus medialis oblique

The single-leg squat assessment is used by CPTs to determine the stability of a person's hip joint, ankle flexibility, and center strength. It may not be appropriate for elderly or obese individuals, who may find it too difficult to perform.

PULLING ASSESSMENT

The pulling assessment is an excellent tool to determine how efficiently a client moves while pulling. The assessment will reveal postural distortions that affect pushing performance. Administer the test on a cable press machine. The client will stand in a split stance with the abdomen drawn in. Have the client perform 20 pulls (rows) in slow, controlled manner. Observe and record any postural distortions

	Overactive muscles	Underactive muscles
An arch in the lower back at the lumbo-pelvic-hip (LPH) complex is evidence of:	Hip flexor complex Erector spinae	All intrinsic core stabilizers (such as the transverse abdominus, multifidus, transversospinalis, internal obliques, and pelvic-floor muscles)
Pulling up of the shoulders is evidence of:	Levator scapulae Sternocleidomastoid Upper trapezius	Mid trapezius Lower trapezius
A head that juts forward is evidence of:	Levator scapulae Sternocleidomastoid Upper trapezius	Deep cervical flexors

Copyright © Mometrix Media. You have been licensed one copy of this document for personal use only. Any other reproduction or redistribution is strictly prohibited. All rights reserved.
This content is provided for test preparation purposes only and does not imply an endorsement by Mometrix of any particular political, scientific, or religious point of view.

PUSHING ASSESSMENT

The pushing assessment is an excellent tool to determine how efficiently a client moves while pushing. The assessment will reveal postural distortions that affect pushing performance. Administer the test on a cable press machine. The client will stand in a split stance with the abdomen drawn in. Have the client perform 20 presses in slow, controlled manner. Observe and record any postural distortions.

	Overactive muscles	Underactive muscles
An arch in the lower back at the lumbo-pelvic-hip (LPH) complex is evidence of:	Hip flexor complex Erector spinae	All intrinsic core stabilizers (such as the transverse abdominus, multifidus, transversospinalis, internal obliques, and pelvic-floor muscles)
Shoulder elevation is evidence of:	Levator scapulae Sternocleidomastoid Upper trapezius	Mid trapezius Lower trapezius
A head that juts forward is evidence of:	Levator scapulae Sternocleidomastoid Upper trapezius	Deep cervical flexors

STRENGTH ASSESSMENTS

DAVIES AND SHARK SKILL TESTS

To administer the Davies test, have the client begin in a push-up position with the hands positioned one yard (3 feet) apart. Instruct the client to move one hand rapidly to touch the other in an alternating fashion while maintaining a push-up position. Record the number of completed in a 15-second period. Repeat three times.

The Davies test evaluates upper-body strength, agility, and stability; it may not be appropriate for people with shoulder problems or injuries.

To give a **shark skill test**, create a 3X3 square grid on the floor numbered one through nine (masking tape works well). Start the client in the center box. Have the client stand on one leg with hands on hips. Have the client hop from the center box to square one, then to the center, then to square two, then to the center, and so on, until the client has hopped into each square. Switch legs and repeat the exercise. Do this four times, twice for each leg, recording the time for performance. Add one-tenth of a second for mistakes, such as the raised foot falling to the ground, stepping into an incorrect square, or the hands dropping.

The shark skill test evaluates lower-body strength and agility as well as a person's muscle coordination; it may not be appropriate for people with lower-extremity problems or injuries.

UPPER- AND LOWER-EXTREMITY STRENGTH ASSESSMENTS

The **bench press** is the standard upper-extremity strength test. The client should warm up with a comfortable weight and then rest for 60 seconds. Add 10 to 20 pounds, have the client do three to five repetitions and then rest for two minutes. Add another 10 to 20 pounds, and have the client do another three to five repetitions. Repeat this progression until the client cannot complete the repetitions. Use the NASM chart to establish the maximum level of intensity for one repetition.

The upper-extremity strength assessment evaluates the maximum level of intensity for one repetition; it is an advanced assessment and is not appropriate for novice clients.

Copyright © Mometrix Media. You have been licensed one copy of this document for personal use only. Any other reproduction or redistribution is strictly prohibited. All rights reserved. This content is provided for test preparation purposes only and does not imply an endorsement by Mometrix of any particular political, scientific, or religious point of view.

The **squat** is the standard lower-extremity strength test. Have the client warm up with a comfortable weight, and then rest for 60 seconds. Put on an additional 30 to 40 pounds, have the client do three to five repetitions, and then rest for two minutes. Add another 30 to 40 pounds, and have the client do another three to five repetitions. Repeat this progression until the client cannot complete the repetitions. Use the NASM chart to establish the maximum level of intensity for one repetition.

The lower-extremity strength assessment evaluates the maximum level of intensity for one squat repetition; it is an advanced assessment and is not appropriate for novice clients.

POSTURAL AND MOVEMENT DYSFUNCTIONS

DECONDITIONED STATES

A deconditioned state is a decline or lack of physical fitness characterized by low stamina, decreased strength, muscle distortions, lack of flexibility, and lack of overall muscle stability and agility. A deconditioned state is not merely being overweight; it describes a decline in physical ability, reduced musculoskeletal strength and capability, and limited cardiorespiratory capacity.

When **sedentary** individuals begin a typical training program, they substantially increase their risk for injury and overwork muscles. It is important to modify typical training programs to ensure that the client increases fitness in a safe and steady manner.

Proprioception is the information transmitted through the body via the senses. A training program that incorporates movements throughout the different planes of motion and through all muscle actions and contractions increases the level of neuromuscular communication throughout the body results in a proprioceptively enriched environment that forces the body to increase its ability to stabilize and balance. The use of a stability ball when doing any number of training exercises creates a proprioceptively challenging environment.

POSTURAL DISTORTION

Muscle imbalances cause **postural distortions**. Imbalanced muscles alter joint mechanics, decrease functionality, and lead to injury. There are three common postural distortions. **Pronated feet and knees** that rotate inward characterize pronation distortion syndrome. An **arch in the lower back** characterizes lower crossed syndrome. **Rounded shoulders and a protruding head** characterize

Copyright © Mometrix Media. You have been licensed one copy of this document for personal use only. Any other reproduction or redistribution is strictly prohibited. All rights reserved. This content is provided for test preparation purposes only and does not imply an endorsement by Mometrix of any particular political, scientific, or religious point of view.

upper crossed syndrome. Each distortion has a number of shortened and lengthened muscles, increased and decreased joint function, and possible injuries.

	Pronation Distortion	Lower Crossed	Upper Crossed
Shortened Muscle	Gastrocnemius, Soleus, Peroneals, Adductors, Iliotibial head, Hip flexor complex, and Biceps femoris (short head)	Gastrocnemius, Soleus, Hip flexor complex, Adductors, Latissimus dorsi, and Erector spinae	Upper trapezius, Levator scapulae, Sternocleidomastoid, Scalenes, Latissimus dorsi, Teres major, and Pectoralis major/minor
Lengthened Muscle	Anterior tibialis, Posterior tibialis, Vastus medialis, Gluteus medius, Gluteus maximus, and Hip external rotators	Anterior tibialis, Posterior tibialis, Gluteus maximus, Gluteus medius, Transversus abdominis, and Internal Oblique	Deep cervical flexors, Serratus anterior, Rhomboids, Mid-trapezius, Lower trapezius, Teres minor, and Infraspinatus
Increased	Knee adduction, Knee internal rotation, Foot pronation, and Foot external rotation	Lumbar extension	Cervical extension and Scapular protraction/elevation
Decreased	Ankle dorsiflexion and Ankle inversion	Hip extension	Shoulder extension and Shoulder external rotation
Possible Injuries	Plantar fasciitis, Posterior tibialis tendonitis (shin splints), Patellar tendonitis, and Low-back pain	Hamstring complex strain, Anterior knee pain, and Low-back pain	Headaches, Biceps tendonitis, Rotator cuff impingement, and Thoracic outlet syndrome

CUMULATIVE INJURY CYCLE

Postural distortions coupled with repetitive motions (even those associated with daily living) result in the kinetic chain not working properly. Poor kinetic chain function affects muscles and connective tissue and confuses the body, which reacts as though these distortions are injuries that require repair. The body will try to fix the problem, resulting in the **cumulative injury cycle**.

This cycle includes the following:

- Muscle imbalance
- Injury to connective tissue
- Inflammation of the injured tissues
- Increased muscle tension and spasms
- Knots in the soft tissue (also called adhesions)
- Altered reciprocal inhibition
- Increased synergistic dominance (when synergist muscles overcompensate for a weak prime mover muscle)
- Altered joint motion

Copyright © Mometrix Media. You have been licensed one copy of this document for personal use only. Any other reproduction or redistribution is strictly prohibited. All rights reserved. This content is provided for test preparation purposes only and does not imply an endorsement by Mometrix of any particular political, scientific, or religious point of view.

Failure to identify and correct this cycle can lead to permanent changes in the body. **Davis's law** states that soft tissue will form or rebuild itself along the lines of any stress, which may run contrary to the natural lines of the muscle, which will inhibit optimal muscle function.

GENERAL ADAPTATION SYNDROME

Hans Selye identified general adaptation syndrome, which states that the body, specifically the kinetic chain, attempts to stay in equilibrium at all times by counteracting any stresses placed on it. There are three types of responses to various stresses:

1. **Alarm reaction**— The body's initial when it is stressed. In this stage, the body responds to unfamiliar stressors with a variety of physiological changes.
2. **Resistance development**—The body has become familiar with the stress mechanism and has begun to develop specific responses to handle and adapt to the stress.
3. **Exhaustion**—Exhaustion occurs when the body has been overwhelmed by a stress mechanism and can no longer cope. Exhaustion can result in damage to the body ranging from emotional wear to physical damage such as stress fractures or muscle tears.

MUSCLE IMBALANCE

Muscle imbalance is sub-optimal lengthening or shortening of the muscle around a joint, which causes improper movement. Distortion of the **kinetic chain** (e.g., an improper length-tension relationship or force-couple relationship) can lead to a muscle imbalance. When there is a muscle imbalance, instead of muscles working together synergistically as they are designed to, one muscle or muscle group works harder than it should, resulting in tightness (overactive muscle), while another muscle or muscle group works less than it should, resulting in weakness (underactive muscle). This cycle can lead to postural distortion and injury.

Muscle distortions are caused by:

- Repetitive motions
- Emotional stress/heightened emotional states
- Stress on the body that affects the kinetic chain
- Cumulative trauma
- Poor nervous system and muscle communication/coordination
- Lack of strength
- Improper physical training

ALTERED RECIPROCAL INHIBITION

Altered reciprocal inhibition refers to an overactive or tight agonist muscle that stifles the proper function of its partner antagonist muscle—as with a tight hip flexor reciprocally inhibiting its antagonist muscle, the hip extensor.

Synergistic dominance occurs when synergist muscles overcompensate for a weak prime mover muscle. This process is the body's backup system, allowing the muscles adjacent to the prime mover to pick up the slack when it is not functioning optimally. Synergistic dominance and altered reciprocal inhibition result in muscle imbalances that affect the kinetic chain.

Arthrokinetic dysfunction refers to alterations to the kinetic chain that change the way joints work. It can also lead to muscle imbalances and other postural distortions.

Copyright © Mometrix Media. You have been licensed one copy of this document for personal use only. Any other reproduction or redistribution is strictly prohibited. All rights reserved. This content is provided for test preparation purposes only and does not imply an endorsement by Mometrix of any particular political, scientific, or religious point of view.

NEUROMUSCULAR EFFICIENCY

Neuromuscular efficiency refers to the body's ability to communicate correct movements properly in response to various stimuli to the nervous system and the muscular system. The result of neuromuscular efficiency is a full, stable kinetic chain.

Muscle spindles and **Golgi tendon organs**, key sensory organs that affect neuromuscular control and efficiency, react to changes in the muscles and have protective mechanisms that react to extreme movement. Muscle spindles detect changes in the length of a muscle and also how quickly the muscle stretches. Golgi tendon organs can sense tension alterations in a muscle and how quickly this tension changes.

Flexibility training challenges these organs in a positive way, increasing neuromuscular efficiency. Autogenic inhibition is an automatic response from the receptors that tells the body to relax the muscle and allow it to stretch. It occurs after a body part receives sufficient stimulation (e.g., a 30-second stretch).

REASSESSMENT

Fitness assessments serve a variety of important functions including determining a baseline fitness level, promoting safety, focusing training, facilitating goal setting, and motivation. As the client progresses through a fitness program, it is important to conduct **reassessments** at regular intervals to measure progress, revise goals, and increase motivation. Ideally, personal trainers should conduct reassessments **monthly**. Re-testing body composition is an excellent way to measure how well the client has progressed. Positive results will motivate the client, and provide evidence that the program is successful. The certified personal trainer should conduct the same fitness tests that were administered initially, but they should be progressed to reflect any improvements in the client's fitness levels.

To effectively meet a client's needs, the concept of reassessment needs to be expanded. A variety of factors should be considered in reassessment, including evolving fitness goals, injury, and lifestyle change. If a client's goals change, their exercise program will need to change as well (SAID Principle). Consistently discussing a client's **goals** allows the trainer to design a program aimed at meeting the evolving goals. If a client is **injured** or recovering from an injury, it is important to reassess the client to determine a safe course of action. **Lifestyle changes** are an overlooked factor that must be re-assessed. A fitness program must fit within a client's lifestyle. As the lifestyle changes, the program may need to change as well. A certified professional trainer should consider the needs of their client first. Consistently reassessing client needs and ensuring that the program is aligned with client needs is an excellent way to achieve this objective.

Copyright © Mometrix Media. You have been licensed one copy of this document for personal use only. Any other reproduction or redistribution is strictly prohibited. All rights reserved.
This content is provided for test preparation purposes only and does not imply an endorsement by Mometrix of any particular political, scientific, or religious point of view.

Program Design and Implementation

In the past, health and fitness professionals worked in a less systematic manner with clients, merely giving clients exercises and tasks that had worked in the past for the trainer or the trainer's other clients. The program was developed by NASM to tailor fitness regimens for **specific clients**, factoring in **special considerations** (such as medical concerns and specific postural distortions or compensations) that might affect the training.

By including these considerations in the program design, following the OPT model, and prescribing the correct exercises (stabilization, strength, or power), the health and fitness professional can work with the client to develop the most efficient regimen, maximize gains, and minimize potential injury. NASM trainers use program design to monitor and tweak acute variables in the regimen, giving it a scientific basis.

ELEMENTS OF PROGRAM DESIGN

According to NASM, program design refers to a systematic process for achieving clients' fitness goals. NASM refers to it as a purposeful system, which includes the following:

- **OPT model**—the foundation of all NASM training. OPT stands for Optimum Performance Training, consisting of a three-pronged approach. These three steps are 1) stability, 2) strength, and 3) power, and they must be applied in that order.
- **Phases of training**—within the OPT model there are further levels of training. A health and fitness professional must know the five phases for proper program design:
  - Phase 1—stabilization endurance training
  - Phase 2—strength endurance training
  - Phase 3—hypertrophy training
  - Phase 4—maximum strength training
  - Phase 5—power training
- **Acute variables**— essential program elements that determine how the body is stressed and influence how the body adapts.
- **Application**—how the acute variables are prescribed, including what exercises will be chosen, how they are to be performed, and how often they are performed.

OPT METHOD

The OPT method of program design gives a certified health and fitness professional a proven method of designing and tracking the activities and improvements of an individual client. Because specific **templates** clearly outline the program, trainers can follow parameters systematically instead of guessing what might work for a particular client.

Having this knowledge gives a CPT a distinct edge over other trainers because a CPT using the OPT method can design a program for nearly any client with any of a wide range of fitness goals, from losing weight to increasing athletic ability.

The OPT program design facilitates troubleshooting a fitness regimen by clearly defining the acute variables in the program, making it easy to alter the program for better results.

Copyright © Mometrix Media. You have been licensed one copy of this document for personal use only. Any other reproduction or redistribution is strictly prohibited. All rights reserved.
This content is provided for test preparation purposes only and does not imply an endorsement by Mometrix of any particular political, scientific, or religious point of view.

ACUTE VARIABLES

An acute variable is an important aspect of exercise training that can be changed to fit a particular client's needs.

NASM details several acute variables:

- **Number of repetitions**—a single complete movement
- **Number of sets**—a single round of exercises
- **Intensity of training**—how hard a person exerts him- or herself during the performance of an exercise compared to their maximum effort level
- **Tempo of training**—how quickly repetitions are performed
- **Length of rest time**—downtime between sets of exercise
- **Volume of training**—the amount of work (training) performed over an extended time
- **Frequency of training**—how often a client is training
- **Duration of training**—how long a given training session lasts, and also how long a client stays in one phase of training
- **Types of exercises**—the specific exercises being chosen for the client

NASM PROGRAM DESIGN CONTINUUM

NASM's program design continuum gives some general guidelines on how to set some of the acute variables involved with fitness training.

For the **muscular endurance/stabilization level**, the continuum recommends that the client perform one to three sets of each exercise for 12 to 25 repetitions. The intensity level is from 50 to 70 percent of the client's one-repetition maximum percent, and rest should not exceed 90 seconds between sets.

For the **hypertrophy level**, the continuum recommends that the client perform three to five sets of each exercise for 6 to 12 repetitions. The intensity level is from 75 to 85 percent of the client's one-repetition maximum percent, and rest should not exceed 60 seconds between sets.

For the **maximal strength level**, the continuum recommends that the client perform four to six sets of each exercise for 1 to 5 repetitions. The intensity level is from 85 to 100 percent of the client's one-repetition maximum percent, and the client rest 3-5 minutes between sets.

For the **power level**, the continuum recommends that the client perform three to six sets of each exercise for 1 to 10 repetitions. The intensity level is from 30 to 45 percent of the client's one-repetition maximum percent, and the client rest 3-5 minutes between sets.

Phase	Repetitions	Sets	Intensity Level	Rest
Muscular endurance/stabilization	12–20	1–3	50–70% of 1RM	0–90 s
Hypertrophy	6–12	3–5	75–85% of 1RM	0–60 s
Maximal strength	1–5	4–6	85–100% of 1RM	3–5 min
Power	1–10	3–6	30–45% of 1RM	3–5 min

ACUTE VARIABLE: REPETITIONS

A repetition is the completion of one motion of a given exercise. It is called a repetition because it is repeated several times in a row to perform a complete set in an exercise routine. This usually entails using a muscle or group of muscles to **contract** and **retract**.

Copyright © Mometrix Media. You have been licensed one copy of this document for personal use only. Any other reproduction or redistribution is strictly prohibited. All rights reserved. This content is provided for test preparation purposes only and does not imply an endorsement by Mometrix of any particular political, scientific, or religious point of view.

The number of repetitions is an important acute variable because it can be tailored to a client's ability level and his or her ultimate fitness goals. More repetitions at a lower weight result in increased muscle endurance, while fewer repetitions at a higher weight can lead to increased muscle mass (hypertrophy) and the ability to move faster with more-explosive power.

Trainers can use the **repetition continuum guidelines** to determine the appropriate number of repetitions to prescribe. While it is best for a client to start with more repetitions at a lower weight and increase to power-building (fewer repetitions at a high weight), it is important to alternate high repetitions and low repetitions once the power level has been achieved to avoid injury.

IDEAL NUMBER OF REPETITIONS

NASM's repetition continuum gives general guidelines for the appropriate number of repetitions for each of the **three main OPT levels**: stabilization, strength, and power.

For **stability exercises**, a larger number of repetitions with a lighter weight load are recommended. Somewhere between twelve and 25 repetitions per set is the standard. The higher end of the spectrum leads to gains in muscle endurance.

For **strength exercises**, a moderate number of repetitions with a moderate weight load are recommended. Somewhere between one and twelve repetitions per set is the standard. The higher end of the spectrum leads to maximum muscle growth.

For **power exercises**, a lower number of repetitions with a higher weight load are recommended. Somewhere between one and ten repetitions per set is standard.

ACUTE VARIABLE: NUMBER OF SETS

A set is a completion of one group of repetitions of a given exercise performed consecutively. Many other acute variables come into play when determining how many sets of one exercise a client should perform. These include the number of repetitions for the client's level of training and the total number of exercises the client will perform in a given workout.

There is a direct relationship between how many individual **repetitions** and how many **sets** should go together. As the number repetitions increase, the number of sets decrease, and vice versa. Exercise intensity is also a factor. For example, if a client is working with heavier weights, fewer repetitions with more sets will be used.

The number of sets also correlates to the client's particular **fitness goals**. When a client is working toward muscle endurance and increased muscle mass, fewer sets consisting of higher repetitions at a lower weight load are best. When a client is working toward strength and power gains, more sets consisting of fewer repetitions at a higher weight load are best.

RECOMMENDED NUMBER OF SETS

The number of sets directly correlates with the number of repetitions and the intensity of the exercise, which often translates into how much weight is used. The number of sets corresponds with the specific fitness gains a client is working toward.

To increase **stability and muscle endurance**, NASM recommends up to three high repetition sets (12 to 25) with light weights.

To increase **muscle mass**, NASM recommends three or four medium repetition sets (8 to 12) with moderately heavy weight.

Copyright © Mometrix Media. You have been licensed one copy of this document for personal use only. Any other reproduction or redistribution is strictly prohibited. All rights reserved. This content is provided for test preparation purposes only and does not imply an endorsement by Mometrix of any particular political, scientific, or religious point of view.

To increase **strength**, NASM recommends four to six low repetition sets (up to five) with maximum weight.

To increase **power**, NASM recommends three to six low repetition sets (up to 10) with weights that weigh 10% of the client's weight.

ACUTE VARIABLE: TRAINING INTENSITY

One way to alter a fitness regimen is by changing the level of **intensity** at which a workout, or its individual component exercises, is performed. Intensity is a scale that reflects how hard an individual is working compared to how hard that particular client can work. Intensity can be **subjective** (e.g., talk test, perceived exertion) or **objective** (e.g., % of 1 rep max, oxygen consumption). Intensity can be measured by the amount of weight lifted and also by how much oxygen the individual is consuming (cardiorespiratory intensity).

The intensity of the work must be balanced with other acute variables, namely the number of **repetitions** and the number of **sets** of an exercise. These two variables will be programmed according to the client's capabilities and goals, and then intensity will be factored in according to the intensity continuum.

Other acute variables can affect the level of intensity. For example, taking little rest between exercises makes the subsequent exercises more intense.

RECOMMENDED INTENSITY

The intensity of the exercise, number of repetitions, and number of sets are directly related and correlate with the specific fitness gains a client is working toward. The following describes NASM's intensity continuum:

- To increase **stability and muscle endurance**, NASM recommends working at from 40 to 70 percent of the client's maximum weight capability, or one-repetition maximum.
- To increase **muscle mass**, NASM recommends working at from 71 to 85 percent of the client's maximum weight capability.
- To increase **strength**, NASM recommends working at from 86 to 100 percent of the client's maximum weight capability.
- To increase **power**, NASM recommends working at less than 50 percent of the client's maximum weight capability or just one-tenth of total body weight if using medicine balls.

ACUTE VARIABLE: REPETITION TEMPO

Tempo refers to how fast one exercise is performed in a set, which can be changed to meet the capabilities and goals of a particular client. NASM uses its **repetition tempo spectrum** as a general guideline for how fast exercises should be performed for the three levels of the OPT model.

For **stabilization-level exercises**, the tempo should remain slow and controlled. This increases stability and endurance while allowing the trainer to observe for postural distortions or compensations. The slower tempo also gives added stimuli to the nervous system and the connective tissue to prepare for more-advanced motion later.

For **strength-level exercises**, the tempo should be somewhere in the middle.

For **power-level exercises**, the tempo should be as quick as can be managed while keeping all muscles under control.

Copyright © Mometrix Media. You have been licensed one copy of this document for personal use only. Any other reproduction or redistribution is strictly prohibited. All rights reserved. This content is provided for test preparation purposes only and does not imply an endorsement by Mometrix of any particular political, scientific, or religious point of view.

ACUTE VARIABLE: REST TIME

Rest time refers to the amount of downtime taken between sets of exercise during a training session. Rest time can affect the energy the body uses during the workout and can be calibrated to meet the capability and goals of a particular client.

To achieve maximum power, for example, it may be necessary to take an extended rest time between sets or exercises to give the body a chance to recover. For muscle building, however, shorter rest times (no more than a minute and a half) are advisable.

Stability-level exercises use oxygen and glucose energy stores.

Strength-level exercises use adenosine triphosphate/creatine phosphate (ATP/CP) and glucose energy stores.

Power-level exercises use ATP/CP energy stores.

RECOMMENDED REST PERIOD

NASM has a **rest interval continuum** that details general guidelines for each main level of the OPT model. Rest time gives the body a chance to recover and restore the energy source needed to continue.

Stability-level exercises should be performed with a relatively short rest period between exercises and sets, which may be anywhere from no time to a minute and a half.

Strength-level exercises can be performed in relatively quick succession (less than a minute of rest) or with a longer rest (up to five minutes).

Power-level exercises should have a lengthier rest period—anywhere from three to five minutes.

Keep in mind that within 30 seconds after a set, adenosine triphosphate/creatine phosphate (ATP/CP) levels will be back up to about half capacity; at a minute, there is almost 90-percent recovery. It can take up to three minutes for these levels to be back at full capacity.

ACUTE VARIABLE: TRAINING VOLUME

Training volume refers to the amount of physical activity performed within a defined time frame. It is important for a health and fitness professional to plot this component out in advance when designing a program to ensure accurate monitoring and to avoid overtraining the client.

The amount a client can train depends on many **factors**, some unrelated to fitness goals or limitations. Lifestyle considerations such as work, family obligations, age, and overall current fitness level will in part dictate how much the client can train. The phase of training will also play a role in determining training volume.

Training volume and the acute variable of **intensity** are closely related; when there is a higher level of one variable, there must be a lower level of the other and vice versa. A person cannot train hard continually because of the risk of overtraining.

RECOMMENDED TRAINING VOLUME

NASM has a volume continuum that details general guidelines for each main level of the OPT model. The **training volume** used will give the desired cellular changes and nervous system changes sought for on each level. Volume is determined by multiplying the number of sets by the number of repetitions.

Copyright © Mometrix Media. You have been licensed one copy of this document for personal use only. Any other reproduction or redistribution is strictly prohibited. All rights reserved.
This content is provided for test preparation purposes only and does not imply an endorsement by Mometrix of any particular political, scientific, or religious point of view.

Stability-level exercises should be performed with a large number of sets and a high number of repetitions. The total number of exercises, determined by multiplying the number of sets with the number of repetitions, should be between 36 and 75.

Strength-level exercises should be more moderate, with the total number of exercises to be determined by multiplying the number of sets by the number of repetitions—between 8 and 36.

Power-level exercises should be at a lower volume, with between 6 and 30 total exercises.

ACUTE VARIABLE: TRAINING FREQUENCY

Training frequency refers to how much training is done within a given period.

The amount a client can train depends on many factors, some unrelated to fitness goals or limitations. Lifestyle considerations such as work, family obligations, age, and overall current fitness level will in part dictate how much the client can train. The phase of training will also play a role in determining training volume.

The underlying **goals** of the client will be the primary factor in determining training frequency. For general fitness goals, a total-body workout two to three times a week may be adequate. If the client is a competitive athlete, however, body-part-specific workouts may occur up to six times a week.

TRAINING VOLUME ADAPTATIONS

The manner in which **training volume** and **intensity levels** are paired can have a great effect on the end results of training.

Benefits of a **high-volume, low-intensity** workout schedule can include:

- An increase in the amount of muscle cross-section
- An increase in base metabolism
- An increase in lean muscle tissue
- Better blood results
- Lower overall body fat

Benefits of a **low-volume, high-intensity** workout schedule can include:

- An increase in how much force a person can deliver
- An increase in nervous-system communication
- An increase in muscle response time

ACUTE VARIABLE: TRAINING DURATION

Training duration can refer to two separate things when it comes to fitness training:

1. Specific to the NASM system of training, training duration can refer to how long a client stays in one of the **OPT phases**. Depending on factors such as beginning fitness level, whether injuries occurred, client motivation, and ultimate goals, a client will usually work in a given phase for a month to two months.
2. Training duration can also refer to the actual amount of time from the beginning to the end of a **workout session**. This is important because training sessions that are too long (exceeding an hour or hour and a half) can result in fatigue and body changes that will negatively impact training.

Copyright © Mometrix Media. You have been licensed one copy of this document for personal use only. Any other reproduction or redistribution is strictly prohibited. All rights reserved. This content is provided for test preparation purposes only and does not imply an endorsement by Mometrix of any particular political, scientific, or religious point of view.

ACUTE VARIABLE: CHOOSING EXERCISES

Choosing exercises in a training routine may seem simple, but it can have a profound effect on the outcome of the program. For example, the choice of exercises will be drastically different for a client who wants to exercise to improve his or her overall health versus those chosen for a person who is a competitive bodybuilder or Olympic athlete.

There are three basic **categories of exercises** (single-joint, multijoint, and total-body), which NASM sorts based on how much of the body is used to perform the exercise. A fitness assessment must be completed, the client's physical history taken, and goals identified to configure this part of the program design for the client. Then the trainer can determine where on the OPT chart to begin the client and which exercises to select from that phase/level of training.

TYPICAL PROGRAM DESIGN

In a typical program design, in which the goal is overall fitness, the following will give a good idea of how to balance several acute variables:

The overall routine should last from about forty-five minutes to an hour, including a warm-up and a cool-down of ten minutes each. Up to seven exercises should be chosen for the client. Three sets of each of the exercises are done, with a dozen repetitions performed for each set. The tempo is moderate, with up to four seconds to perform the main motion, two beats to release, and only one beat before starting the next repetition.

PRINCIPLE OF SPECIFICITY

The principle of specificity states that the body will specifically adapt to particular stresses it is exposed to. This means that the exercises selected should be picked with an eye toward the client's specific goals. For example, if the client is an Olympic bodybuilder, upper-body and arm strength will be the focus for that client.

NASM's exercise selection continuum gives some general guidelines as to what types of exercises work best for different training levels. For the **stability level**, any of the three main types of exercise (single-joint, multijoint, and total-body) should be performed in a slow, deliberate manner in an unstable environment. For the **strength level** of the OPT model, the same three exercises can be used. For the **power level** of the OPT model, total-body exercises are ideal, performed in a fast, forceful motion.

EXAMPLES OF EXERCISES

For stability and strength, any of the three general types of exercises are effective. For power, total-body exercises work best.

Exercises appropriate for the **stability level** include stability-ball exercises such as the crunch, chest press, or hamstring roll as well as one-leg balance exercises, such as any of NASM's step-up exercises.

Exercises appropriate for the **strength level** include squats, presses, and cable rowing.

Exercises appropriate for the **power level** include medicine-ball exercises, such as overhead throws or presses. Jumps are also effective; tuck jumps and box jumps are ideal.

Keep the **progression continuum** in mind as a client progresses: the floor, then a sports beam, and then a foam roll or balance disc is an ideal progression of instability to help develop neuromuscular coordination.

Copyright © Mometrix Media. You have been licensed one copy of this document for personal use only. Any other reproduction or redistribution is strictly prohibited. All rights reserved. This content is provided for test preparation purposes only and does not imply an endorsement by Mometrix of any particular political, scientific, or religious point of view.

TRAINING PLANS

Periodization is the basic concept behind NASM's approach to program design. It is a systematic way of changing up a client's training routine, so his or her body does not plateau but continues to make progress toward fitness goals while avoiding overtraining and overuse injuries.

A **training plan** is a comprehensive written plan that considers all acute variables, the client's assessments, and the client's goals. It views the overall approach to training from long- and short-term perspectives.

An **annual plan**, as the name implies, details the training plan for an entire year, giving the trainer a good overview while giving the client a visual tool to help him or her see exactly how the OPT plan will be implemented.

PERIODIZATION

Periodization of a training regimen is highly effective because it prevents the negative impact of general adaptation syndrome. Specifically, it assures that the same routine is not employed to the point that the body learns to cope, thus reducing ongoing training gains.

Periodization can improve **fitness gains** while reducing **injuries** from repetitive actions. It also gives variations in training type, volume, and frequency, opening the door for more interesting and thoughtful programs that keep the client motivated and involved.

Even though periodization has been shown to work well, many health and fitness professionals do not use it in their training programs. This means that the training programs they use are repetitive, which can result in overuse injuries and a plateau effect in training. These results, in turn, can lead to low client motivation and cessation of regular training.

SCIENTIFIC RESEARCH

Many scientific studies support the idea that an integrated training program, such as the one adopted by NASM, is the ideal way to train clients to maximize gains while minimizing injuries and other barriers.

B. Tan found that changing the variables in a men's resistance-training program encouraged ongoing adaptations while minimizing injury.

W.J. Kraemer and N.A. Ratamess determined that well-thought-out strength-training programs using periodized training methods not only increased physiological benefits but also showed better performance improvements when compared to nonperiodized regimens.

M.R. Rhea discovered that daily tweaking of a training program's variables resulted in better improvements than changing them monthly. This researcher also found that ongoing increases in training volume, coinciding with decreases in intensity, were the best method for increasing the endurance of muscles.

PERIODIZATION APPROACH AND OPT SYSTEM

For each period of training, which can also be referred to as a phase, there is a corresponding OPT level. The period model includes a **preliminary phase** (or anatomic adaptation), a **muscle-building phase** (or hypertrophy adaptation), a **power-building phase** (or a maximum-strength adaptation), and an **explosive-power phase**.

The levels of OPT are stabilization, strength, and power.

Copyright © Mometrix Media. You have been licensed one copy of this document for personal use only. Any other reproduction or redistribution is strictly prohibited. All rights reserved. This content is provided for test preparation purposes only and does not imply an endorsement by Mometrix of any particular political, scientific, or religious point of view.

NASM likens the OPT model to a staircase. Each of the OPT levels is a series of steps, with each step representing a specific phase of that level. Periodization consists of taking the client not just straight up the staircase, but up and down in a particular design according to his or her specific goals and capabilities. This is done to avoid **general adaptation syndrome**, in which not varying from the same routine leads to a plateau effect.

PHASES OF TRAINING

The **stabilization level** of the OPT model has one phase of training: stabilization endurance, which focuses on stabilizing the kinetic chain, core musculature, and connective tissue and increasing cardiorespiratory and muscular endurance.

The **strength level** of the OPT model has three phases: strength endurance, hypertrophy, and maximal strength. During the strength-endurance phase, the client's strength and stabilization endurance will improve, and they may experience hypertrophy. The hypertrophy phase focuses on building muscle mass. The maximal-strength phase focuses on increasing the load placed on the body's tissues. Per NASM, the strength period has several goals. The first goal of the strength period is to improve the core's ability to stabilize the pelvis and spine when they are exposed to heavy weight. To promote weight loss or hypertrophy, the strength phase aims to increase the load-bearing capabilities of muscles, tendons, ligaments, and joints by increasing the training volume and increasing metabolic demand. To promote maximal strength, the body increases motor unit recruitment, frequency of motor unit recruitment, and motor unit synchronization. .

The **power level** of the OPT model has one phase: the power phase, in which the main goal is to increase the speed at which maximum force can be produced.

STABILIZATION LEVEL

Stabilization training is the cornerstone of the OPT model; without stabilizing the kinetic chain and working through body compensations and postural distortions, more-advanced training will be reduced in effectiveness and may result in injury.

Stabilization specifically seeks to correct muscle imbalances, repair kinetic-chain distortions, increase cardiorespiratory and muscular endurance, and ease connective tissues (such as ligaments and tendons) into increased activity.

Stabilization training focuses on increasing **proprioceptive demand**. Performing low-intensity exercises for high repetitions in a controlled, unstable environment increases proprioceptive demand. This is particularly useful for out-of-shape, overweight, or older clients. The level of instability is increased to progress the client.

The stabilization level has one phase: **stabilization endurance**.

STRENGTH LEVEL

Strength training is an important part of the OPT model, helping clients progress and achieve a variety of different fitness goals. It follows stabilization training, which helps prepare the body for more-advanced strength training.

The main goal of the strength level is to accomplish several **adaptations in strength**, including increased endurance, building muscle mass, and increasing how much weight or stress the body can handle. This is accomplished through increasing the number of exercises, performing more repetitions, adding sets, and increasing intensity.

Copyright © Mometrix Media. You have been licensed one copy of this document for personal use only. Any other reproduction or redistribution is strictly prohibited. All rights reserved.
This content is provided for test preparation purposes only and does not imply an endorsement by Mometrix of any particular political, scientific, or religious point of view.

The strength level is essential for anyone who wants to increase metabolism, promote higher bone density, and build muscle mass.

The strength level has three different phases of training. These are called **strength endurance**, **hypertrophy**, and **maximal strength**.

POWER LEVEL

Power or reactive training is not a necessary component of NASM's OPT model and is reserved for athletes or clients with advanced fitness goals. Power training focuses on increasing a client's ability to produce explosive but controlled movement at a high rate of speed (velocity).

The CPT increases the amount of weight client must move, the speed at which this load is moved, or both to progress a client through the power phase of training. Light and heavy loads must be used at high rates of speed to maximize power training. This helps the body increase its level of neuromuscular efficiency, or the method in which the brain communicates with the nervous system and muscles.

The power level has one phase of training: the **power phase**.

PHASES

PHASE 1: STABILIZATION ENDURANCE PHASE

The first phase of training in the OPT model is stabilization endurance training. This is the ideal phase for clients who are new to training, overweight, or elderly. While beneficial for all clients, those who wish to increase their base fitness level and lose body fat will gain the most benefit from this phase.

The primary goals of this phase are increasing stability, muscular endurance, neuromuscular efficiency of the core musculature and improving intermuscular and intramuscular coordination. It is important that training occur in a slow, systematic manner to prepare connective tissue, which has fewer blood vessels and less vascular support than muscle tissue and thus adapts more slowly to increased activity.

Accomplishing these goals reduces injury risk, maintains client interest, and sustains motivation.

PHASE 2: STRENGTH ENDURANCE PHASE

The second phase of training is strength endurance training. This phase eases the client into strength training from the stabilization phase of training, continuing to work on core stabilization while increasing endurance and beginning to build muscle mass. This is accomplished by performing a superset consisting of a stable exercise with a similar one that maximizes proprioceptive instability (controlled instability). This results in a high volume of work, which helps the client progress through the phase.

For a client who is seeking to improve base-level fitness or reduce body fat, acute variables can be tweaked when phase 1 has been completed. If the client seeks to improve lean muscle mass and overall athletic ability, repetitions should be reduced, and intensity should be increased, over a four-week period.

PHASE 3: HYPERTROPHY PHASE

The third phase of training is the hypertrophy phase. This phase focuses on increasing muscle mass, accomplished by performing a high volume of work with short rest intervals. This encourages the body to compensate through the growth of additional muscle tissue.

112

Copyright © Mometrix Media. You have been licensed one copy of this document for personal use only. Any other reproduction or redistribution is strictly prohibited. All rights reserved. This content is provided for test preparation purposes only and does not imply an endorsement by Mometrix of any particular political, scientific, or religious point of view.

The hypertrophy phase is initiated after the client has successfully progressed through phases 1 and 2. To increase lean muscle mass and overall athletic ability, increase intensity and training volume while reducing repetitions over a period of four weeks. Upon completion of phase 3, the client should be progressed (to phases 4 and 5) or cycled backward through phases 1 and 2. This creates the periodization scheme that helps reduce injury and maximize gains.

PHASE 4: MAXIMAL STRENGTH TRAINING PHASE

The fourth phase of training is the maximal strength phase, which increases the ability of the body to cope with a higher weight or workload. This is done by focusing on the neuromuscular system—improving communication between the brain, nervous system, and muscles—and how fast the muscles can respond to stimulus. This phase can also act as an excellent foundation for power training.

The focus of the phase should be on placing an increased load on the body to achieve these goals. The client should remain in this phase of training for approximately four weeks before progressing to phase 5 or cycling back to stabilization exercises (phases 1 and 2).

PHASE 5: POWER TRAINING PHASE

The fifth phase of training is the power training phase. The main focus of power training is to increase the rate of force production by pairing a strength exercise with a power exercise. Basic strength exercises are performed at the upper range of intensity (from 80 to 100 percent), while speed drills are performed as quickly as can be managed while maintaining proper form, but at a lower intensity level (from 30 to 50 percent). This creates two combinations that increase power: 1) high weight with intense, powerful movement, and 2) low weight with rapid movement.

Progression by tweaking acute variables should only be performed if the client has successfully progressed through the other levels of OPT.

A client should remain in this phase for approximately four weeks and then return to stabilization exercises (phases 1 and 2).

TIME FRAME

The **stabilization level** of the OPT model consists of one phase: strength endurance. This phase of training should be performed for approximately four weeks to allow for an increase in stabilization of the core musculature as well as muscular endurance.

The **strength level** of the OPT model consists of three phases: strength endurance, hypertrophy, and maximal strength. Each of these phases should be performed for four weeks.

The **power level** of the OPT model consists of one phase: power. This phase is optional, as only a client attempting to increase explosive power would benefit from power level training. For clients who are bodybuilders, athletes, or have specific power goals, this phase should be progressed through for approximately four weeks before returning to earlier phases of training.

FITNESS GOALS

REDUCING OVERALL PERCENTAGE OF BODY FAT

To reduce the overall percentage of body fat, a client must use more energy than he or she consumes. The best way to accomplish this is through a two-pronged approach: **increasing calorie-burning muscle** while **increasing calorie expenditure** through cardiorespiratory exercise.

Copyright © Mometrix Media. You have been licensed one copy of this document for personal use only. Any other reproduction or redistribution is strictly prohibited. All rights reserved. This content is provided for test preparation purposes only and does not imply an endorsement by Mometrix of any particular political, scientific, or religious point of view.

Because the client does not wish to maximize muscle mass or build explosive power, he or she will only need to be progressed through the first two phases of training: stabilization and strength endurance. The client should spend approximately four weeks in each phase, and then go back and forth between the two phases.

A sample plan could include working out three days a week for a month in phase one, and then three days a week for a month in the second phase. These workouts include cardiorespiratory exercises and weight training, with simple flexibility exercises done daily, if desired.

INCREASING THE AMOUNT OF LEAN MUSCLE MASS

To increase lean muscle mass, a client must take in more energy than he or she burns to gain weight in the form of muscle. The best way to accomplish this is by ingesting more **high-quality proteins** while increasing the overall **volume of training**, which will help the body create additional muscle fibers.

Because hypertrophy is the main goal, the client will need to be progressed through three, and possibly four phases of the OPT model: stabilization endurance, strength endurance, hypertrophy, and maximal strength.

The client begins by spending approximately four weeks in phase 1 to prepare for the more-advanced training. After four weeks in phase 2, the client can progress to a month in phase 3. Depending on the client's goals, he or she can revert to phase 2 and cycle through phases 2 and 3 or work up to phase 4 and then cycle between phases 2, 3, and 4.

IMPROVING OVERALL BASE LEVEL OF FITNESS

Improving base level fitness requires making strides in several different areas, including endurance, strength, and power. This will require the client to be systematically taken through **four phases** of the OPT model, including stabilization endurance, strength endurance, maximal strength, and power: The first two phases and the final phase are the most vital for this particular goal. Because the client is not seeking to build maximum muscle mass, phase 4 (hypertrophy) can be bypassed.

The client should be taken through each of these phases (1, 2, 3, and 5) for approximately four weeks each, after which phases 1, 2, and 5 should be systematically alternated in a manner known as **undulating periodization**. In undulating periodization, the three phases are alternated weekly instead of monthly.

FITNESS TECHNOLOGY

The fitness industry is ever evolving, and there are a variety of products on the market. It is important for a prospective trainer to have knowledge of the **available products** to guide their client and answer any questions that may arise and to incorporate them where beneficial. Among the more common products on the market are heart rate monitors, performance trackers, calorie counters. Each of these products has pros and cons. Ultimately, these tools should be used as **supplements**, and are not suitable as replacements for certified professionals. No device can provide the level of expertise that a qualified trainer can.

Measuring **heart rate** is an effective method for determining exercise intensity. Traditionally, this has been measured using a watch with a second hand (or a stopwatch) with fingers placed on the wrist or neck. While this is sufficient for most individuals, it is not accurate, and it is difficult to administer while exercise is in progress. There are a variety of heart rate monitors that claim to provide accurate readings in real time. Recorded measurements can be displayed on the device itself, or on a linked device such as a cell phone. Monitors can be worn across the chest or around

Copyright © Mometrix Media. You have been licensed one copy of this document for personal use only. Any other reproduction or redistribution is strictly prohibited. All rights reserved. This content is provided for test preparation purposes only and does not imply an endorsement by Mometrix of any particular political, scientific, or religious point of view.

the wrist. The sensors around the chest tend to provide a more accurate measurement, but they are less convenient. Wrist sensors tend to be more comfortable and convenient, but they are typically less accurate. Accurate heart rate measurements are effective for athletes with advanced fitness goals, and they are especially useful for interval training.

For clients with a **weight-loss goal**, it is important to track how many calories they are burning. There are many products on the market that measure calories burned, most of which use a heart rate sensor and an algorithm that considers height, weight, and age among other factors. While knowledge of calories burned can be useful, it is important to remember that these devices are not always accurate. Inaccurate calorie counts can be problematic if they cause a client to overeat on the mistaken belief that they can consume additional calories.

Performance trackers typically measure physical activity such as steps taken. Performance trackers are good at tracking how active the client is and can provide motivation to stay active through alerts, goals, and other tools. Although not based on science, the idea of taking 10,000 steps a day has gained popularity, and performance trackers are helpful in assisting the client in reaching this goal. Inaccuracy plagues performance trackers, and it is important to alert clients to this fact.

Copyright © Mometrix Media. You have been licensed one copy of this document for personal use only. Any other reproduction or redistribution is strictly prohibited. All rights reserved. This content is provided for test preparation purposes only and does not imply an endorsement by Mometrix of any particular political, scientific, or religious point of view.

OPT Model

To address the wide spectrum of fitness needs the modern training client demands, NASM uses an integrated, progressive system that incorporates many different training techniques, such as:

- Cardiovascular training
- Stretching
- Coordination
- Strength or resistance training
- Balance

These methods are introduced in a progressive manner, using the **OPT method**, which takes a client through levels of training commensurate with ability and improved performance.

By using a wide variety of training techniques introduced on a gradient, a client will experience **physiological benefits** (e.g., higher bone density and enhanced lung function), **physical benefits** (e.g., weight loss), and **increased ability to perform** (e.g., enhanced flexibility and increased strength).

The OPT model consists of three distinct levels: stabilization, strength, and power. The client should complete a phase before progressing to the next phase.

1. The **Stabilization phase** assesses and addresses specific weaknesses in a client and improves those areas first. This stage improves neuromuscular communication and lays a foundation for more-intense training. It includes phase 1: stabilization endurance training.
2. The **Strength phase** strengthens prime movers and sustains the stabilization endurance that the first phase developed. It includes three phases: strength endurance training (Phase 2), hypertrophy training (Phase 3), and maximal strength training (Phase 4). Strength endurance training increases strength and endurance. Hypertrophy training increases the size of muscle fibers. Maximum strength training increases the body's ability to handle heavy loads.
3. The **Power phase** increases the body's ability to create maximum force as rapidly as possible. It includes phase 5: power training.

STABILIZATION LEVEL

The stabilization level is the first phase of the OPT model. The primary goals of this phase are:

- Enhanced muscle suppleness and flexibility
- Increased joint balance
- Increased muscle endurance
- Improved posture
- Improved neurological/muscular coordination

The **training strategies** employed for this phase of stabilization training include:

- Using light weights at a high number of repetitions
- Using increased proprioception (such as with a balance ball) to challenge the nervous system and increase balance and neuromuscular efficiency
- Using flexibility training to address problem areas

Because each level of NASM's Optimum Performance Training (OPT) model has different overall goals, the trainer should select exercises that promote the goals of the phase.

Copyright © Mometrix Media. You have been licensed one copy of this document for personal use only. Any other reproduction or redistribution is strictly prohibited. All rights reserved. This content is provided for test preparation purposes only and does not imply an endorsement by Mometrix of any particular political, scientific, or religious point of view.

Some ideal exercises for the stabilization level include:

- **Floor prone cobra**—performed by lying on the flat on the floor on the stomach with the arms down by the sides. Keeping the core muscles firm, lift the torso off the ground for two seconds.
- **Quadruped arm/opposite leg raise**—performed by lying on the stomach flat on the floor with the arms over the head. Keeping the core muscles firm, raise the opposite leg and arm off the ground, hold for 2 to 4 seconds, and then switch sides.
- **Prone iso-abs** (also known as a plank)—performed by resting on the forearms (with the elbows at ninety degrees) while holding the body in a rigid position using the core muscles.

STRENGTH LEVEL

The strength level includes phases 2, 3, and 4 of the OPT model. The primary goals of *phase 2* (strength endurance training) include:

- Increased lean muscle
- Increased joint balance
- Increased endurance
- Enhanced strength in prime mover muscles

The **training strategies** employed for this phase of strength training include:

- Using midrange weights and a comparable number of repetitions
- Using flexibility training for activity
- Using superset training (a dual combination of exercises with no rest time in between)

The primary goal of **Phase 3** (hypertrophy) is:

- Increasing muscle size

The **training strategies** employed for this phase of strength training include:

- Using flexibility training for activity
- Many sets of heavy weights for a midlevel number of repetitions (fewer than 10)

Phase 4 is an optional phase of the OPT model. The primary goals of *phase 4* (maximum strength training) are as follows:

- Increase top level of force
- Enhance neuromuscular efficiency

The **training strategies** employed for this phase of strength training include:

- Using flexibility training for activity
- Heavy weights at a low number of repetitions (fewer than 5)

Copyright © Mometrix Media. You have been licensed one copy of this document for personal use only. Any other reproduction or redistribution is strictly prohibited. All rights reserved.
This content is provided for test preparation purposes only and does not imply an endorsement by Mometrix of any particular political, scientific, or religious point of view.

POWER LEVEL

The power level is the fifth phase of the OPT model. This level is optional and requires successful completion of the stabilization and strength levels.

The primary goals of **Phase 5** (power training) are as follows:

- Increased strength of prime mover muscles
- Increased strength at higher speeds
- Increased ability to produce higher levels of force
- Enhanced neuromuscular efficiency

The **training strategies** employed for this phase of strength training include:

- Using flexibility training for high levels of activity and movement
- Performing repetitions as quickly as safely viable
- Using superset training (a dual combination of exercises with no down time in between)

IMPLEMENTATION

After conducting a full range of fitness assessments, the trainer will design an effective fitness program using the OPT program template. The **NASM Program Template** is a special form that helps the trainer design an integrated program that improves all functional abilities (e.g., flexibility, stability, strength, balance, speed, agility, and quickness). The template contains sections to prescribe exercises in the primary training modalities (e.g., warm-up, core/balance/plyometric training, speed, agility and quickness (SAQ) drills, resistance training, and cool-down). The template also has sections for sets, repetitions, tempo, and rest. Each training session should follow the OPT template to ensure adequate progression.

Copyright © Mometrix Media. You have been licensed one copy of this document for personal use only. Any other reproduction or redistribution is strictly prohibited. All rights reserved. This content is provided for test preparation purposes only and does not imply an endorsement by Mometrix of any particular political, scientific, or religious point of view.

Flexibility Training

Flexibility training prevents various neuromuscular injuries and corrects movement inefficiencies by including exercises and activities that improve a person's ability to move efficiently. Efficient movement is especially important in a training program to increase joint and muscle mobility for physical activity and to counteract postural imbalances caused by over- and underactive muscles that have lost their flexibility, which inhibits the proper movement of surrounding muscles and muscle groups.

Flexibility Training Benefits

Increase	Decrease	Maintain
Joint range of motion	Excessive tension	Normal muscle length
Neuromuscular efficiency	Joint stress	
Muscle function		
Flexibility of musculotendinous junction		

IMPORTANT TERMS

Flexibility refers to the level to which a person can extend the muscles and soft tissues, allowing the joint a full range of motion.

Dynamic functional flexibility refers to the cycle of flexibility that comes from extensibility, which allows for a wide range of motion of a joint, coupled with optimal communication between the nervous system and the muscles.

Extensibility refers to the general ability of muscles and soft body tissues to stretch or be elastic.

Dynamic range of motion refers to the body's ability to move freely in all planes of movement coupled with the ability of the nervous system to handle and control these movements in a safe manner.

Flexibility training seeks to improve all of these different areas to increase flexibility and extensibility to accommodate a better range of motion. This improves posture and blood flow and can decrease the incidence of injury.

> **Review Video: Important Terms**
> Visit mometrix.com/academy and enter code: 909745

MULTIPLANAR FLEXIBILITY

Multiplanar flexibility refers to the flexibility that allows the joints, muscles, and soft tissue to extend into all planes of motion.

For the **biceps femoris**, multiplanar flexibility refers to:

- Frontal plane—flexibility needed for optimal adduction of the hip
- Transverse plane—flexibility needed for optimal rotation of the knee and hip
- Sagittal plane—flexibility needed for optimal hip flexion and extension of the knee

Copyright © Mometrix Media. You have been licensed one copy of this document for personal use only. Any other reproduction or redistribution is strictly prohibited. All rights reserved.
This content is provided for test preparation purposes only and does not imply an endorsement by Mometrix of any particular political, scientific, or religious point of view.

For the **gastrocnemius**, multiplanar flexibility refers to:

- Frontal plane—flexibility needed for optimal calcaneus inversion
- Transverse plane—flexibility needed for optimal rotation of the femur
- Sagittal plane—flexibility needed for optimal ankle dorsiflexion

For the **latissimus dorsi**, multiplanar flexibility refers to:

- Frontal plane—flexibility needed for optimal shoulder abduction
- Transverse plane—flexibility needed for optimal rotation of the humerus
- Sagittal plane—flexibility needed for optimal shoulder flexion

SCIENTIFIC APPROACH

Flexibility training, one important component of a balanced, integrated training program, has many benefits:

- Improving extensibility of muscles and soft tissue
- Alleviating stress on joints
- Improving overall range of motion
- Lowering muscle tension
- Correcting or maintaining proper muscle lengths

Pattern overload is damage resulting from repeatedly doing the same activity, repeatedly stressing the muscles and joints. The activities associated with daily living and repeatedly using the same physical training routine cause pattern overload. Incorporating flexibility training into an integrated training program can help introduce varied forms of movement into a person's routine and combat muscle imbalances that may result from pattern overload.

FLEXIBILITY CONTINUUM

Much like the different stages in the OPT model; flexibility training should likewise take a progressive approach. By introducing different types of flexibility training over time, a CPT can help a client maximize results, minimize injuries, and avoid potential pitfalls of repetitive training routines.

The following are the three stages of flexibility training:

1. **Corrective flexibility** addresses basic problems such as joint range of motion, muscle imbalance, joint mobility issues, using self-myofascial release, and static stretching techniques.
2. **Active flexibility** improves extensibility of soft tissues and neuromuscular system communication through reciprocal inhibition, using stretches that work the muscles and joints through a range of motion. It employs self-myofascial release and active-isolated stretching.
3. **Functional flexibility** takes active flexibility to the next level, using stretching techniques that move through all planes of motion to simulate correct muscle use and stretching. It employs self-myofascial release and dynamic stretching.

SELF-MYOFASCIAL RELEASE

Self-myofascial release refers to a system of stretching that targets the communication system between the nervous system and the body's **fascia**, or connective tissue. A foam roller applies light

Copyright © Mometrix Media. You have been licensed one copy of this document for personal use only. Any other reproduction or redistribution is strictly prohibited. All rights reserved. This content is provided for test preparation purposes only and does not imply an endorsement by Mometrix of any particular political, scientific, or religious point of view.

pressure to the muscle where there is an adhesion. The goal is to stimulate the Golgi tendon organs, induce autogenic inhibition, and allow the body to release the knot.

Self-myofascial release requires an application of pressure to the knot for at least 30 seconds, giving the Golgi tendon organs time to react to the pressure. Self-myofascial release is an element of all stages of flexibility training to help reprogram the soft tissue of the body.

LATISSIMUS DORSI AND PIRIFORMIS MUSCLES

To perform self-myofascial release on the **latissimus dorsi**, the client lies on his or her side on the floor. The foam roll rests along the upper torso close to the armpit, with the lower arm raised parallel to the ground. The client should gently roll on the foam roll to find a knot on the muscle, holding the position for at least 30 seconds until there is some sensation of release or relief.

To perform self-myofascial release on the **piriformis**, the client sits on the floor with knees bent. The client should cross one leg over the other, with the ankle resting on the top of the knee, and use one arm for balance. The client should place the foam roll under his rear end and lean toward the side with the leg that is up, finding a tender spot on the posterior hip area. The client gently rolls on the foam roll, holding the position for at least 30 seconds until there is some sensation of release or relief.

ADDUCTORS, GASTROCNEMIUS, AND SOLEUS

The client should lie in a prone position, with the arms bent in front for support to perform self-myofascial release on the **adductors**. Have the client position one leg toward the side, with the foot parallel to the floor. Have the client place the foam roll under his or her extended leg near the groin area. The client should gently roll on the foam roll, find a tender spot, and hold the position for at least 30 seconds until there is some sensation of release or relief.

To perform self-myofascial release on the **gastrocnemius** and **soleus**, the client should begin by sitting down on the floor with the legs extended in front. The calves rest on the foam roll, with one leg on top of the other. The client should gently roll on the foam roll, find a tender spot, and hold the position for at least 30 seconds until there is some sensation of release or relief.

TENSOR FASCIA LATA/ILIOTIBIAL (TFL/IT) BAND

To perform self-myofascial release on the **TFL/IT band**, have the client lie on his or her side on the floor. The client can bend the lower arm underneath for support, with the torso elevated off the ground. Have the client place the foam roll underneath the lower leg above the knee but below the hip, and then cross the top leg over and in front of the other leg, so it is on the floor just in front of the knee. The client should gently roll on the foam roll, find a tender spot, and hold the position for at least 30 seconds until there is some sensation of release or relief.

STATIC STRETCHING

Static stretching is familiar to most people. A static stretch involves placing the muscle under steady tension for 20 to 30 seconds to encourage a release or stretch.

Static stretching works through **autogenic inhibition**, which automatically occurs when the Golgi tendon receptors and muscle spindles activate and trigger a relaxation reflex in the muscles. Performing one or two sets of a stretch lasting at least 20 seconds gives the body's receptors time to react to the stress of the stretch.

Static stretching decreases **muscle-spindle reactions** and lessens the chance of injury caused by a muscle-spindle protective reaction on chronically tight muscles before activity.

Copyright © Mometrix Media. You have been licensed one copy of this document for personal use only. Any other reproduction or redistribution is strictly prohibited. All rights reserved. This content is provided for test preparation purposes only and does not imply an endorsement by Mometrix of any particular political, scientific, or religious point of view.

PSOAS AND THE GASTROCNEMIUS

To perform a static stretch for the **psoas**, the client stands in a forward lunge. The back leg should then rotate inward. Have the client raise the arm on the same side as the back leg and rotate the hip in the direction of that arm, pressing forward to give the hips a stretch. The client holds the stretch for at least 20 seconds; repeat on the other side.

To perform a static stretch for the **gastrocnemius**, the client lunges with both hands on a wall and arms slightly bent for support. Have the client lean forward to stretch the back leg, making sure to keep the feet pointing forward and not allowing them to roll in on the arches. Hold this stretch for at least 20 seconds, and repeat on the other side.

HIP FLEXORS

The client performs a kneeling **hip-flexor stretch** on a small floor mat. Have the client kneel on the mat with one knee with the other knee bent in front of the body. The kneeling position is optimal for stretching the rectus femoris muscle because it crosses both target areas (the knee and the hip). The client raises the arm on the side of the bent knee straight into the air and then presses the hip forward toward the side of the raised arm. The client should feel the stretch on the front of the hip. Instruct the client to hold the stretch for at least 20 seconds; repeat on the other side.

LATISSIMUS DORSI

To perform the **latissimus dorsi ball stretch**, you will need a large stability ball. Place the ball on the floor, and have the client get on the floor next to it on his or her hands and knees. Have the client place one arm on the ball with the arm bent at a 90-degree angle. The thumb should be facing up. Pulling the core muscles in and bending the hips to rotate up, the client slowly rolls the ball away from the body by extending the arm straight. Instruct the client to hold the stretch for at least 20 seconds; repeat on the opposite side.

Should this stretch result in uncomfortable sensations in the shoulder, decrease the intensity by having the client place his or her palm down on the ball instead of having the thumb up in the air.

ADDUCTORS

To perform a **standing adductor stretch**, have the client stand straight up with hands on hips and feet in a wide stance, well beyond shoulder-width distance apart (this is very important to get the best stretch). Have the client bend one knee and move the other leg back so it is approximately six inches behind the front foot. Be sure both feet are on the ground, pointing straight forward (the back leg will be bent at the ankle). Have the client slide sideways toward the bent leg to give the straight leg a flex in the upper interior groin area. Have the client hold this position for at least 20 seconds; repeat on the opposite side.

PECTORALS

To perform a **static pectoral-wall stretch**, find a stationary object for the client to lean against (a doorway works well). Have the client stand in a lunge position with arms placed at right angles out from the body and lean against the object. Be sure the shoulder-to-elbow area stays flat, and the shoulders stay pressed down during the stretch to maximize its effect. Have the client lean forward into the doorway until a stretch can be felt in the front shoulder muscles. Have the client hold the stretch for at least 20 seconds; repeat for a second set.

UPPER TRAPEZIUS/SCALENE MUSCLES

To perform the **static upper trapezius/scalene stretch**, the client begins in an upright, standing position with feet shoulder-width apart. Check the client's posture, and make sure the body is in

Copyright © Mometrix Media. You have been licensed one copy of this document for personal use only. Any other reproduction or redistribution is strictly prohibited. All rights reserved. This content is provided for test preparation purposes only and does not imply an endorsement by Mometrix of any particular political, scientific, or religious point of view.

optimal alignment. The client extends one arm out slightly away from the body and slightly behind the torso. Have the client gently tilt the head away from the extended arm, pressing the scapula on the side the arm is extended. Be sure the client keeps the shoulders pressed down to increase the effectiveness of the stretch, which will be felt behind the shoulder blade. Hold the stretch for at least 20 seconds, and repeat on the other side.

ACTIVE-ISOLATED STRETCHING

Active-isolated stretching is designed to trigger reciprocal inhibition by actively moving a joint through its full range of motion. Agonist and synergist muscles are activated in these stretches.

These types of stretches are very effective as a warm-up for other training or sports activity. A set of five to ten, held for a minimal period (one or two seconds), helps warm up the body and prepare the muscles for activity.

Some examples of active-isolated stretching include:

- Active pectoral wall stretch
- Active upright adductor stretch
- Active kneeling quad stretch
- Active supine biceps femoris stretch

UPPER GASTROCNEMIUS

To perform the **active upper-gastrocnemius stretch** with pronation and supination, have the client stand facing a wall or other sturdy, flat surface. The client leans forward against the wall and raises one leg. The standing leg is stretched out straight behind. The raised leg should be bent at the knee. Keeping the back foot flat on the ground, rotate the bent leg open to the side, then closed across the other knee like a gate swinging open and closed. Have the client act in a fully controlled, quick manner (one to two seconds). The hip should be the source of the motion, not the leg or knee. Perform a set of ten to fifteen on each side.

BICEPS FEMORIS

To perform the **active supine biceps femoris stretch**, have the client lie flat supine on the floor. One knee is raised so the thigh is perpendicular to the floor, and the leg is bent at a right angle. Have the client hold the back of the raised leg with the corresponding arm, and then quickly stretch the leg up, holding for one to two seconds. Make sure this is done in a completely controlled manner. To maximize the stretch, shift the hip on the stretching side inward a bit before extending the leg. Do a set of ten to fifteen on each side.

PSOAS

To perform the **active standing psoas stretch**, have the client stand in a forward lunge. The back leg should then be rotated inward. The client raises the arm on the same side as the back leg and rotates the hip in the direction of that arm, pressing forward to give the hips a stretch as he or she steps forward quickly, but in a controlled manner. Make sure the buttocks are tight when moving into the stretch to maximize effectiveness. Have the client hold the stretch in the hip for one to two seconds, and repeat on the other side. Do a set of ten to fifteen on each side.

HIP FLEXORS

To perform the **active kneeling hip-flexor stretch**, have the client kneel on the ground on a small mat. One knee should be down and the other steadying the body at a 90-degree angle in front of the torso. Raise the arm on the same side as the lower knee straight into the air and rotate the hip

123

Copyright © Mometrix Media. You have been licensed one copy of this document for personal use only. Any other reproduction or redistribution is strictly prohibited. All rights reserved.
This content is provided for test preparation purposes only and does not imply an endorsement by Mometrix of any particular political, scientific, or religious point of view.

inward. Have the client contract the gluteals on the side being stretched while rotating the hips backward. The client slowly leans forward until a stretch can be felt in the front hip, and then bends to the side and rotates the hip back. Have the client hold the stretch in the hip for one to two seconds, and repeat on the other side. Do a set of ten to fifteen on each side.

ADDUCTORS AND THE LATISSIMUS DORSI

To perform an **active standing adductor stretch**, have the client stand straight up with hands on hips and feet in a wide stance; well beyond shoulder-width distance apart (this is very important to get the best stretch). Have the client bend one knee and move the other leg back so it is approximately six inches behind the front foot. Keep both feet on the ground and pointed straight forward (the back leg will be bent at the ankle). Have the client quickly (but in a controlled manner) slide sideways toward the bent leg to give the straight leg a flex in the upper interior groin area, holding the stretch for one to two seconds. Do a set of ten to fifteen on both sides.

LATISSIMUS DORSI

To perform the **active latissimus-dorsi ball stretch**, you will need a large stability ball. Place the ball on the floor, and have the client get on the floor next to it, on his or her hands and knees. The client places one arm on the ball, with the arm bent at an approximately 90-degree angle. The thumb should be facing up. Pulling the core muscles in and bending the hips to rotate up, the client quickly (but in a controlled manner) rolls the ball away from the body by extending the arm straight, holding the stretch for one to two seconds. A set of five to ten repetitions should be performed on each side.

The movement should emanate from the hips moving into an upward (posterior) tilt, not from the arms or hands.

PECTORALS

It is best to perform an **active pectoral-wall stretch** in an open doorway (although any stationary place a client can lean against as instructed will work just as well). Have the client stand in a lunge with both arms placed at right angles out from the body and lean into the door frame. Be sure the shoulder-to-elbow area stays flat, and the shoulders stay pressed down to maximize the effects of the stretch. The client leans forward in a quick but controlled manner into the doorway until a stretch can be felt in the front shoulder muscles. Have the client hold the stretch for one to two seconds. Have the client perform a set of five to ten repetitions of this stretch.

Make sure the client pulls back the shoulder blades when performing the stretch to maximize its effectiveness.

UPPER TRAPEZIUS/SCALENE MUSCLES

To perform the **static upper-trapezius/scalene stretch**, the client begins in an upright standing position with feet shoulder-width apart. Check the client's posture, and make sure the body is in optimal alignment. Have the client extend one arm out slightly away from the body and slightly behind the torso. The client gently tilts their head away from the extended arm, quickly but in a controlled manner, pressing the scapula on the side the arm is extended. Be sure the client keeps the shoulders pressed down to increase the effectiveness of the stretch. The stretch will be felt behind the shoulder blade. Hold the stretch for one to two seconds. A set of five to ten repetitions is performed on each side.

If the client's hand is numb or tingles, the tilt of the head should be decreased.

Copyright © Mometrix Media. You have been licensed one copy of this document for personal use only. Any other reproduction or redistribution is strictly prohibited. All rights reserved. This content is provided for test preparation purposes only and does not imply an endorsement by Mometrix of any particular political, scientific, or religious point of view.

DYNAMIC STRETCHING

Dynamic stretching is a form of highly active stretching that maximizes the body's production of force and movement through the various planes of motion to increase the extensibility of a joint and its surrounding muscles through **reciprocal inhibition**. For a client in good physical condition (with good flexibility, strength, and balance) dynamic stretching can be a beneficial warm-up regimen. It is best used on clients that have progressed well through lower levels and phases of training and have no postural distortions.

Dynamic stretching can be performed in a rotation of anywhere from three to ten different stretches, with ten repetitions of each stretch. Some examples of dynamic stretching include tube walking and prisoner squats.

PRISONER SQUAT

To perform a prisoner squat, the client stands straight up with both arms bent outward at the shoulders, touching the ears. Feet should be shoulder-width apart, and toes should face straight forward. Have the client bend into a squat, careful to keep perfect form without postural distortions or compensations; make sure the toes stay forward and the knees stay in line with the toes. The client straightens the knees and hips, so he or she is standing straight up, rising all the way up onto the toes. Have the client return to the original position and repeat the action 10 times.

MULTIPLANAR LUNGE

To perform a multiplanar lunge, the client begins by standing straight up, hands on hips, with feet shoulder-width apart. Make sure the client has proper alignment and maintains it throughout the stretch, keeping toes straight forward through the lunges and keeping knees in line with the toes. The client steps forward into a deep lunge, bending the knees and hips to the floor. Repeat this action ten times on each side. The client switches to side lunges, doing ten repetitions on each side. Finally, the client performs turning lunges, stepping forward and twisting at the hips—ten repetitions on each side.

SINGLE-LEG SQUAT TOUCHDOWN

To perform a single-leg squat touchdown, the client stands straight up, with hands on hips and one leg raised off the ground in front of the body approximately six inches off the ground. With the client maintaining proper form, have him or her squat down on the standing leg, reach across the body with the opposite arm, and touch the standing foot while maintaining balance. Have the client keep their balance by pulling in the core muscles and tightening the buttocks. Perform ten repetitions on each side. Make sure the knees are aligned with the toes to maximize the benefits of the stretch.

MEDICINE BALL CHOP AND LIFT

To perform the medicine ball chop and lift dynamic stretch, you will need a medicine ball of a size and weight appropriate for the particular client. The client begins standing straight up with feet a bit more than shoulder-width apart. He or she turns one leg inward, so the toes point perpendicular to the other foot and bends the knee of that leg. Have the client bend over the straight leg with the medicine ball extending toward the floor. The client straightens all the way up while twisting the ball across the body and above the head. The client returns to the original position and repeats ten times for each side.

TUBE WALKING

Tube walking is a dynamic stretching exercise performed using a length of rubber exercise tubing. To perform tube walking from side to side, begin by having the client place tubing around both legs

125

Copyright © Mometrix Media. You have been licensed one copy of this document for personal use only. Any other reproduction or redistribution is strictly prohibited. All rights reserved. This content is provided for test preparation purposes only and does not imply an endorsement by Mometrix of any particular political, scientific, or religious point of view.

just above the ankles. The client stands straight up with hands on hips and feet shoulder-width apart. The knees should be slightly bent and pliable, and the toes should face straight forward. Keeping good body alignment, the client pulls in the core muscles and then takes ten little steps to the side. Be sure the knees do not rotate inward and the toes point forward. Have the client repeat the exercise in the opposite direction.

SPECIFIC STRETCHING TECHNIQUE AND STRENGTHENING EXERCISES

If the client exhibits a **feet-turning-out compensation** when viewed from behind, it is likely that he or she has the following tight or overactive muscles:

- Biceps femoris
- Soleus
- Lateral gastrocnemius

Additionally, the following muscles are likely weak, or underactive:

- Popliteus
- Gracilis
- Soleus
- Medial gastrocnemius
- Medial hamstring

Performing self-myofascial release and static stretching on the **biceps femoris** and the **gastrocnemius**—and performing single-leg balance reaches as a strengthening exercise—can help alleviate these problems.

If the client exhibits a **knees-moving-inward compensation** when viewed from behind, it is likely that he or she has the following tight or overactive muscles:

- Biceps femoris
- Tensor fascia lata
- Adductor complex
- Vastus lateralis

Additionally, the following muscles are likely weak or underactive:

- Gluteus maximus
- Gluteus medius
- Vastus medialis oblique

Performing self-myofascial release and static stretching on the **tensor fascia lata/iliotibial (TFL/IT) band** and the **adductors** and performing side-by-side tube walking as a strengthening exercise can help alleviate these problems.

If the client exhibits an **excessive forward lean** in the lumbo-pelvic-hip (LPH) complex when viewed from the side, it is a sign of a muscle imbalance that must be addressed by the CPT. It is likely that he or she has the following tight or overactive muscles:

- Abdominals
- Hip flexors

Copyright © Mometrix Media. You have been licensed one copy of this document for personal use only. Any other reproduction or redistribution is strictly prohibited. All rights reserved. This content is provided for test preparation purposes only and does not imply an endorsement by Mometrix of any particular political, scientific, or religious point of view.

- Soleus
- Gastrocnemius

Additionally, the following muscles are likely weak or underactive:

- Erector spinae
- Gluteus maximus
- Anterior tibialis

Performing self-myofascial release and static stretching on the **hip flexor complex** and the **piriformis** and performing ball squats as a strengthening exercise can help alleviate these problems.

If the client exhibits a **low-back-arching compensation** in the lumbo-pelvic-hip (LPH) complex when viewed from the side, it is a sign of a muscle imbalance that must be addressed by the CPT. It is likely that he or she has the following tight or overactive muscles:

- Hip flexor complex
- Latissimus dorsi
- Erector spinae

Additionally, the following muscles are likely weak or underactive:

- Core stabilizers
- Hamstrings
- Gluteus maximus

Performing self-myofascial release and static stretching on the **erector spinae, hip flexors, and the hip flexor complex** and performing ball squats as a strengthening exercise can help alleviate these problems.

If the client exhibits an **arms-slumping shoulder compensation** when viewed from the side, it is likely that he or she has the following tight or overactive muscles:

- Teres major
- Pectoralis major
- Latissimus dorsi

Additionally, the following muscles are likely weak or underactive:

- Rhomboids
- Mid trapezius
- Lower trapezius
- Rotator cuff

Performing self-myofascial release and static stretching on the **thoracic spine** and the **latissimus dorsi** and performing squat-to-row exercises for strengthening can help alleviate these problems.

Copyright © Mometrix Media. You have been licensed one copy of this document for personal use only. Any other reproduction or redistribution is strictly prohibited. All rights reserved. This content is provided for test preparation purposes only and does not imply an endorsement by Mometrix of any particular political, scientific, or religious point of view.

If the client exhibits a **scrunching-up-of-the-shoulders compensation** when a pushing/pulling assessment is viewed from the side, it is likely that he or she has the following tight or overactive muscles:

- Levator scapulae
- Upper trapezius
- Upper scalene

Additionally, the following muscles are likely weak or underactive:

- Rhomboids
- Mid trapezius
- Lower trapezius
- Rotator cuff

Performing self-myofascial release and static stretching on the **upper scalene** and the **upper trapezius** and performing ball cobra exercises for strengthening can help alleviate these problems.

If the client compensates by **jutting the head forward** when a pushing/pulling assessment is viewed from the side, it is likely that he or she has the following tight or overactive muscles:

- Levator scapulae
- Upper trapezius
- Upper scalene

Additionally, the following muscles are likely weak or underactive:

- Deep cervical flexors

Performing self-myofascial release and static stretching on the **upper scalene** and the **upper trapezius** can help alleviate this problem. Keeping the head soft and in a neutral position when performing all activities can help strengthen the weak muscles.

Copyright © Mometrix Media. You have been licensed one copy of this document for personal use only. Any other reproduction or redistribution is strictly prohibited. All rights reserved. This content is provided for test preparation purposes only and does not imply an endorsement by Mometrix of any particular political, scientific, or religious point of view.

Cardiorespiratory Training

Integrated cardiorespiratory training is any activity that places positive, controlled stress on the cardiorespiratory system. Because this is a very simple definition, nearly **any activity** can be considered integrated cardiorespiratory training. Walking, running, sports activity, and lifting weights are examples of integrated cardiorespiratory training. Activities also include exercises that require mechanical implements such as a treadmill (often a foundation of the gym experience).

Cardiorespiratory training can be used as a separate component of a workout when incorporated as a warm-up or cool-down and as the main part of the workout itself.

WARM-UP

A warm-up is a preparatory action taken that readies the body to perform physically. There are two types of warm-ups:

1. A general warm-up consists of low-level activity meant to get the body prepared for general activities. Running around a track or on a treadmill before weight training is considered a general warm-up.
2. A specific warm-up focuses on the activity that follows and prepares the body for the specific stresses it will be placed under. Performing some isometric exercises such as push-ups before weight training is considered a specific warm-up.

BENEFITS OF A WARM-UP

A warm-up benefits a cardiorespiratory workout in the following ways:

1. Mentally prepares a person for physical activity.
2. Increases the temperature of the body and its tissues, which increases the body's metabolism in preparation for physical activity and makes soft tissue more amenable to stretching.
3. Increases the activity level of the heart and lungs, which prepares these organs for more activity, and increases blood flow and oxygen flow.

It has not been conclusively demonstrated that warm-ups prevent injury, but they have benefits and should be performed before an activity is undertaken. It has been demonstrated that warm-ups have the potential to reduce **neuromuscular fatigue**. When a person exercises, lactic acid builds up in the muscles and can accumulate over subsequent training sessions. Warm-ups may help inhibit the buildup of lactic acid in the muscles, thereby reducing neuromuscular fatigue.

LENGTH OF WARM-UP

Ideally, a warm-up should last around **ten minutes**, although this time can be shortened or lengthened depending on the particular client and the activity that will be undertaken. The warm-up should include general and specific elements, engaging the body in cardiorespiratory activity and taxing some of the main muscle groups that the main workout will target.

For novice clients, the warm-up may last for a good portion of the entire workout for the first several sessions as they become accustomed to some of the exercises used for stabilization. After the client gets used to these introductory exercises and techniques, he or she can do them on his or her own before working with the trainer each session. This can usually commence after three sessions at the discretion of the health and fitness professional. This will leave more time to work on more-substantive fitness areas one-on-one.

Copyright © Mometrix Media. You have been licensed one copy of this document for personal use only. Any other reproduction or redistribution is strictly prohibited. All rights reserved. This content is provided for test preparation purposes only and does not imply an endorsement by Mometrix of any particular political, scientific, or religious point of view.

WARM-UP ROUTINES

A warm-up for an individual at the **stabilization level** includes the following:

- Five to ten minutes of cardiorespiratory training, such as running on a treadmill, pedaling on a stationary bike, or walking on a stair climber.
- Five to ten minutes of static stretching, focusing on the leg muscles.
- Five to ten minutes of self-myofascial release exercises.

A warm-up for an individual working at the **strength level** includes the following:

- Five to ten minutes of cardiorespiratory training, such as running on a treadmill, pedaling on a stationary bike, or walking on a stair climber.
- Five to ten minutes of active-isolated stretching, focusing on the leg muscles.
- Five to ten minutes of self-myofascial release exercises.

A warm-up for an individual at the **power level** includes the following:

- Five to ten minutes of dynamic stretching, such as tube walking or prisoner squats.
- Five to ten minutes of self-myofascial release exercises.

COOL-DOWN

A cool-down is a low-intensity activity performed after a training session that helps transition the body back to regular heart and breathing rates. An ideal cool-down lasts from five to ten minutes.

Benefits of a cool-down include:

- Slows the cardiorespiratory system
- Decreases the body's temperature
- Restores the proper muscle length and tension
- Decreases the risk of light-headedness or feinting
- Facilitates the return to the body's normal functionality

A cool-down should include a **reduction in activity level**, taking a higher-rate cardiorespiratory training activity down to approximately half the heart rate level for a few minutes. This reduces the stress on the body on a gradient and also helps prevent blood from collecting in the lower extremities, which can lead to a client becoming dizzy and perhaps even fainting.

A cool-down should also incorporate **static stretching** and **self-myofascial release** to maximize muscle extensibility and release lactic acid from the muscles after a workout to reduce soreness.

A client should be able to perform his or her own cool-down after approximately three sessions, at the discretion of the health and fitness professional. This will allow more time for the client and trainer to focus on the substantive portion of the workout one-on-one.

BENEFITS OF CARDIORESPIRATORY TRAINING

Cardiorespiratory training can increase general fitness levels and help control weight. It can decrease many chronic problems and give a person an emotional outlet that helps improve mental well-being and sleep patterns.

Copyright © Mometrix Media. You have been licensed one copy of this document for personal use only. Any other reproduction or redistribution is strictly prohibited. All rights reserved. This content is provided for test preparation purposes only and does not imply an endorsement by Mometrix of any particular political, scientific, or religious point of view.

Cardiorespiratory training **increases** the following:

- Muscle extensibility
- General performance of all activities, from daily activities to sports and fitness activities
- Immune system function
- Glucose tolerance
- Blood work
- Bone density

Cardiorespiratory training **decreases** the following:

- General tiredness
- Overweight
- Mental stress symptoms, from depression to anxiety
- Chronic illnesses
- Diabetes
- High blood pressure
- Heart disease

HEALTH- VS. FITNESS-RELATED BENEFITS

Cardiorespiratory activity has **health-related benefits** as well as **fitness-related benefits**. Moderate cardiorespiratory can produce marked improvement in overall health, even if it is not accompanied by measurable gains in fitness level. Cardiorespiratory training needs to be more intense to confer fitness benefits.

Cardiorespiratory training can have a **positive cumulative effect** in the following areas:

- Decrease in the resting and exercising heart rate
- Increase in VO2 maximum, cardiac volume, stroke output, and the ability of muscles to process oxygen

F.I.T.T.E. FACTORS

The acronym F.I.T.T.E. stands for the following:

- **Frequency**—the number of training sessions conducted within a specific time, (e.g., one week)
- **Intensity**—how physically demanding an activity is. For improved health, moderate level activity is recommended. For improved fitness levels, a higher intensity level is recommended.
- **Time**—duration of time spent engaged in an activity. For improved health, 30 minutes a day is a good time frame. For increased fitness levels, more time is recommended.
- **Type**—the precise activity being undertaken.
- **Enjoyment**—how fun or pleasant a given activity is.

Enjoyment (the E in NASM's F.I.T.T.E. Factors for cardiorespiratory training) is often overlooked when putting together a cardiorespiratory routine for a particular client. It is important to create a program that considers the needs and interests of the individual client to encourage the client to stick with the program. When the activities are geared toward the client's personality, likes, and dislikes, he or she is more likely to continue with the training regimen and derive full benefit from

Copyright © Mometrix Media. You have been licensed one copy of this document for personal use only. Any other reproduction or redistribution is strictly prohibited. All rights reserved. This content is provided for test preparation purposes only and does not imply an endorsement by Mometrix of any particular political, scientific, or religious point of view.

the consistent application of training. It can also ensure that the client is happy with the CPT's work, leading to potential referrals.

IMPROVED HEALTH FITNESS PARAMETERS

NASM recommends the following cardiorespiratory-training guidelines for improved general health:

- **Frequency**—Five to seven sessions per week
- **Intensity**—Moderate
- **Time**—Up to 30 minutes daily, which can be broken into shorter segments
- **Type**—Any activity that will get heart and respiratory rates up, such as walking or jogging, or even working around the house
- **Enjoyment**—The more enjoyable the activity, the better

NASM recommends the following cardiorespiratory-training guidelines for improved fitness:

- **Frequency**—Three to five sessions per week
- **Intensity**—Measured by heart rate maximum (between 60 and 90 percent) or VO2 maximum (40 to 85 percent)
- **Time**—Twenty minutes to an hour per session
- **Type**—Any activity that will increase heart and respiratory rates
- **Enjoyment**—The more enjoyable the activity, the better

FAT-BURNING ZONE

The law of thermodynamics states that body fat can only be **burned** when the body is using more energy than it is consuming. This is important because many clients begin exercising with a goal of improving their aesthetic appeal (e.g., they seek to lose fat and look better). The idea of a fat-burning zone is a misconception based on a misunderstanding of metabolism. While it is true that during lower intensity exercise the body burns a greater percentage of calories from fat than it does from carbohydrates, this does not constitute an ideal fat-burning zone. As exercise intensity increases, a greater percentage of calories will be burned from carbohydrates, but a greater number of calories will be burned overall, including more calories from fat.

CALORIE USAGE

Measuring respiratory gasses with a metabolic analyzer by way of indirect calorimetry can reveal the amount of oxygen and carbon dioxide exchanged in the lungs, which usually correlates with the amounts of the same gasses used by body tissues. This shows a person's **respiratory exchange ratio** (RER), which could then be used to determine the percentage of **carbohydrates** being burned versus the percentage of **fat** being burned. The RER represents a comparison of the carbon dioxide produced to the amount of oxygen taken in. The higher the RER, the higher is the level of carbohydrates being burned.

EPOC

EPOC stands for **Excess Postexercise Oxygen Consumption**—the increased need for oxygen after exercise, which raises metabolism, resulting in more calories burned. This phenomenon is a result of the body working to return to its initial state: lowering the heart rate, refilling energy stores, and cooling off body tissue. The intensity of a workout has a direct impact on EPOC, and breaking a workout into two sessions may also help maximize the effects of this phenomenon.

Copyright © Mometrix Media. You have been licensed one copy of this document for personal use only. Any other reproduction or redistribution is strictly prohibited. All rights reserved. This content is provided for test preparation purposes only and does not imply an endorsement by Mometrix of any particular political, scientific, or religious point of view.

FAT-BURNING REGIMEN

Because of the law of thermodynamics, the **overall expenditure of calories** is the most important factor to consider when a health and fitness professional implements into a training regimen. A person must burn more calories than he or she consumes.

Because the body attempts to conserve energy as a general rule, it is important to maximize calorie burning to maximize excess post exercise oxygen consumption (EPOC), which encourages the body to continue to burn calories after the training session is over through increased metabolic activity.

GENERAL ADAPTATION SYNDROME AND THE PRINCIPLE OF SPECIFICITY

When designing a cardiorespiratory program for a client, it is important to remember **general adaptation syndrome**—the body's ability to cope gradually with stresses placed upon it. The principle of specificity is an important concept that a CPT must understand to enact the desired change in a client. The body will adapt in response to the particular stresses it is subjected to. Cardiorespiratory exercises must be varied in type, intensity, and frequency to prevent the body from adapting to a routine and to force the body to progress through a fitness program. This is especially relevant if fitness goals, and not just general health goals, are the client's primary objective. Stage training and circuit training are good ways to incorporate varied cardiorespiratory training into a client's exercise routine.

STAGE TRAINING

Stage training is a systematic approach to cardiorespiratory training that gives the body enough time to heal and recuperate while varying the routine enough to avoid general adaptation syndrome (the stage in which the body becomes used to an exercise routine and fails to continue progressing toward fitness goals).

NASM's stage-training progression is presented in **three stages** based on a person's heart rate and RER. These three stages go with the three phases of the OPT model (stabilization, strength, and power). Each stage is meant to act as a platform for the next progressive stage.

HEART RATE ZONES

Zone one encompasses an RER of 0.80 to 0.90, representing a 65- to 75-percent heart rate maximum. The aerobic energy system is engaged and burning fatty acids and glycogen to perform at this level. Lighter exercise, such as walking, falls under zone one.

Zone two encompasses an RER of 0.95 to 1.0, representing a 76- to 85-percent heart rate maximum. The aerobic and anaerobic energy systems are engaged and burning glycogen and lactic acid to perform at this level. Moderate exercise, such as jogging, falls under zone two.

Zone three encompasses an RER of 1.1, representing an 86 to 90 percent heart rate maximum. The anaerobic energy system is engaged and burning glycogen and adenosine triphosphate/creatine phosphate (ATP/CP) to perform at this level. Higher-intensity activity, such as running sprints, falls under zone three.

Zone	RER	% of HR Max	Energy System	Examples
One	0.8-0.9	65-75%	Aerobic	Walking, light jogging
Two	0.95-1.0	76-85%	Aerobic/Anaerobic	Group exercise, spinning
Three	1.1	86-95%	Anaerobic	Sprinting

Copyright © Mometrix Media. You have been licensed one copy of this document for personal use only. Any other reproduction or redistribution is strictly prohibited. All rights reserved. This content is provided for test preparation purposes only and does not imply an endorsement by Mometrix of any particular political, scientific, or religious point of view.

Stage I, which correlates with zone one, is best for a relatively new client still in the stabilization level of OPT. Stage I increases blood flow to the body and creates a platform from which the client can progress.

Stage II, which correlates with zone two, is best for a client who has progressed to the strength level of OPT. Stage II pushes the body to burn more calories and raises the anaerobic threshold to meet advanced fitness goals.

Stage III, which correlates with zone three, is best for a client that has progressed to an advanced level of training. Stage III increases the amount, intensity, and speed of the workout.

Implementing Stage I (Stabilization Level) Cardiorespiratory Training

Stage I is a beginning phase and should follow a gradual progression. The goal is for the client to be able to perform up to 30 minutes of exercise at 65 to 75 percent of maximal heart rate, keeping the body in an aerobic state and taxing only the target system.

Some beginning clients may only be able to handle this workload for a few minutes at a time. Start the client off in five-minute increments until he or she can handle thirty-minute sessions three times a week. This could take a few months' time, but it is important to progress a client at a manageable rate to achieve the desired effects and properly prepare the body for stage II.

Implementing Stage II (Strength Level) Cardiorespiratory Training

Stage II is a median phase designed for those who have progressed beyond the beginning workloads of stage I. The ideal goal is for the client to be able to push their body to work in aerobic and anaerobic states, as revealed by the client's heart rate.

Intervals are added to the workout to change the intensity of the workout periodically to accomplish this. Work the client through zone one, with the heart rate at 60- to 75-percent of maximum capacity, and then zone two, with the heart rate at 80- to 85-percent of maximum capacity.

Adding stage II interval training to a client's workout regimen: To begin stage II interval training, a client starts with a five- to ten-minute cardiorespiratory training warm-up in zone one. The trainer pushes the client into a higher heart rate zone—zone two—by gradually increasing the workload or intensity of the activity over the course of one minute. After this one-minute interval, the client should return to zone one for another five-minute period. This pattern should be repeated until three one-minute, zone-two intervals have been performed. A short cool-down of a few minutes ends the session.

If a client is unable to reach a zone-two heart rate or maintain it for the entire minute-long interval, modified interval training can be used until the client can perform the standard progression.

If the client cannot hit the higher heart rate zone, take the highest number he or she was able to attain and calibrate this as an 85-percent heart rate. Subtract 5 percent from this number and use this as the target zone-two heart rate until the client can eventually achieve the higher number.

If the client's heart rate exceeds the target heart rate, but he or she can recover when the interval is over, adjust the target rate by adding a few beats to the target number.

Copyright © Mometrix Media. You have been licensed one copy of this document for personal use only. Any other reproduction or redistribution is strictly prohibited. All rights reserved. This content is provided for test preparation purposes only and does not imply an endorsement by Mometrix of any particular political, scientific, or religious point of view.

IMPLEMENTING STAGE III (POWER LEVEL) CARDIORESPIRATORY TRAINING

Stage III is an advanced phase designed for those who have progressed beyond the intermediate workloads of stage II. The ideal goal is for the client to be able to push their body to work primarily in the anaerobic system, as revealed by the client's heart rate.

Intervals are added to the workout to change the intensity of the workout periodically to accomplish this. Progressively work the client through zones one through three, with the heart rate being pushed to up to 85- to 90-percent maximum capacity through the use of specific intervals.

Adding stage III interval training: To begin with stage III interval training, the client starts with a five- to ten-minute cardiorespiratory warm-up in zone one. The trainer pushes the client into a higher heart rate zone (zone two) by gradually increasing the workload or intensity of the activity over the course of two minutes. The trainer then takes the client directly into zone three with a one-minute interval at an increased intensity. A three-minute interval at a lower intensity should be used to transition the client back to his or her zone-two heart rate, followed by a ten-minute cool down in zone one.

COORDINATING STAGES

Stage training should be approached in a systematic and staggered manner, so the client's body does not adapt to the routine and fail to continue progressing toward fitness goals. This means that a **rotation** of stage I, stage II, and stage III should be employed. This ensures that the client will not overtrain or become burned out, and the risk of injury is minimized.

The client's **metabolism** will increase as they are able to perform varying levels of activity and intensity. A monthly plan might include stage I, stage II, and stage III on alternating days, two days of rest, followed by a downward progression consisting of stage II, stage I, and stage III on alternating days finishing with two days of rest. The cycle is then repeated.

CIRCUIT TRAINING

Circuit training is a weight-training method that involves performing different types of weight training in rapid succession, so the heart rate stays elevated throughout the routine. A client can perform weight training and a cardiorespiratory workout without spending twice as much time doing each component separately. Circuit training is a very effective workout regimen that can improve a person's level of fitness and increase metabolism by boosting excess post-exercise oxygen consumption (EPOC) and increasing muscle mass.

Some common circuit-training exercises include chest presses, triceps extensions, biceps curls, and overhead presses.

A client who may respond to circuit training the best is one who is averse to traditional forms of cardiorespiratory training, such as running or aerobics, but enjoys weight training. By capitalizing on the client's enjoyment of weight training and stacking the exercises in a rapid-fire sequence, the client can get still get the benefits of a cardiorespiratory workout without even noticing. This goes hand in hand with NASM's F.I.T.T.E. Factors, which stress finding activities the client enjoys to maximize compliance with the program and overall mental and emotional benefits.

REST PERIOD

Studies have shown that waiting 20 seconds between circuit-training sets can produce higher levels of excess post-exercise oxygen consumption (EPOC), while waiting 60 seconds between sets results in a higher overall calorie burn for the circuit-training session. However, this could be misleading, as the higher calorie burn may result from the training session being longer in duration. Whichever

135

Copyright © Mometrix Media. You have been licensed one copy of this document for personal use only. Any other reproduction or redistribution is strictly prohibited. All rights reserved. This content is provided for test preparation purposes only and does not imply an endorsement by Mometrix of any particular political, scientific, or religious point of view.

rest period a CPT chooses when designing a circuit-training routine for a client, he or she should be careful not to extend the rest period; resting for more than three minutes can negate the beneficial effects of circuit training entirely.

CIRCUIT TRAINING AND STAGE TRAINING

A systematic approach to a client's workout regimen can be used, incorporating stage training and circuit training for maximum results.

For a **beginner client**, this could include a warm-up and cool-down consisting of about 10 minutes of flexibility work (self-myofascial release and stretching exercises) with about 10 minutes of stage I cardiorespiratory training, followed by 20 minutes of circuit-training cardio, and another 10 minutes of stage-training cardio.

Time ranges can be determined by the trainer, with sections of the routine cut down to five minutes if, for example, the client's heart rate is exceeding the target maximum during stage training.

For an **intermediate client** who is past the basic level of training, this could include a warm-up and cool-down consisting of ten minutes of flexibility work (self-myofascial release and stretching exercises), about 10 minutes of stage II cardiorespiratory training, followed by 20 minutes of circuit-training cardio, and another 10 minutes of stage-training cardio.

Time ranges can be determined by the trainer, with sections of the routine cut down to five minutes if the client's heart rate is exceeding the target maximum during stage training, for example.

For an **advanced-level client**, include a warm-up and cool-down of about 10 minutes of flexibility work (self-myofascial release and stretching exercises) with about 10 minutes of stage III cardiorespiratory training, followed by 20 minutes of circuit-training cardiorespiratory training, and finally 10 minutes of stage II cardiorespiratory training.

Time ranges can be determined by the trainer, with sections of the routine cut down to five minutes if, for example, the client's heart rate is exceeding the target maximum during stage training.

CARDIORESPIRATORY ACTIVITIES FOR SPECIFIC SITUATIONS

Because all cardiorespiratory exercises and activities require the client to move, it is important to consider how this movement occurs and whether it is ideal for that particular client.

For a client who exhibits **rounded shoulders or a protruded head postural distortion**, it is important to keep an eye on the following and troubleshoot when necessary:

- Do not allow a client to lean forward excessively on cardiorespiratory training equipment such as a treadmill; watch for overreliance on handles, which can lead to further postural problems.
- Watch for proper form on all equipment, including bikes and elliptical trainers.
- Make sure watching television or using electronic equipment (e.g., MP3 player) is not affecting the client's posture as he or she works.

Copyright © Mometrix Media. You have been licensed one copy of this document for personal use only. Any other reproduction or redistribution is strictly prohibited. All rights reserved. This content is provided for test preparation purposes only and does not imply an endorsement by Mometrix of any particular political, scientific, or religious point of view.

For a client who exhibits an **excessive lower-back-arch postural distortion**, it is important to keep an eye on the following and troubleshoot when necessary:

- Keep running or walking at a manageable speed, so the client does not attempt to compensate by extending his or her stride, aggravating this postural distortion.
- Consider avoiding stair steppers or stationary bicycles when beginning to train with that client, because these may exacerbate the postural distortion from the outset.
- Add extra flexibility exercises that target this particular area.

For a client whose **feet rotate out and knees bend in**, it is important to keep an eye on the following and troubleshoot when necessary:

- Watch for proper form on all cardiorespiratory machines, as it will be easy for the ankle and knee joints to flex improperly during use.
- Consider alternate cardiorespiratory exercise sources other than stair steppers or treadmills on incline mode when beginning to train with this client, because these may exacerbate the postural distortion from the outset.
- Add extra flexibility exercises that target these particular areas.

Copyright © Mometrix Media. You have been licensed one copy of this document for personal use only. Any other reproduction or redistribution is strictly prohibited. All rights reserved.
This content is provided for test preparation purposes only and does not imply an endorsement by Mometrix of any particular political, scientific, or religious point of view.

Core Stabilization Training

The core is the center of the human body. It is composed of skeletal components such as the lumbo-pelvic-hip (LPH) complex, the lower spine, and the corresponding musculature which consists of twenty-nine muscles that attach to the LPH complex.

The **core musculature** is composed of two sets of muscles: the movement and stabilization systems. As the name of each implies, the movement system is the primary source of core motion, while the stabilization system helps maintain the structural integrity of the LPH complex and cervical spine.

The core acts as the **center of motion and gravity** for the entire body; much of the body's power is generated from this region.

STABILIZATION SYSTEM AND MOVEMENT SYSTEM

The **core musculature systems** work together to stabilize the central skeletal system, act as the center of gravity, and initiate much of the body's motion. This is accomplished by absorbing shock and distributing weight appropriately among other functions. It is important to address the stabilization system first to create the groundwork from which to build to train these muscles to work synergistically. This will strengthen a client's core and allow further strengthening of the movement-system muscles.

The **stabilization system**, divided into the local and global systems, keeps the core skeletal systems in place and working properly. The local stabilization system provides support to the abdomen by providing variable tension between structural (skeletal) components. The local stabilization system is composed of the following muscles:

- Transversus abdominis
- Internal oblique
- Lumbar multifidus
- Pelvic floor muscles
- Diaphragm

The **global stabilization system** supports the dynamic connection of the pelvis to the spine. The global stabilization system is composed of the following muscles:

- Quadratus lumborum
- Psoas major
- External oblique
- Parts of the internal oblique
- Rectus abdominis
- Gluteus medius
- Adductor magnus
- Adductor longus
- Adductor brevis
- Gracilis
- Pectineus

The stabilization system of the core musculature is made up mainly of **slow-twitch muscles** that work best under a sustained stress (up to 20 seconds) to get the desired result of heightened

138

Copyright © Mometrix Media. You have been licensed one copy of this document for personal use only. Any other reproduction or redistribution is strictly prohibited. All rights reserved. This content is provided for test preparation purposes only and does not imply an endorsement by Mometrix of any particular political, scientific, or religious point of view.

intramuscular coordination, which is the ability of the nervous system to effectively and efficiently communicate within the muscle. This is important to promote stabilization of the LPH complex.

The **movement system**, which acts as the primary source of core motion and action, is composed of the following muscles, which lie lower in the hips and upper legs:

- Hip muscles
  - Adductors
  - Abductors
- Hamstrings
- Quadriceps
- Latissimus dorsi

The movement system works in concert with the stabilization system to move the **LPH complex**. This means that there must be high levels of intermuscular coordination, which is the ability of the nervous system to communicate effectively and efficiently between different muscles so they can work together properly.

Many people may have strong movement system muscles working with weak stabilization muscles. It is the job of the stabilization system to hold the **skeletal system** in proper position. If the powerful muscles acting on top of the skeletal system are not fully controlled, a person is vulnerable to injuries, compensations, postural distortions, and improper muscle interactions (such as synergistic dominance). These can lead to improper movement and, ultimately, injury. It is important to train and strengthen these deep-stabilization muscles to ensure optimal kinetic-chain communication and function.

CORE MUSCULATURE

The core musculature is vital because it helps insulate the spine from external forces and injury, and it is the source point of most major movement of the body. Training these muscles is important to increase strength, flexibility, body stability, and force production. This requires a systematic approach that follows NASM's Optimum Performance Training (OPT) model of stability, strength, and power phases.

The **stability phase** of core training aims at creating a supporting musculature system for the lumbo-pelvic-hip (LPH) complex. The **strength phase** of core training aims to improve strength by addressing how the muscles communicate and move efficiently. The **power phase** of core training aims to increase how much explosive force the muscles can produce at a given time by the muscles of the LPH complex.

CHRONIC BACK PAIN

Approximately 8 percent of American adults suffer from **chronic back pain**. This is often caused by limited strength and control of the stabilization muscles such as the diaphragm, pelvic-floor muscles, transversus abdominis, and internal obliques.

Performing abdominal exercises to strengthen the movement system muscles without proper stabilization strength can stress the underlying structures by increase pressure and exerting force on the spine. This can lead to damaged spinal disks and spinal ligaments. The solution is to make sure that the stabilization muscles are trained in a **progressive manner** along with the movement system muscles so that they can begin to work synergistically.

Copyright © Mometrix Media. You have been licensed one copy of this document for personal use only. Any other reproduction or redistribution is strictly prohibited. All rights reserved.
This content is provided for test preparation purposes only and does not imply an endorsement by Mometrix of any particular political, scientific, or religious point of view.

DRAWING-IN MANEUVER

Performing two simple exercises—the **drawing-in maneuver** and **bracing**— before core training increases pelvic stabilization. The drawing-in maneuver improves the performance of the local stabilization system. The easiest way to perform the exercise in a controlled and measurable manner is to have the client get on the floor on all fours, with knees and hands shoulder-width apart. Have the client concentrate on the abdominals at the belly button, and then pull in the abs from the belly button toward the spine. Bracing strengthens the global movement system. Bracing stabilizes the body by contracting the core (abdomen), lower back, and buttocks muscles simultaneously.

Performing these exercises before other abdominal work will help maintain the lumbo-pelvic-hip (LPH) complex in a neutral position during a training session.

TRAINING THE CORE MUSCULATURE SYSTEMS

The core musculature has several important functions, including protecting the spine from the stresses and forces of everyday life. A training program should focus on increasing strength and power in the LPH complex to meet the demands placed on the body. Greater muscle control and increased strength make for a more efficient kinetic chain with ideal neuromuscular efficiency.

Stabilization training follows the OPT model, consisting of three levels of core training exercises including stabilization, strength, and power levels.

STABILIZATION TRAINING EXERCISES
MARCHING EXERCISE

To perform the marching exercise, the client lies on the floor with knees bent at a 90-degree angle. Feet should be flat on the floor, and arms should be straight down at the side of the body.

Using the drawing-in maneuver, the client lifts one foot off the floor while maintaining perfect form. The client holds this position for a few seconds and then lowers the foot back to the floor. Repeat the exercise while using the opposite foot.

The key to this exercise is to make sure the client stays drawn-in during the exercise this targets muscles that ensure the core stabilization muscles are being worked.

TWO-LEG FLOOR BRIDGE EXERCISE

Have the client lie on the floor with knees bent at a 90-degree angle. Feet should be flat on the floor, and arms should be straight down at the side of the body. Make sure toes are pointing forward.

The client should perform the drawing-in maneuver and shift the hips up off the ground, lifting the rear end off the ground, creating a plank with the torso, in which the shoulders, hips, and knees are aligned. Have the client slowly lower back to the starting position.

The key to this exercise is to make sure the client does not overextend the hips and thrust the lower back into an overextended position, which places the wrong kind of stress on the spine.

PRONE COBRA FLOOR EXERCISE

Begin the prone cobra floor exercise by having client lie face down on the floor with arms extended at the sides of the body and the palms of the hands down.

Have the client perform the drawing-in maneuver and press down toward the floor with contracted gluteal muscles. While contracting the shoulder muscles together, lift the chest off the floor and

140

Copyright © Mometrix Media. You have been licensed one copy of this document for personal use only. Any other reproduction or redistribution is strictly prohibited. All rights reserved. This content is provided for test preparation purposes only and does not imply an endorsement by Mometrix of any particular political, scientific, or religious point of view.

raise the arms. Have the client hold for a few seconds, and then lower the chest, chin, and arms back to the ground.

The key to this exercise is to make sure the client does not overextend the chest and arms and put the lower back into an overextended position, which places the wrong kind of stress on the spine.

PRONE ISO-AB EXERCISE

The prone iso-ab exercise is also known as a **plank**. The client lies flat on the floor as if preparing for a push-up, and then performs the drawing-in maneuver. Contracting the gluteal muscles, have the client push up off the ground, leaning on arms bent at a 90-degree angle. Have the client hold for a few seconds, and then return the entire body to the floor.

If this position is too advanced, the exercise can also be performed in a full push-up position, or a modified push-up position with the knees bent on the ground.

STRENGTH-TRAINING EXERCISES

BALL CRUNCH EXERCISE

For the ball crunch exercise, a large stability ball is used. The client lays on the ball with his or her back on the ball and legs bent over the edge at a right angle. Have the client bend the arms at the elbow and place the hands behind the head. The client should perform the drawing-in maneuver to prepare the core. He or she performs an abdominal crunch, lifting up off the ball with a movement that emanates from between the shoulder blades, and then returns to starting position.

To maximize the benefit from this exercise and maintain proper form, be sure the client presses the chin toward the chest during the exercise.

BACK EXTENSION EXERCISE

For the back-extension exercise, a back-extension bench is used. The client positions him- or herself over the bench with the body facing downward. Have the client bend the arms at the elbow and place the hands behind the head. The client should perform the drawing-in maneuver to prepare the core, slowly pull the torso up, so the body comes to a straight-line position, and then return to the starting position.

To maximize the benefit from this exercise and maintain proper form, be sure that the client keeps all major points of the body aligned—from the knees to the hips to the shoulders—watching to prevent hyperextension of the lower back.

REVERSE CRUNCH EXERCISE

For the reverse crunch exercise, a weight bench is used. The client lays on his or her back on the bench with the legs bent at a right angle at the hip and a 45-degree angle at the knees. Have the client grip the weight bench with both hands at about ear level. The client should perform the drawing-in maneuver to prepare the core muscles. He or she then slowly pulls the hips upward off the bench, pulling the knees in toward the torso. The client slowly returns to the starting position in a controlled manner.

To maximize the benefit of this exercise and maintain proper form, be sure the client maintains control of the legs throughout the exercise, taking care not to use the legs to create momentum; rather, the movement should emanate from the core muscles. This will help ensure the safety of the lower back.

Copyright © Mometrix Media. You have been licensed one copy of this document for personal use only. Any other reproduction or redistribution is strictly prohibited. All rights reserved.
This content is provided for test preparation purposes only and does not imply an endorsement by Mometrix of any particular political, scientific, or religious point of view.

CABLE ROTATION EXERCISE

For the cable rotation exercise, a cable machine is used. The client stands with feet shoulder-width apart and both arms extended out from the body at waist level. Have the client hold the cable in one hand, and then cross the other hand over the body to also hold the cable, without twisting the torso. The client should perform the drawing-in maneuver to prepare the core muscles and then twist at the hips, allowing the knee to rotate in as the body twists. The core muscles and gluteus maximus should be the primary working muscles. The client returns to the starting position in a slow and controlled manner.

To maximize the benefit from this exercise and maintain proper form, be sure that the client maintains extension in the hips, knees, and ankles. This will protect the lower back from hyperextension and unnecessary stress.

POWER-TRAINING EXERCISES

ROTATION CHEST PASS EXERCISE

For the rotation chest pass exercise, a weighted medicine ball and a partner are needed. The client stands with feet shoulder-width apart and knees bent. Have him or her hold the medicine ball at chest level, with the elbows bent out evenly at each side. The client should perform the drawing-in maneuver to prepare the core muscles, and then have the client pivot one leg as he or she pushes the ball out to the side rapidly with power to the partner (or at a wall if no other person is available). The core muscles and the gluteus maximus should be the primary muscles used during this exercise. The partner can perform the same exercise or just toss the ball back so the exercise can be repeated.

To maximize the benefit from this exercise and to maintain proper form, be sure that the client maintains extension in the hips, knees, and ankles. This will protect the lower back from hyperextension and unnecessary stress.

STABILITY BALL/MEDICINE BALL PULLOVER THROW

For the stability ball/medicine ball pullover throw exercise, a stability ball, and a weighted medicine ball will be needed along with a partner, if available. Have the client lie back on the stability ball with knees hanging over the edge at a right angle and feet resting on the floor. The client extends the arms over the head, holding the medicine ball in both hands. The client should perform the drawing-in maneuver to prepare the core muscles and tuck the chin into the body as he or she does a rapid crunch, pulling the medicine ball forward over the head and tossing it with power to a partner or at a wall if no partner is available. All of the core muscles and the gluteus maximus are activated during this exercise.

Make sure the client keeps the lower back supported during this exercise and uses the core muscles, not momentum from the arms, to perform this exercise to protect the lower back from hyperextension.

FRONT MEDICINE-BALL OBLIQUE THROW EXERCISE

For the front medicine-ball oblique throw, a weighted medicine ball and a partner will be needed. Have the client stand facing either the partner or a wall, with feet shoulder-width apart. Have the client bend the knees and hold the medicine ball with both hands on the outside of one knee. The torso should be slightly twisted to that side. The client should perform the drawing-in maneuver to prepare the core muscles. In a rapid lifting motion, the client straightens and throws the ball forward with force, with arms extending straight out at about ear level.

Copyright © Mometrix Media. You have been licensed one copy of this document for personal use only. Any other reproduction or redistribution is strictly prohibited. All rights reserved. This content is provided for test preparation purposes only and does not imply an endorsement by Mometrix of any particular political, scientific, or religious point of view.

This exercise can be performed in repetitions on each side or in an alternating fashion. Be sure that the client keeps the hips, knees, and ankles properly flexed and that the back is not hyperextended.

WOODCHOP THROW EXERCISE

For the woodchop throw exercise, a weighted medicine ball will be needed. Have the client stand with their feet shoulder-width apart. The client holds the medicine ball in both hands and raises it over the head to one side, pivoting the opposite foot and twisting the torso at the hips. The client should perform the drawing-in maneuver to prepare the core muscles. In a rapid descending motion, the client crosses the body with the medicine ball and throws it down toward the opposite foot, shifting from one foot to the other.

This exercise can be performed in repetitions on each side or in an alternating fashion.

SOCCER THROW EXERCISE

The soccer throw requires a weighted medicine ball. Have the client stand with their feet shoulder-width apart. The client holds the medicine ball in both hands and raises it overhead. The client should perform the drawing-in maneuver to prepare the core muscles. In a rapid descending motion, the client tosses the medicine ball to the floor and allows the arms to follow through.

BALANCE

Balance is the ability to maintain the body in a particular position, which is essential to all movement activities. Balance is not a singular ability, but it is a component of all motion and works in conjunction with the kinetic chain and movement systems of the body.

While balance is often approached as a static process, it is a **dynamic** one. Balance requires that a person is able to increase or decrease force to the correct location in the body at the correct moment and in the correct plane of motion. The ability to accomplish this is directly related to a person's stability, strength, and power capabilities.

To **maintain balance**, a person must use all parts of the kinetic chain and many different neurological avenues that require optimal force-couple relationships and length-tension relationships, joint stability and efficiency, and muscular and neurological coordination.

Copyright © Mometrix Media. You have been licensed one copy of this document for personal use only. Any other reproduction or redistribution is strictly prohibited. All rights reserved.
This content is provided for test preparation purposes only and does not imply an endorsement by Mometrix of any particular political, scientific, or religious point of view.

Balance Training

Effective balance training continually challenges a person's ability to maintain equilibrium and balance threshold. The **balance threshold** is how far the body can move away from the center of gravity while still maintaining equilibrium. The best way to challenge this is through all planes of motion and through activities that keep the client a little off kilter, thus encouraging the correct neural pathways to increase communication, ultimately resulting in increased reaction time and neuromuscular coordination.

It is very important that challenges to the client's balance be **controllable and progressive**. The client should be challenged by a combination of factors which will increase in difficulty. Some factors involved are:

- The number of arms or legs in use
- The stability of the client's support (e.g. floor, balance beam, or half foam roll)
- The speed of the exercise
- The complexity of the exercise

For example, the basic progression for **proprioceptive exercise** is:

- Position the client on the floor with no implements
- The client uses half of a foam roll, placed rounded-side-down on the floor
- The client uses an Airex balance pad placed on the floor
- The client uses a balance disc placed on the floor

SCIENTIFIC RATIONALE

Balance training is essential to the improvement of **dynamic joint stabilization**, which is the body's ability to support a joint during any given movement. This can be accomplished by introducing multisensory conditions while a client is performing basic exercises. This helps the client become aware of his or her body balance and also helps the body start to program in biomechanically correct movement patterns. A proper progression through the Optimum Performance Training (OPT) levels is vital to avoid movement compensations and poor form during particular exercises.

The posterior tibialis and the peroneus longus stabilize the foot and ankle complex. The glutes and the adductor complex stabilize the hip joint. The rotator cuff stabilizes the humerus on the glenoid fossa.

MULTISENSORY CONDITIONS

Multisensory conditions refer to a training environment that provides varying sensory input to stimulate the body's **mechanoreceptors** and **proprioceptors**. This provides a wealth of input to the body's neurological system, increasing the communication between the neurological and muscular systems. The body's ability to rapidly respond to balance challenges increases, allowing a person to maintain a high degree of balance even when equilibrium is challenged.

Controlled instability refers to the manner in which challenges to a client's balance should be introduced. By creating an environment that offers a progression of instability, starting with the flat floor and ending with a balance disc, a health and fitness professional gives the client a little bit of instability at a time. This allows the client to approach exercises and increase stability gradually, in a controlled manner, while maintaining proper form and avoiding movement compensations that might otherwise result.

Copyright © Mometrix Media. You have been licensed one copy of this document for personal use only. Any other reproduction or redistribution is strictly prohibited. All rights reserved.
This content is provided for test preparation purposes only and does not imply an endorsement by Mometrix of any particular political, scientific, or religious point of view.

BALANCE AND JOINT DYSFUNCTION

When an individual suffers from **joint dysfunction**, there will be an accompanying **balance** problem. This is because joint dysfunction is symptomatic, as well as a cause, of a host of other problems that affect balance. These include an unfortunate cycle of injury: basic muscle inhibition, which leads to injury to the joint itself, which in turn leads to swelling of the joint and ultimately to altered ability of the body to translate sensory input to proper movement. This can all lead to dysfunction in the kinetic chain, creating faulty movement patterns that disrupt not only basic movement, but also overall ability to maintain body equilibrium or balance. This can result from many different issues, including synergistic dominance or slow prime mover activation.

LEVELS OF BALANCE TRAINING

Like all aspects of a systematic, progressive fitness-training regimen, the three basic levels of NASM's OPT fitness model—stabilization, strength, and power—are built into balance training.

Stabilization balance exercises include:

- Single-leg lift and chop
- Single-leg hip rotation (internal and external)
- Single-leg balance
- Single-leg throw and catch
- Single-leg balance reach

Strength balance exercises include:

- Single-leg Romanian deadlift
- Single-leg squat
- Single-leg squat touchdown
- Multiplanar Lunge to balance
- Multiplanar Step-up to balance

Power balance exercises include:

- Multiplanar Single-leg box hop-down with stabilization
- Multiplanar Single-leg box hop-up with stabilization
- Multiplanar (transverse, frontal, and sagittal) hop with stabilization

BALANCE-TRAINING: STABILIZATION-LEVEL EXERCISES
SINGLE-LEG BALANCE EXERCISE

To perform the single-leg balance exercise, have the client stand up straight with the feet positioned shoulder-width apart and the toes facing straight forward. Hands should be placed on the hips, and upper-body posture should include chest lifted and the shoulders back. The client should perform the drawing-in maneuver to prepare the core muscles. He or she then slightly lifts one leg up off the floor by bending the leg at the knee. Have the client balance on one foot for up to 20 seconds, keeping the shoulders, hips, and ankles in alignment, returning the foot to the floor in a slow, controlled manner.

To maximize the effectiveness of this exercise, have the client keep the gluteus maximus of the balancing leg in contracted mode for the duration of the balancing time.

Copyright © Mometrix Media. You have been licensed one copy of this document for personal use only. Any other reproduction or redistribution is strictly prohibited. All rights reserved. This content is provided for test preparation purposes only and does not imply an endorsement by Mometrix of any particular political, scientific, or religious point of view.

SINGLE-LEG BALANCE REACH EXERCISE

To perform the single-leg balance reach exercise, the client stands up straight with the feet shoulder-width apart and the toes facing straight forward. Hands should be placed on the hips. Upper-body posture includes chest lifted and shoulders back. Have the client perform the drawing-in maneuver to prepare the core muscles, slightly lift one leg up off the floor by bending the leg at the knee, and then straighten the leg, so it is stretched directly in front of the body. He or she holds this position for two beats then slowly returns to the original position. This exercise can be repeated without setting the foot down.

This exercise can also be progressed to different planes of motion. To work in the frontal plane, have the client extend the leg out to the side of the body; to work in the transverse plane, have the client reach behind the body with the leg, turning the torso in the direction of the extended leg.

SINGLE-LEG HIP INTERNAL AND EXTERNAL ROTATION EXERCISE

To perform the single-leg hip internal and external rotation exercise, the client stands up straight with the feet shoulder-width apart and facing straight forward. Hands should be placed on the hips; upper-body posture includes chest lifted and shoulders back. The client should perform the drawing-in maneuver to prepare the core muscles, and then slightly lift one leg up off the floor by bending the leg at the knee. Have the client turn the body at the hip, first inward then outward, for two beats in each direction, and then slowly return to the original position. This exercise can be performed in a set on one leg, or by alternating legs.

Make sure the client maintains a neutral hip position to avoid unnecessary strain to the lower back.

SINGLE-LEG LIFT AND CHOP EXERCISE

For the single-leg lift and chop exercise, a weighted medicine ball is used. The client stands up straight with the feet shoulder-width apart and the toes facing straight forward. Hands should be placed on the hips. Upper-body posture includes chest lifted and shoulders back. The client should perform the drawing-in maneuver to prepare the core muscles, and then slightly lift one leg up off the floor by bending the leg at the knee. Have the client hold the medicine ball in both hands, extended over the head to the same side as the raised leg, and then swing the ball downward to the opposite side of the body, holding there for two beats.

To maximize the effectiveness of this exercise, have the client keep the knee in line with the toes of the raised leg.

SINGLE-LEG SQUAT TOUCHDOWN EXERCISE

For the single-leg squat touchdown, a weighted medicine ball is used. Have the client stand up straight with the feet shoulder-width apart and the toes facing straight forward. Hands should be placed on the hips, and upper-body posture should include chest lifted and shoulders back. The client should perform the drawing-in maneuver to prepare the core muscles, and then slightly lift one leg up off the floor by bending it at the knee. From this position, the client should squat and reach down diagonally with the hand from the same side as the lifted leg and touch the opposite ankle. He or she then returns to the starting position, using the core muscles and gluteus maximus to maintain balance on the way up.

If the ankle proves too difficult for the client to reach, have him or her reach to a point higher up on the leg and work lower as they progress.

Copyright © Mometrix Media. You have been licensed one copy of this document for personal use only. Any other reproduction or redistribution is strictly prohibited. All rights reserved. This content is provided for test preparation purposes only and does not imply an endorsement by Mometrix of any particular political, scientific, or religious point of view.

BALANCE-TRAINING: STRENGTH-LEVEL EXERCISES
SINGLE-LEG SQUAT EXERCISE

For the single-leg squat exercise, the client stands up straight with the feet shoulder-width apart and the toes facing straight forward. Hands should be placed on the hips; upper-body posture includes chest lifted and shoulders back. The client should perform the drawing-in maneuver to prepare the core muscles, and then slightly lift one leg up off the floor by bending at the knee. Have the client slowly perform a squat on one leg, just to the point where alignment starts to go out; hold for two beats.

To maximize the effectiveness of this exercise, the client should keep the knee in line with the toes of the raised leg.

SINGLE-LEG ROMANIAN DEADLIFT EXERCISE

For the single-leg Romanian deadlift exercise, a weighted medicine ball is used. The client stands up straight with the feet shoulder-width apart and the toes facing straight forward. Hands should be placed on the hips. Upper-body posture includes chest lifted and shoulders back. The client should perform the drawing-in maneuver to prepare the core muscles, and then slightly lift one leg up off the floor by bending the leg at the knee, to about ankle level. Have the client reach directly down and touch the top of the lifted foot. He or she should return to the starting position, using the core muscles and gluteus maximus to maintain balance on the way up.

If the top of the foot proves too difficult for the client to reach, have him or her reach to a point higher up on the leg and work lower as they progress.

MULTIPLANAR STEP-UP TO BALANCE EXERCISE

For the step-up to balance exercise, an exercise step is needed. Have the client begin by facing the exercise step, with feet placed shoulder-width apart. Hands should be placed on the hips. Upper-body posture includes chest lifted and shoulders back. The client should perform the drawing-in maneuver to prepare the core muscles, and then step up onto the exercise step with one foot. With toes pointing forward and hips straight, the client balances over the one foot, with the other foot up, leg bent at a 90-degree angle at the knee. After holding for two beats, the client slowly returns the lifted foot to the ground and returns to the original starting position.

MULTIPLANAR LUNGE TO BALANCE EXERCISE

To perform the lunge to balance exercise, have the client stand up straight with the feet positioned shoulder-width apart and the toes facing straight forward. Hands should be placed on the hips. Upper-body posture includes chest lifted and shoulders back. The client should perform the drawing-in maneuver to prepare the core muscles. He or she lunges forward in a deep lunge, with the back knee bending to the ground. Pushing off hard from the front leg, the client should return to an upright position, balancing on the back leg alone, while the formerly front leg is bent at a 90-degree angle.

This exercise can also be performed in different planes, with a side lunge to work in the frontal plane, and a turning lunge to work in the transverse plane.

Make sure the client's back is not hyperextended during these lunges. If the hip muscles are overactive, a shallower lunge is advisable.

Copyright © Mometrix Media. You have been licensed one copy of this document for personal use only. Any other reproduction or redistribution is strictly prohibited. All rights reserved. This content is provided for test preparation purposes only and does not imply an endorsement by Mometrix of any particular political, scientific, or religious point of view.

BALANCE-TRAINING: POWER-LEVEL EXERCISES

MULTIPLANAR HOP WITH STABILIZATION EXERCISE

For the multiplanar hop with stabilization exercise, an agility ladder is used. Place the agility ladder flat on the ground, and have the client stand at one end, with the feet positioned shoulder-width apart. Hands should be placed on the hips. Upper-body posture includes chest lifted and shoulders back. Have the client perform the drawing-in maneuver to prepare the core muscles, and then slightly lift one leg by bending at the knee. The client hops forward with the raised foot into the first slot of the agility ladder, landing on the balancing leg, and holds this position for up to five beats. Then have the client hop backward, again switching the feet.

This exercise can be performed in all planes of motion. To work in the sagittal plane, have the client begin with his or her back facing the agility ladder and hop backward. To work in the transverse plane, have the client stand next to the agility ladder and hop sideways.

MULTIPLANAR SINGLE-LEG BOX HOP-UP WITH STABILIZATION EXERCISE

For the single-leg box hop-up with stabilization exercise, an exercise step will be used. Have the client begin by facing the exercise step, with the feet positioned shoulder-width apart. Hands should be placed on the hips. Upper-body posture should include chest lifted and shoulders back. The client should perform the drawing-in maneuver to prepare the core muscles, and then slightly lift one leg by bending at the knee. From that position, have the client jump up onto the box with both feet, landing with knees bent slightly and feet pointing forward. Repeat the exercise using either the same start foot or by alternating feet.

This exercise can also be performed in the transverse and frontal planes.

MULTIPLANAR SINGLE-LEG BOX HOP-DOWN WITH STABILIZATION EXERCISE

For the single-leg box hop-down with stabilization exercise, an exercise step is used. The client begins by standing atop the exercise step, with the feet positioned shoulder-width apart. Hands should be placed on the hips. Upper-body posture includes chest lifted and shoulders back. The client should perform the drawing-in maneuver to prepare the core muscles, and then slightly lift one leg by bending at the knee. From that position, have the client jump down to the floor from the box, landing on both feet, with knees bent slightly and feet pointing forward. Repeat the exercise by using the same start foot or by alternating the feet.

This exercise can also be performed in the transverse and frontal planes.

IMPLEMENTING BALANCE-TRAINING REGIMENS

The best way to implement a balance-training regimen is by following NASM's **Optimum Performance Training (OPT) model**. Usually, the correct balance-training level will correspond to the current overall training level the client is in (e.g., a stability-level client should work on stability-level balance exercises).

Three sets of **stabilization balance exercises** should be performed for as many as four exercises; each set should include 12 to 20 repetitions. The pace of the exercises should be slow and controlled, with up to 90 seconds of rest between each set.

Select as many as four **strength balance exercises** and perform two to three sets of each, with eight to twelve repetitions per set. The exercises should be performed at a medium pace, with up to a minute of rest between each set.

Copyright © Mometrix Media. You have been licensed one copy of this document for personal use only. Any other reproduction or redistribution is strictly prohibited. All rights reserved. This content is provided for test preparation purposes only and does not imply an endorsement by Mometrix of any particular political, scientific, or religious point of view.

Power balance exercises should be performed in two or three sets of up to two exercises, with between eight to a dozen repetitions each. The pace of the exercises should be fully controlled, holding the end pose for up to five beats, with up to a minute of rest between each set.

OPT Level	Phase	Balance Exercise	Reps	Sets	Rest
Stabilization	1	1 – 4 balance stabilization	12 – 20 6 – 10 (SL)	1 - 3	0 – 90 s
Strength	2	1 – 3 balance strength	8 - 12	2 - 3	0 – 60 s
Hypertrophy	3	0 – 4 balance strength	8 - 12	2 - 3	0 – 60 s
Maximal Strength	4	0 – 3 balance strength	8 - 12	2 - 3	0 – 60 s
Power	5	0 – 2 balance power	8 - 12	2 - 3	0 – 60 s

Copyright © Mometrix Media. You have been licensed one copy of this document for personal use only. Any other reproduction or redistribution is strictly prohibited. All rights reserved. This content is provided for test preparation purposes only and does not imply an endorsement by Mometrix of any particular political, scientific, or religious point of view.

Reactive Training

Reactive or **power training** is the third level on NASM's OPT model. Reactive training comprises rapid-fire exercises that increase the body's ability to produce maximum force quickly. Before a client attempts reactive-training exercises, he or she should have progressed through the first two levels of the OPT model, stabilization, and strength. Once the client builds sufficient strength and balance, he or she can engage in power-level activities.

To increase a person's ability to create explosive muscle force, a trainer must incorporate **plyometric exercises** that have an eccentric contraction coupled with a powerful concentric contraction. Plyometrics will increase the ability of the nervous system and muscular system to communicate efficiently and produce maximum force.

INTEGRATED PERFORMANCE PARADIGM

Reactive training gives a person the ability to program rapid, correct movement patterns into their muscles and neural pathways. This gives all components of the kinetic chain, including the muscles, ligaments, and tendons, the ability to become stronger for all activities, whether daily living or athletic in nature. A body can only react as quickly as its level of coordination will allow. The outcome is to improve a person's ability to react quickly in an efficient, high-energy way; this is commonly called **rate of force production**. Due to the perception that reactive training increases injury risk, it is often left out of a traditional training program. However, if the client properly progresses through the first two levels of the OPT model, and his or her particular needs are assessed and built into the training routine, power-level training can be effectively and safely incorporated into that client's overall goals.

LEVELS OF REACTIVE TRAINING

Like all aspects of a systematic, progressive fitness training regimen, the three basic levels of NASM's OPT fitness model—stabilization, strength, and power—are built into reactive training.

Stabilization reactive exercises include:

- Multiplanar jump with stabilization
- Squat jump with stabilization
- Box jump-down with stabilization
- Box jump-up with stabilization

Strength reactive exercises include:

- Tuck jump
- Squat jump
- Power step-up
- Butt kick

Power reactive exercises include:

- Proprioceptive plyometrics
- Single-leg power step-up
- Ice skater

Copyright © Mometrix Media. You have been licensed one copy of this document for personal use only. Any other reproduction or redistribution is strictly prohibited. All rights reserved.
This content is provided for test preparation purposes only and does not imply an endorsement by Mometrix of any particular political, scientific, or religious point of view.

SPOTTING TECHNIQUES

The principle of **progressive overload** suggests that the body only meets fitness goals when sufficiently challenged. It is important to challenge the body's limits to improve fitness, but there is an inherent injury risk associated with this practice. **Spotting** can significantly reduce this risk. When spotting, a trainer provides the client with a minimal amount of assistance to ensure they complete the repetition or set.

Spotting can occur anywhere within the range of motion. In the early stages of a lift, the trainer can provide assistance to ensure that the client can begin the movement safely. During the lift, the trainer can help the client through any difficult or "sticking" points. At the end of the lift, the trainer can help the client safely return the weight to the end position. When spotting, it is important to provide only as much assistance as the client needs. The trainer should not be performing the movement for the client. Before the exercise begins, the trainer should discuss what the spot. If a spot requires physical contact, the client should be made aware, and the trainer should obtain consent to make physical contact.

REACTIVE-TRAINING: STABILIZATION-LEVEL EXERCISES

SQUAT JUMP WITH STABILIZATION

The client begins the squat jump with stabilization exercise by standing with the feet positioned shoulder-width apart and the toes facing straight forward. The client should perform the drawing-in maneuver to prepare the core muscles and to tighten the gluteus maximus. Have the client bend as though sitting down in a chair, with arms straightened behind the body. Then the client jumps straight up, with arms going straight up over the head and legs extending straight. Have the client land in the same knees-bent position, with arms returning to the starting position, and hold for up to five seconds.

BOX JUMP-UP WITH STABILIZATION EXERCISE

For the box jump-up with stabilization exercise, an exercise step is used. The client begins by facing the exercise step with the feet positioned shoulder-width apart. Arms should be straight and held in line with the torso. Upper-body posture includes chest lifted and shoulders back. The client should perform the drawing-in maneuver to prepare the core muscles and then bend the knees deeply as though sitting down in a chair. From that position, the client jumps up onto the box with both feet, landing with knees bent and feet pointing forward. Repeat the exercise using either the same starting foot or by alternating the feet.

This exercise can also be performed in the transverse and frontal planes.

BOX JUMP-DOWN WITH STABILIZATION EXERCISE

For the box jump-down with stabilization exercise, an exercise step is used. The client begins standing atop the step; feet are placed shoulder-width apart. Arms should be straight and held in line with the torso. Upper-body posture includes chest lifted and shoulders back. The client should perform the drawing-in maneuver to prepare the core muscles and then bend the knees deeply as though sitting down in a chair. From that position, have the client jump down off of the box with both feet, landing with knees bent and feet pointing forward. Repeat the exercise using either the same starting foot or by alternating feet.

This exercise can also be performed in the transverse and frontal planes.

Copyright © Mometrix Media. You have been licensed one copy of this document for personal use only. Any other reproduction or redistribution is strictly prohibited. All rights reserved. This content is provided for test preparation purposes only and does not imply an endorsement by Mometrix of any particular political, scientific, or religious point of view.

HORIZONTAL JUMP WITH STABILIZATION EXERCISE

The client begins the horizontal jump with stabilization exercise by standing atop the exercise step, with the feet positioned shoulder-width apart. Arms should be straight and held in line with the torso. Upper-body posture includes chest lifted and shoulders back. The client should perform the drawing-in maneuver to prepare the core muscles and then bend the knees deeply as though sitting down in a chair. From that position, have the client jump straight ahead as far as he or she can. The client finishes with knees bent, feet facing forward, and arms straight and held parallel to the bent knees. Have the client hold the end position for up to five beats.

This exercise can also be performed in the transverse and frontal planes. Make sure that the client lands gently to help the body properly absorb the shock of the exercise.

REACTIVE-TRAINING: STRENGTH-LEVEL EXERCISES

SQUAT JUMP EXERCISE

The client begins the squat jump exercise by standing with the feet positioned shoulder-width apart and the toes facing straight forward. The client should perform the drawing-in maneuver to prepare the core muscles and to tighten the gluteus maximus. The client bends as though sitting down in a chair, with arms straightened behind the body. The client jumps straight up, with arms going straight up over the head and the legs extending straight. Have the client land in the same knees-bent position, with arms returning to the starting position. As soon as the client has landed, he or she should perform another squat jump, again ending in the starting position.

TUCK JUMP EXERCISE

The client begins the tuck jump exercise by standing with the feet positioned shoulder-width apart and the toes facing straight forward. The client should perform the drawing-in maneuver to prepare the core muscles and to tighten the gluteus maximus. The client bends as though sitting down in a chair, with arms straightened behind the body. Have the client jump straight up with the body and arms staying in the same position, but keep the legs bent in and under the body. The client lands in the same knees-bent position, with arms returning to the starting position. As soon as the client has landed, he or she should perform another tuck jump, again ending in the starting position.

Make sure the client maintains proper form throughout the exercise and lands gently to avoid unnecessary shock to the body.

BUTT KICK JUMP EXERCISE

For the butt kick jump, the client begins by standing with the feet positioned shoulder-width apart and the toes facing straight forward. The client should perform the drawing-in maneuver to prepare the core muscles and to tighten the gluteus maximus. Have the client bend as though sitting down in a chair, with arms straightened behind the body. The client jumps straight up, with the body and arms straightening up and the legs bending in rapidly under the buttocks. He or she lands in the same knees-bent position, with arms returning to the starting position. As soon as the client has landed, he or she should perform another butt kick jump, again ending in the starting position.

Make sure the client maintains proper form throughout the exercise and lands gently to avoid unnecessary shock to the body.

POWER STEP-UP EXERCISE

For the power step-up exercise, an exercise step will be needed. The client begins facing the step, with the feet positioned shoulder-width apart and the toes facing straight forward. The client

Copyright © Mometrix Media. You have been licensed one copy of this document for personal use only. Any other reproduction or redistribution is strictly prohibited. All rights reserved. This content is provided for test preparation purposes only and does not imply an endorsement by Mometrix of any particular political, scientific, or religious point of view.

should perform the drawing-in maneuver to prepare the core muscles and to tighten the gluteus maximus. Have the client step up onto the box with one foot, and then push up off of the box with force, extending both legs straight while in the air. The client lands in the starting position and performs another step up right away.

To maintain proper alignment and maximize the effectiveness of the exercise, make sure the client keeps the knees and feet lined up before the step-up motion and during landing.

REACTIVE-TRAINING: POWER-LEVEL EXERCISES

ICE SKATER EXERCISE

For the ice skater exercise, an agility ladder is used. Lay the agility ladder flat on the floor, and have the client begin by standing in front of the ladder, facing away from it with the feet positioned shoulder-width apart. The client bends the knees deeply and leans the torso forward, lifting the inside leg slightly in a posture resembling that of a speed skater. The client should perform the drawing-in maneuver to prepare the core muscles, and then jump from the balancing leg to the raised leg in a sideways motion, parallel to the agility ladder. The client jumps back and forth in the same manner as quickly as he or she can while maintaining proper form.

SINGLE-LEG POWER STEP-UP EXERCISE

For the single-leg power step-up exercise, an exercise step will be needed. The client begins facing the step, with feet shoulder-width apart and the toes facing straight ahead. The client should perform the drawing-in maneuver to prepare the core muscles and to tighten the gluteus maximus. Have the client step up onto the box with one foot then push up off of the box with force and extend both legs straight while in the air. The client lands on the stepping leg and then performs another step up right away.

To maintain proper alignment and maximize the effectiveness of the exercise, make sure the client keeps the knees and feet lined up before the step-up motion and during landing.

PROPRIOCEPTIVE PLYOMETRICS EXERCISE

For the proprioceptive plyometrics exercise, five-disc cones are needed. (If no disc cones are available, any relatively flat item, even masking tape, can be used.) Lay the disc cones in a T formation on the ground, and have the client stand by them with feet shoulder-width apart. The client should perform the drawing-in maneuver to prepare the core muscles and to tighten the gluteus maximus, and then bend the knees slightly. Instruct the client to either hop on a single leg or jump on both feet in various patterns over, across, and through the cone formation. Be sure that the client maintains proper alignment of the knees and ankles, and there is no hyperextension of the lower back.

IMPLEMENTING REACTIVE-TRAINING REGIMENS

The best way to implement a reactive-training regimen is by following NASM's **OPT model**. Usually, the correct reactive-training level will correspond to the current overall training level the client is in (e.g., a stability-level client should work on stability-level balance exercises).

Stabilization reactive exercises are performed in up to three sets of up to two exercises, with from between five to eight repetitions each. The pace of the exercises should be slow and controlled, with up to 90 seconds of rest between each set.

Copyright © Mometrix Media. You have been licensed one copy of this document for personal use only. Any other reproduction or redistribution is strictly prohibited. All rights reserved.
This content is provided for test preparation purposes only and does not imply an endorsement by Mometrix of any particular political, scientific, or religious point of view.

Strength reactive exercises are performed in two or three sets of up to four exercises, with from between eight to ten repetitions each. The pace of the exercises should be medium, with up to a minute of rest between each set.

Power reactive exercises are performed in two or three sets of up to two exercises, with from between eight to a dozen repetitions each. The pace of the exercises should be as quick as possible while maintaining control, with up to a minute of rest between each set.

Copyright © Mometrix Media. You have been licensed one copy of this document for personal use only. Any other reproduction or redistribution is strictly prohibited. All rights reserved. This content is provided for test preparation purposes only and does not imply an endorsement by Mometrix of any particular political, scientific, or religious point of view.

SAQ Training

SAQ refers to speed, agility, and quickness training. It follows NASM's OPT model.

Speed is a term used to describe a person's aptitude for straight-ahead swiftness. Speed includes front side and backside mechanics, which refer to the triple flexion of the front and back legs, respectively.

Agility is a term used to describe a person's aptitude for beginning or stopping motion quickly.

Quickness is a term used to describe how fast a person can react to external stimulus and alter his or her position in response.

POSITIONING

Proper running mechanics are essential to optimal kinetic chain efficiency. Consider the following kinetic chain checkpoints:

- **Head**—The head should remain in alignment with the hip complex and be maintained in a neutral position, without extension or compensation.
- **LPH complex**—The lumbo-pelvic-hip (LPH) complex should remain neutral, with a slight lean ahead when accelerating.
- **Knees**—The knees should always face forward. If the knee rotates inward, an increase in stability exercises and a decrease in activities that may lead to injury are required.
- **Feet/ankles**—The feet should always face forward and be in a dorsiflexed position upon impact with the ground. Watch for improper internal rotation, which can lead to injury.

IMPLEMENT SAQ TRAINING REGIMENS

The best way to implement an SAQ-training regimen is by following NASM's **OPT model**. Usually, the correct SAQ training level will correspond to the current overall training level the client is in—for example, stability-level clients should work on stability-level exercises.

Stabilization SAQ exercises are performed in up to two sets of up to six exercises, of half an agility ladder, with up to 60 seconds of rest between each ladder drill and up to 90 seconds for cone drills.

Strength SAQ exercises should be performed in up to four sets of up to nine exercises, of half an agility ladder, with up to 60 seconds of rest between each ladder drill and up to 90 seconds for cone drills.

Copyright © Mometrix Media. You have been licensed one copy of this document for personal use only. Any other reproduction or redistribution is strictly prohibited. All rights reserved. This content is provided for test preparation purposes only and does not imply an endorsement by Mometrix of any particular political, scientific, or religious point of view.

Power SAQ exercises should be performed in up to six sets of up to nine exercises, of half an agility ladder, with up to 60 seconds of rest between each ladder drill and up to 90 seconds for cone drills.

OPT Level	Drills	Horizontal inertia	Unpredictability	Example Exercises	Sets	Reps	Resting period
Stabilization	4-6	limited	limited	Cone Shuffles, Agility ladder drills	1-2	2-3	0-60 s
Strength	6-8	moderate	limited	5-10-5, T-Drill, Box drill, Stand Up to Figure 8	3-4	3-5	0-60 s
Power	6-10	maximal	moderate	Modified Box Drill, Partner Mirror Drill, Timed drills	3-5	3-5	0-90 s

SAQ TRAINING: STRENGTH LEVEL EXERCISES
ONE-INS EXERCISE

The one-ins exercise requires a speed ladder and is one of a series of NASM speed-ladder drills specifically designed to improve speed, agility, and quickness.

To perform this exercise, lay the speed ladder down on the ground. The client begins at either end of the ladder. The client should perform the drawing-in maneuver to prepare the core muscles. The client quickly runs through the speed ladder, with one foot stepping in each of the squares. Be sure the client maintains proper form, with feet, knees, hips, and shoulders all facing forward and arms bending at the elbows for each step.

TWO-INS EXERCISE

The two-ins exercise requires a speed ladder and is one of a series of NASM speed-ladder drills specifically designed to improve speed, agility, and quickness.

To perform this exercise, lay the speed ladder down on the ground. The client begins at either end of the ladder. The client should perform the drawing-in maneuver to prepare the core muscles, and then he or she quickly performs the following progression: Step with one foot into a square, and then land with both feet in the same square. Step with the same beginning foot into the next square, and then land with both feet in the same square. Repeat to the end of the ladder, and then do another set beginning with the opposite foot.

SIDE SHUFFLE EXERCISE

The side shuffle exercise requires a speed ladder and is one of a series of NASM speed-ladder drills specifically designed to improve speed, agility, and quickness.

To perform this exercise, lay the speed ladder down on the ground. The client begins at either end of the ladder, facing forward. The client should perform the drawing-in maneuver to prepare the core muscles, and then take a sideways step into the first square of the ladder with the foot closest to the ladder. The other foot should follow into the same square. Then a sideways step with the leading foot is taken into the next square, with the other foot following. Repeat to the end of the ladder, and then do another set in the opposite direction.

Copyright © Mometrix Media. You have been licensed one copy of this document for personal use only. Any other reproduction or redistribution is strictly prohibited. All rights reserved. This content is provided for test preparation purposes only and does not imply an endorsement by Mometrix of any particular political, scientific, or religious point of view.

IN-IN-OUT-OUT EXERCISE

The in-in-out-out exercise requires a speed ladder and is one of a series of NASM speed-ladder drills specifically designed to improve speed, agility, and quickness (SAQ).

To perform this exercise, lay the speed ladder down on the ground. The client begins at either end of the ladder. The client should perform the drawing-in maneuver to prepare the core muscles. He or she quickly performs the following progression: Hop forward into the first square with both feet together, into the second square with both feet together, and then hop with both feet apart, straddling the ladder, for two sections. Repeat to the end of the ladder, and then perform another set in the opposite direction. Repeat as quickly as possible while maintaining proper form.

IN-IN-OUT EXERCISE

The in-in-out exercise requires a speed ladder and is one of a series of NASM speed-ladder drills specifically designed to improve speed, agility, and quickness.

To perform this exercise, lay the speed ladder down on the ground. The in-in-out exercise is also known as a zigzag due to the motion the feet make along the speed ladder.

The client begins standing next to the ladder. The client should perform the drawing-in maneuver to prepare the core muscles, and then quickly perform the following progression: Step with the foot closest to the ladder into the square diagonal to the starting position, and then bring the other foot into that square as well. Have the client step out of the opposite side of the ladder to a position diagonal to the starting point with the first foot and then with the second foot. Repeat this progression to the end of the ladder as quickly as possible while maintaining proper form.

ALI SHUFFLE (WASHING MACHINE) EXERCISE

The Ali shuffle requires a speed ladder and is one of a series of NASM speed-ladder drills specifically designed to improve speed, agility, and quickness.

To perform this exercise, lay the speed ladder on the ground.

The client begins by standing on the ladder, with the squares running to the right. The client should perform the drawing-in maneuver to prepare the core muscles, then quickly perform the following progression: In a jogging motion step with the right foot into the first square, and then follow with the left. Step with the right foot into the square to the right, followed by the left. Step with the right foot backward out of the ladder, followed by the left. Step sideways to the right with the right foot, followed by the left. Repeat this progression to the end of the ladder as quickly as possible while maintaining proper form.

SAQ TRAINING: STRENGTH-LEVEL DRILLS
5-10-5 DRILL

The 5-10-5 drill requires three cones and is one of a series of NASM cone drills specifically designed to improve speed, agility, and quickness.

Place three cones an equal distance apart in a straight line across 10 yards of floor space. The client begins at the middle cone, which will be designated as the start and finish point for the drill.

First, have the client sprint from the center cone to one far cone. Then the client sprints from that cone to the cone at the far end. Lastly, the client sprints back to the center cone. Repeat this progression as the client's template dictates, making sure that the client maintains proper form throughout the exercise.

Copyright © Mometrix Media. You have been licensed one copy of this document for personal use only. Any other reproduction or redistribution is strictly prohibited. All rights reserved. This content is provided for test preparation purposes only and does not imply an endorsement by Mometrix of any particular political, scientific, or religious point of view.

BOX DRILL

The box drill requires four cones and is one of a series of NASM cone drills specifically designed to improve speed, agility, and quickness.

Place four cones in a square, with each side ten yards in length. The client begins at the lower-right corner and performs a different action along each side of the square. First, have the client perform a sprint straight forward to the top-right cone. Then the client side shuffles (hopping with feet open, then closed, then open, then closed) to the top-left cone. The client then backpedals to the bottom-left cone. Lastly, the client performs a grapevine motion (step right, step over with the left, step right, step behind with the left) back to the starting cone. Repeat this drill in the opposite direction, making sure the client maintains proper form throughout the exercise.

T-DRILL

The T-drill exercise requires four cones and is one of a series of NASM cone drills specifically designed to improve speed, agility, and quickness.

Place the cones in a T formation: the start/end cone will be the bottom-center point. Place the second cone five yards straight ahead, and then place the last two cones five yards to each side of the second cone.

The client begins at the start cone and sprints forward to cone two. The client then side shuffles to the left-hand cone. The client performs a grapevine all the way to the other side to the right-hand cone. Then the client side shuffles back to the center cone. Finally, have the client sprint back to the start position.

Repeat this drill in the opposite direction, making sure that the client maintains proper form throughout the exercise.

L.E.F.T. DRILL

The L.E.F.T. drill requires two cones and is one of a series of NASM cone drills specifically designed to improve speed, agility, and quickness.

Place two cones ten yards apart. This exercise consists of having the client travel back and forth between the two cones performing different movements. Beginning with the left-hand cone, the client first sprints straight across to the other cone. Next, have him or her backpedal to the starting cone. The client side shuffles to the far cone and side shuffles back to the start cone. The client performs a grapevine to the far cone and back again to the starting cone. Finally, the client finishes the exercise with one more sprint to the far cone.

Make sure the client maintains proper form throughout the exercise.

Copyright © Mometrix Media. You have been licensed one copy of this document for personal use only. Any other reproduction or redistribution is strictly prohibited. All rights reserved. This content is provided for test preparation purposes only and does not imply an endorsement by Mometrix of any particular political, scientific, or religious point of view.

Integrated Resistance Training

FINAL COMPONENT

The final component of an integrated training program is **resistance training**—weight lifting and other similar exercises. Building muscle is an important component of a fitness regimen because it improves a person's ability across the OPT spectrum, increasing stabilization, strength, and power-producing capabilities. It is also the part of the training routine most often associated with the typical workout.

While this aspect of training is often viewed as the central element, it is but one part of an overall fitness scheme. To properly program resistance training into a fitness regimen, the trainer must understand how to get results, which requires knowing common **barriers** such as the principle of adaptation and general adaptation syndrome.

PRINCIPLE OF ADAPTATION

The principle of adaptation may be the most important physiological concept for a health and fitness professional to know and understand. This principle outlines how the human body will **change** (adapt) to meet additional demands placed upon it from outside stresses to the best of its ability. Because training is usually used as a means of achieving adaptation, whether in the form of weight loss, increased strength or endurance, this principle is the key to all training activities.

It is also important to understand the flip side of this principle: Because the body will adapt to additional stresses, a trainer must vary the method in which stresses are applied, so the body will continue to adapt and not hit a performance plateau.

BENEFITS

A **resistance-training program** can offer a host of benefits derived from the body's ability to adapt to the additional stimuli placed upon it. These adaptations are a function of the general adaptation syndrome and the principle of specificity, which dictate that the body will adapt to the specific forces placed upon it.

Performance benefits include:

- Additional endurance
- Additional explosive strength (power)
- Additional strength in the tissues (muscle, ligament, and tendon)

Physiological benefits include:

- Heightened metabolism
- Improved bone density
- Heightened cardiovascular ability
- Improvements to the hormonal (endocrine) system
- Less body fat
- More lean muscle

Copyright © Mometrix Media. You have been licensed one copy of this document for personal use only. Any other reproduction or redistribution is strictly prohibited. All rights reserved. This content is provided for test preparation purposes only and does not imply an endorsement by Mometrix of any particular political, scientific, or religious point of view.

GENERAL ADAPTATION SYNDROME
STAGES

The alarm reaction stage, resistance development stage, and exhaustion stage are the three stages of **general adaptation syndrome**. Each causes a very specific reaction in the body, and they must be understood to maximize training gains.

- The **alarm reaction stage** is the body's first response to new stimuli. An alarm reaction related to fitness training might be increased oxygen intake or blood flow to the stressed site.
- The **resistance development stage** is the stage in which the body specifically adapts to a particular stimulus, meaning the body learns to cope without making any significant gains. The takeaway from this stage is that the body needs to be continuously challenged to reach new levels of fitness
- **Exhaustion** refers to the body's inability to cope properly with repeated stimuli over time, causing a breakdown in proper function.

Stage	Reaction
Alarm reaction	Initial reaction to stressor such as increased oxygen and blood supply to the necessary areas of the body
Resistance development	Increased functional capacity to adapt to stressor such as increasing motor unit recruitment
Exhaustion	A prolonged intolerable stressor produces fatigue and leads to a breakdown in the system or injury

ALARM REACTION STAGE

Exercise places **stress** on bones, joints, muscles, connective tissues, and the nervous system. When a deconditioned individual begins exercising, the body undergoes a number of physiological changes in response. Increased supply of blood and oxygen and, improved neural recruitment are examples of the body's physiologic responses to exercise. This is referred to as the **alarm reaction stage**.

RESISTANCE DEVELOPMENT STAGE

In the resistance-development phase of general adaptation syndrome, the body becomes accustomed to a new stress placed upon it and creates a **generalized response** to handle this stress. After the initial response, which will manifest as a gain in fitness training (such as being able to run a lap more quickly), the body will not increase in ability unless further stress is placed upon it.

Although many fitness professionals are aware of GAS, they don't always address it properly when designing a program for a client. Often in resistance training, a trainer will merely add more weight to an exercise. While this is one way of changing the stress placed on the body, it is not the only way. It is important to change the number of repetitions and the tempo at which they are performed, along with other elements that are addressed under NASM's program-design parameters.

EXHAUSTION STAGE

When there is an ongoing stress on the body, even a positive one, as is the case with fitness training, the body will adapt to a certain extent and then potentially become **exhausted** or incapable of

Copyright © Mometrix Media. You have been licensed one copy of this document for personal use only. Any other reproduction or redistribution is strictly prohibited. All rights reserved. This content is provided for test preparation purposes only and does not imply an endorsement by Mometrix of any particular political, scientific, or religious point of view.

continuing to cope with the stress. This can lead to a variety of problems such as stress fractures, tears and strains, joint weakness, and general tiredness.

Exhaustion can disrupt a training regimen due to **injury** as well as through client **apathy**: A client who is not experiencing ongoing improvement may become disinterested and lose the motivation to continue.

Reducing incidence: it is important for a trainer to recognize that there are many tissues used in a given workout and take steps to prevent exhaustion and its related injuries in resistance training. These fibers have differing levels of blood flow and therefore may adapt to increased stimulus at different rates. To reduce repetitive stress and increase the range of stress placed on the different tissues, whether muscle, ligament, or tendons, varying weights and tempos should be used as well as different exercises that span all of the planes of movement.

PRINCIPLE OF SPECIFICITY

The principle of specificity is frequently referred to by an alternate name, the **specific adaptation to imposed demands (SAID) principle,** which simply states that a person's body will learn to cope with added stresses placed on it.

The takeaway from this principle is that the body will adapt to meet the demands that are placed on it. The trainer must design a program that challenges the client's body to adapt in the desired fashion.

The OPT model is used to address this issue. It includes **stabilization** (which includes stabilization endurance), **strength** (which includes strength endurance, hypertrophy, and maximal strength), and **power** (which includes the power phase).

METABOLIC, MECHANICAL, AND NEUROMUSCULAR SPECIFICITY

Metabolic, mechanical, and neuromuscular specificity refer to different types of stimuli that can be placed on the body to cause an adaptation reaction.

- **Metabolic specificity** describes the amount of energy demanded of the body—how much energy a workout requires, which can vary depending on the length of time spent training or the intensity at which training is performed.
- **Mechanical specificity** describes the amount of weight or the types of activities demanded of the body—how much resistance is being applied and in what number of repetitions.
- **Neuromuscular specificity** describes how fast a given exercise is performed.

ACHIEVING GOALS

The principle of specificity can be used to help a client achieve specific **goals** based on the fact that the body adapts to the specific demands that are placed on it. That is, doing specific exercises and activities ultimately makes it easier to perform those same activities as the body meets the specific demands placed upon it. As an example, if a client is training to run a marathon, incorporating running into their training regimen would be essential to prepare the body to adapt to it.

However, the principle of specificity also tells us that repeating the same activity over and over without adding systematic training to help complementary body tissues (such as ligaments and tendons) adapt can lead to injury or exhaustion. This creates a **barrier** for a client attempting to achieve a specific goal.

Copyright © Mometrix Media. You have been licensed one copy of this document for personal use only. Any other reproduction or redistribution is strictly prohibited. All rights reserved. This content is provided for test preparation purposes only and does not imply an endorsement by Mometrix of any particular political, scientific, or religious point of view.

GOAL OF RESISTANCE-TRAINING

The primary goal of resistance training is to create **adaptations** in the body relating to strength. This, and more, can be accomplished by increasing the client's overall endurance, creating more lean muscle mass, or by assisting in reducing overall body fat.

With a systematic, integrated approach, the health and fitness professional can help a client maximize the adaptations of all different types of body tissues and minimize exhaustion resulting from general adaptation syndrome, allowing the client to train longer without injury or kinetic-chain compensations.

STRENGTH

Strength is defined as the ability of the body to overcome an exterior force through internal tension. This can come in the form of stabilizing, enduring, balancing, or creating explosive power.

Traditional training programs have focused too much on single-muscle hypertrophy, or building muscle in a single muscle group, working only in one plane of motion. For example, a classic resistance-training program might include a large number of biceps curls. This approach fails to recognize that muscles work in more than one way (e.g., concentrically, isometrically, and eccentrically).

NASM's approach differs in that it works in multiple planes of motion, uses multiple exercises, varies repetitions, changes tempo, and works not only the specific muscle but also the supporting tissues to create overall adaptations while minimizing injury or exhaustion.

MAXIMIZING STRENGTH GAINS

As with all elements of NASM's integrated training regimen, the **OPT model** should be followed when creating a resistance-training routine to maximize gains in strength. Exercises should follow the order of the OPT model (stabilization, strength, and power) to create the sought-after neuromuscular adaptations. Each phase focuses on exercises designed to have a specific effect on the neuromuscular system.

For the **stabilization phase**, specific adaptations include muscular endurance and overall stability. For the **strength phase**, specific adaptations include strength-endurance, building muscle mass (hypertrophy), and creating the highest amount of strength possible (maximal strength). For the **power phase**, there are no additional specific adaptations other than creating explosive power (Power can be understood as a force over a time.)

STABILIZATION LEVEL

The stabilization level of training is vital to help strengthen the underlying musculature and create a strong foundation for all movement. Stabilization is the key to a novice client's success because it addresses the communication of the neuromuscular system—how the brain and nerves tell the muscles to move.

Muscular endurance and stability are the two specific adaptations of this level:

- **Endurance** refers to the length of time a muscle can work. This is important because if the body cannot endure ongoing stressors, form and function will deteriorate, potentially leading to injury.

Copyright © Mometrix Media. You have been licensed one copy of this document for personal use only. Any other reproduction or redistribution is strictly prohibited. All rights reserved. This content is provided for test preparation purposes only and does not imply an endorsement by Mometrix of any particular political, scientific, or religious point of view.

- **Stability** refers to the body's ability to maintain proper postural form while working or moving. This requires muscle endurance (which is why the endurance phase precedes the stability phase) and proper neuromuscular communication to assure the correct muscles are being called upon to perform a given task.

STRENGTH LEVEL

The strength level of the OPT model focusses on achieving higher levels of strength capability and neuromuscular efficiency. There are three specific adaptations to the strength level of resistance training: strength-endurance, hypertrophy, and maximal strength. Each phase should be approached in order as the stages are progressive. **Strength endurance** refers to the length of time a person can maintain a given level of force. **Hypertrophy** refers to building the size of muscles, exercising them isometrically, concentrically, and eccentrically in all planes of motion. **Maximal strength** refers to training that encourages the top number of muscle fibers and motor units to work to create top levels of force.

POWER LEVEL

The power level of the OPT model is designed to help the client achieve explosive force production as quickly as possible. This requires completion of the stabilization and strength levels to establish a proper muscular foundation and the amount of strength needed for such tasks, while concurrently training the neuromuscular system to communicate efficiently enough to handle the demands of power movement.

The **power phase** improves the body's ability to produce force by activating more motor units, improving the synchronization between them, and increasing the activation speed. The primary goal is to increase the **speed** at which movement occurs, so the client is better equipped to handle daily activities or sports-related or other functional activities. This can be accomplished by adding either more speed, velocity, force, or weight.

TYPES OF RESISTANCE-TRAINING SYSTEMS

There are many different types of resistance-training systems. Resistance-training systems were initially appealing to people looking to maximize hypertrophy, such as bodybuilders. Systems include:

- **Single-set**—doing one set of a given exercise
- **Multiple-set**—doing multiple sets of a given exercise
- **Vertical loading**—progressing through the exercises that have been programmed on the OPT template in a vertical fashion
- **Horizontal loading**—performing all the desired sets of each exercise before going on to the next exercise
- **Circuit training**—performing all exercises one after another without stopping in between
- **Superset**—doing two sets of the same exercise without stopping in between
- **Pyramid**—adding more weight, or taking weight off, with each set
- **Drop sets**—Perform a set to failure, remove a small amount of weight, continue with the set
- **Peripheral heart action**—Modified circuit training that alternates between upper and lower body exercises
- **Split routine**—focusing on different areas of the body for separate training sessions

SINGLE-SET RESISTANCE-TRAINING SYSTEM

As the name implies, the single-set resistance-training system involves performing one set of each given exercise. A set includes eight to twelve repetitions performed at a moderate pace. The single-

Copyright © Mometrix Media. You have been licensed one copy of this document for personal use only. Any other reproduction or redistribution is strictly prohibited. All rights reserved.
This content is provided for test preparation purposes only and does not imply an endorsement by Mometrix of any particular political, scientific, or religious point of view.

set training routine is seen as appropriate for a beginning-level client and may not provide enough challenge for an intermediate- or advanced-level client to attain desired strength goals.

While single-set training is sometimes dismissed within the health and fitness industry, it can be ideal for **beginner clients** who need simple training exercises that do not overtax their bodies as they move through the stabilization level of the OPT model. This method can help avoid overtraining and injury for these clients.

MULTIPLE-SET RESISTANCE-TRAINING SYSTEM

The multiple-set resistance-training system involves performing several sets of several different exercises over the course of a workout. This training approach has been in vogue since the 1940s. The number of sets and repetitions depends on the training level of the client and his or her ultimate goals. While a client at any level can be placed in a multiple-set resistance-training routine, it is particularly beneficial for **advanced clients** looking for significant strength and hypertrophy gains.

Health and fitness professionals should be cautious with multiple-set resistance training, taking care not to over-train a client through overuse of areas of the body, leading to exhaustion and possible injury. This is especially likely with novice clients whose body tissues have not been fully conditioned through the steps of the OPT model.

PYRAMID RESISTANCE-TRAINING SYSTEM

The pyramid resistance-training system involves increasing or decreasing the weight after each set. When **adding weight**, anywhere from ten to twelve repetitions per set are recommended. Weight should be added incrementally until the client can only perform a few repetitions at that level.

When **subtracting weight**, fewer repetitions per set are recommended; the heaviest sets should involve about two repetitions, and the lightest set should include four to six repetitions.

This system can also be adapted to a higher number of repetitions (up to 20) by correspondingly decreasing the overall starting and ending weights.

SUPERSET RESISTANCE-TRAINING SYSTEM

A superset involves performing two or more exercises in succession. This can be accomplished in two ways: by using compound sets or by using tri-sets. A **compound set** works the antagonist muscles of a muscle group one right after the other. This is an effective way to maximize training time. A **tri-set** uses three different exercises to work the same muscle group or body area. Tri-sets can also be modified as a bi-set, or two exercises to work one area.

Supersets should be performed in rapid succession without a rest between sets. Usually, supersets entail eight to twelve repetitions per set, although this can be modified by performing a higher number of repetitions at a lighter weight load. Superset training is very effective for those seeking maximal hypertrophy and strength gains, such as Olympic weight lifters or competitive bodybuilders.

CIRCUIT-TRAINING RESISTANCE-TRAINING SYSTEM

The circuit-training resistance-training system involves many different exercises performed in rapid succession. The short rest between sets gives not only weight-training benefits but also a cardiovascular workout. In the workout programming, the number of sets, the number of repetitions, and the amount of rest between sets can all be adjusted. Sets can be single, double, or

Copyright © Mometrix Media. You have been licensed one copy of this document for personal use only. Any other reproduction or redistribution is strictly prohibited. All rights reserved. This content is provided for test preparation purposes only and does not imply an endorsement by Mometrix of any particular political, scientific, or religious point of view.

triple; repetitions can range from eight to a dozen. Rest periods can be short (10 to 15 seconds—just long enough to set up the next exercise) but should be no longer than one minute.

Because this is a rapid workout that provides weight training and cardiorespiratory benefits, it is a very good option for those with limited time to train.

PHA Resistance-Training System

The peripheral heart action (PHA) resistance-training system is circuit training that alternates between upper body and lower body exercises. PHA training can improve circulation because it distributes blood flow through the upper and lower extremities. The client can perform a wide range of repetitions depending on the ultimate training goal (8 on the low end and 20 on the high end). This may be an ideal part of a program aimed at changing body composition.

Split-Routine System

The split-routine training system splits the body into different regions to be trained during different training sessions. This can be ideal for athletes that have specific track and field events, such as shot-putters, or those seeking maximum hypertrophy, such as bodybuilders. Adequate recovery time is need for each body region trained.

Vertical and Horizontal Loading Resistance-Training Systems

Vertical loading, a resistance-training system favored by NASM, travels down the NASM training template in a vertical manner and cycles through body parts in the following manner: whole body, pectoral area, back area, upper arms/shoulders, front arm (biceps), back arm (triceps), and lower extremities. A full rotation is performed, and then the client can begin at the top again. If the exercises are done in rapid succession, this can also become a circuit-style resistance-training routine.

Horizontal loading exhausts one region of the body at a time before working out another region. This is a very popular method of resistance training, but it can waste time with extended rest between sets. If minimal rest is used, horizontal loading can be an effective method of maximizing strength and hypertrophy gains.

Total-Body: Stabilization-Level Exercises
Ball Squat/Curl-to-Press Exercise
For the ball squat/curl-to-press, a stability ball and dumbbells are used.

Have the client stand facing away from a wall, with the stability ball pressed up against the wall by his or her lower back. The client holds the dumbbells in both hands and then rolls down the wall in a squat. The toes should be pointed forward, and the feet are placed shoulder-width apart.

As the client rolls up on the ball and straightens the legs out of the squat, he or she curls the dumbbells up by bending the arms fully at the elbow, and then continues to lift the dumbbells into full extension over the head, with the palms facing away from the wall.

Be sure that the core musculature is engaged at all times and the feet, knees, and hips stay in proper forward alignment.

Multiplanar Step-Up Balance to Overhead Press Exercise
For the multiplanar step-up balance to overhead press, an exercise step and dumbbells are used.

Copyright © Mometrix Media. You have been licensed one copy of this document for personal use only. Any other reproduction or redistribution is strictly prohibited. All rights reserved. This content is provided for test preparation purposes only and does not imply an endorsement by Mometrix of any particular political, scientific, or religious point of view.

The client stands in front of the step with the dumbbells in both hands. Have the client place one foot on the step, so the leg is bent at the knee. The client should step up onto the box with the raised leg, fully straightening it as the other leg is brought up and bent at a right angle at the knee, resulting in the client balancing on the stepping leg. At the same time, the client curls the dumbbells up by bending the arms fully at the elbow and then continues to lift the dumbbells into full extension over the head, with the palms facing forward.

Be sure that the core musculature is engaged at all times and the feet, knees, and hips stay in proper forward alignment.

TOTAL-BODY: STRENGTH-LEVEL EXERCISES
LUNGE TO TWO-ARM DUMBBELL PRESS EXERCISE

For the lunge to two-arm dumbbell press, two dumbbells will be needed.

The client stands with the legs shoulder-width apart and the dumbbells in both hands at the sides of the body. The hands should be turned in toward the body. Have the client step into a deep lunge with one foot forward. Both legs should be bent at right angles. From there, the client pushes hard back into the starting position, while moving the arms through a full curl, and then straightening them up fully overhead. Repeat and lunge with opposite foot.

Be sure the core musculature is engaged at all times and the feet, knees, and hips stay in proper forward alignment to engage the correct muscle groups and avoid unnecessary strain on the lower back.

SQUAT TO TWO-ARM PRESS EXERCISE

For the squat to two-arm press, two dumbbells are used.

The client stands with the feet shoulder-width apart and the dumbbells in both hands, which should rest at the client's sides. The client should activate the core muscles by performing the drawing-in maneuver. Keeping the back straight, have the client bend the knees as if he or she is sitting in a chair. Using the gluteal muscles, the client straightens into a standing position while bending the arms at the elbows into a full curl. This motion is then continued with the arms fully extended over the head.

Be sure that the core musculature is engaged at all times and the feet, knees, and hips stay in proper forward alignment to engage the correct muscle groups and avoid unnecessary strain on the lower back.

TOTAL-BODY: POWER-LEVEL EXERCISES
TWO-ARM PUSH PRESS EXERCISE

For the two-arm push press, two dumbbells are used.

Have the client stand with the feet shoulder-width apart and the dumbbells in both hands, which should rest at his or her sides. The client should activate the core muscles by performing the drawing-in maneuver. Keeping the back straight, the client raises the dumbbells up to his or her ears, with the elbows bent and the palms of the hands facing forward. As the client fully extends the arms up over the head, he or she steps forward with one leg. The forward leg should remain bent, and the back leg should be rotated inward at the hip and knee. The foot should be flexed with the heel off the ground.

Copyright © Mometrix Media. You have been licensed one copy of this document for personal use only. Any other reproduction or redistribution is strictly prohibited. All rights reserved. This content is provided for test preparation purposes only and does not imply an endorsement by Mometrix of any particular political, scientific, or religious point of view.

Be sure that the core musculature is engaged at all times and the feet, knees, and hips stay in proper forward alignment to engage the correct muscle groups and avoid unnecessary strain on the lower back.

BARBELL CLEAN EXERCISE

For the barbell clean, a lightly weighted barbell will be needed.

Have the client bend behind the barbell, with knees fully bent and hands gripping the barbell with knuckles facing forward. The feet should be shoulder-width apart. The client should activate the core muscles by performing the drawing-in maneuver. Keeping the back straight, the client raises the barbell by bending straight up at the elbow (not in a curl). When the bar is at chest level, the elbows fully bend, so the barbell is under the chin. This is a reverse curl: The palms should be facing forward, not in toward the client.

Be sure that the core musculature is engaged at all times and the feet, knees, and hips stay in proper forward alignment to engage the correct muscle groups and avoid unnecessary strain on the lower back.

VERTICAL-LOADING: STABILIZATION-LEVEL EXERCISES

BALL DUMBBELL CHEST PRESS

For the ball dumbbell chest press, a stability ball and dumbbells are used.

Place the ball on the ground, and have the client lie face up on the ball, with the upper back resting on the ball and the lower body bent at a right angle at the knees, feet facing forward. The client holds the dumbbells straight up, which will be directly in front of him- or herself at chest level. Palms should be pointed forward or down to the client's recumbent position.

The client bends the arms at the elbows, lowering the dumbbells into a press position, and then straighten them back out in front of the body.

Be sure the core musculature is engaged at all times and the feet, knees, and hips stay in proper forward alignment to engage the correct muscle groups and avoid unnecessary strain on the lower back.

PUSH-UP EXERCISE

The client starts in a classic push-up position: The legs are closed, the feet are together, the arms are shoulder-width apart, and the palms are flat and pointing up. The client should perform the drawing-in maneuver, tightening the core musculature to maintain a strong plank position to challenge these muscles and to avoid unnecessary stress to the lower back. Have the client bend his or her arms at the elbows and lower down as far as possible while maintaining proper form.

To make this exercise easier, have the client position on the knees or press off of a bench or wall instead of the ground.

To make this exercise harder, have the client position the feet on a stability ball or place the hands on medicine or stability balls.

Copyright © Mometrix Media. You have been licensed one copy of this document for personal use only. Any other reproduction or redistribution is strictly prohibited. All rights reserved.
This content is provided for test preparation purposes only and does not imply an endorsement by Mometrix of any particular political, scientific, or religious point of view.

STANDING CABLE ROW BACK EXERCISE

A cable machine is used for the standing cable row.

The client stands facing the cable machine with the feet shoulder-width apart and one foot about eighteen inches in front of the other foot. Both knees should be slightly bent. Have the client grip the cables with arms fully extended straight in front at chest height. The hands should face inward. The client pulls straight back, bends the elbows, and presses the shoulder blades down. Have the client slowly release and return to the original position. Be sure that proper posture is maintained; do not allow the shoulders to rise or the head to press forward.

This exercise can be performed in a seated position to make it easier. The arms can be alternated while standing on two feet or the exercise could be performed on one foot to make this exercise more challenging.

BALL DUMBBELL ROW BACK EXERCISE

For the ball dumbbell row, a stability ball and a set of dumbbells are used.

Have the client lie on his or her stomach on the ball. The body should be in a plank position, with the core musculature activated and the body flat and extended. The client holds the dumbbells just off the ground in front of him- or herself, with arms fully extended straight ahead at shoulder level. The palms of the hands should face the ground. Have the client perform a row motion by pulling the dumbbells straight back toward his or her body, bending the elbows and pressing the shoulder blades down.

To make this exercise easier, the client bends over the ball instead of laying on it. To make this exercise more difficult, try alternating the arms or performing the exercise one arm per set.

SINGLE-LEG DUMBBELL SCAPTION SHOULDER EXERCISE

For the single-leg dumbbell scaption, two dumbbells are used.

The client stands in a neutral position, with hips, knees, and feet facing front. Have the client hold the dumbbells in both hands, which should be facing forward and held in a low V slightly away from the body. The client should perform the drawing-in maneuver to activate the core musculature and gluteals. Then have him or her raise one foot slightly off the ground and balance on the other foot.

The client slowly raises the dumbbells out to either side by lifting the arms so the body is in a T pose. The thumbs should face the ceiling. Have the client slowly release and return to the starting position.

To make this exercise easier, the client performs the exercise sitting down or standing on both feet. To make this exercise more difficult, the client alternates arms or uses only one arm per set.

SEATED STABILITY-BALL MILITARY PRESS SHOULDER EXERCISE

For the seated stability-ball military press, a stability ball and two dumbbells are used.

The client sits on the ball in a neutral position, with hips, knees, and feet facing forward. Have the client hold the dumbbells in both hands, which should be raised to form right angles at the elbows, with the dumbbells at ear level; the hands should face forward.

The client should perform the drawing-in maneuver to activate the core musculature. Make sure the client maintains proper posture to avoid unnecessary stress to the lower back. Have the client

Copyright © Mometrix Media. You have been licensed one copy of this document for personal use only. Any other reproduction or redistribution is strictly prohibited. All rights reserved.
This content is provided for test preparation purposes only and does not imply an endorsement by Mometrix of any particular political, scientific, or religious point of view.

raise the dumbbells over his or her head by straightening the arms; the hands should continue to face forward throughout the motion. The client slowly releases and returns to the starting position.

To make this exercise easier, the client sits on a stable surface. To make this exercise harder, the client alternates arms or uses only one arm per set.

SEATED DUMBBELL SHOULDER PRESS EXERCISE

For the seated dumbbell shoulder press, a weight bench and two dumbbells are used.

The client sits in a neutral position, with hips, knees, and feet facing forward, on a weight bench that has the seat back raised. Knees are bent at right angles, and feet are flat on the floor. Have the client hold the dumbbells in both hands, which should be raised to form right angles at the elbows, with the dumbbells at ear level; the hands should face forward.

The client should perform the drawing-in maneuver to activate the core musculature. Make sure the client keeps proper posture to avoid unnecessary stress on the lower back. Have the client raise the dumbbells over his or her head by straightening the arms; the hands should continue to face forward throughout the motion. The client slowly releases and returns to the starting position.

Watch out for postural compensations, especially the head protruding forward; correct this immediately.

SINGLE-LEG DUMBBELL CURL BICEPS EXERCISE

For the single-leg dumbbell curl, a set of dumbbells is used.

The client begins in a neutral position, with the hips, knees, and feet facing forward. Have the client hold the dumbbells in a low V formation, with the arms held slightly away from the body. The hands face forward and slightly outward. The client should perform the drawing-in maneuver to activate the core musculature and to tighten the gluteals. The client raises one foot slightly off the ground and balances on the opposite leg while bending at the elbow and lifting the dumbbells into full curls. The client slowly releases and returns to the starting position. Be sure the client keeps the shoulder blades pressed down during the exercise.

To make this exercise easier, the client stands on both feet. To make this exercise more difficult, the client alternates arms or uses only one arm per set.

SINGLE-LEG BARBELL CURL BICEPS EXERCISE

For the single-leg barbell curl, a weighted barbell is used.

The client begins in a neutral position, with the hips, knees, and feet facing forward. Have the client hold the barbell with arms fully extended and resting near the tops of the thighs. The palms of the hands face forward. The client should perform the drawing-in maneuver to activate the core musculature and tighten the gluteals. The client raises one foot slightly off the ground and balances on the opposite leg while bending at the elbow and lifting the barbell into a full curl. Have the client slowly release and return to the starting position. Be sure the client keeps the shoulder blades pressed down during the exercise.

To make this exercise easier, the client stands on both feet. To make this exercise more difficult, the client alternates arms or uses only one arm per set.

Copyright © Mometrix Media. You have been licensed one copy of this document for personal use only. Any other reproduction or redistribution is strictly prohibited. All rights reserved. This content is provided for test preparation purposes only and does not imply an endorsement by Mometrix of any particular political, scientific, or religious point of view.

SUPINE BALL DUMBBELL TRICEPS EXTENSION EXERCISE

For the supine ball dumbbell triceps extension, a stability ball and set of dumbbells are used.

The client lies on the stability ball with the mid-back resting on the ball, the lower torso balanced off the edge of the ball, and the legs bent at the knee in a right angle. Have the client hold the dumbbells in both hands, which should be held straight up, or in front in the recumbent position, with arms fully extended at shoulder level. The palms should face inward, toward each other.

The client should perform the drawing-in maneuver to activate the core musculature; make sure proper posture is maintained to avoid unnecessary strain on the lower back. The client bends the elbows toward the head, making a right angle. Have the client slowly release and return to the original position.

To make this exercise easier, the client performs it on a stable surface. To make this exercise harder, the client alternates arms or uses one arm per set.

PRONE BALL DUMBBELL TRICEPS EXTENSION EXERCISE

For the prone ball dumbbell triceps extension, a stability ball and a set of dumbbells are used.

The client lies on his or her stomach on the stability ball, with the legs straight back and toes resting on the floor. Have the client hold the dumbbells in both hands with the upper arms held close to the body and bent at a right angle at the elbow. The palms should face inward, toward the stability ball.

The client should perform the drawing-in maneuver to activate the core musculature; make sure proper posture is maintained to avoid unnecessary strain on the lower back. The client straightens the arms straight back, so they are in a straight line with the body. Have the client slowly release and return to the original position.

To make this exercise easier, the client performs it standing up. To make this exercise harder, the client alternates arms or uses one arm per set.

BALL SQUAT LEG EXERCISE

For the ball squat, a stability ball and a set of dumbbells are used.

The client presses the stability ball up against a wall with his or her mid-back. Have the client stand in a neutral position, with hips, knees, and feet facing forward. The dumbbells are held at the client's sides, with the hands facing inward. The client should perform the drawing-in maneuver to activate the core musculature. The client rolls down the wall on the ball by bending at the knees until they are almost at a right angle. Have the client slowly roll back up to the starting position.

To make this exercise easier, the client bends less or holds on to a fixed object while squatting. To make this exercise more difficult, the client omits the stability ball; observe for kinetic-chain compensations and correct immediately.

MULTIPLANAR STEP-UP TO BALANCE

For the multiplanar step-up to balance, an exercise step and a set of dumbbells are used.

The client stands in front of the step in a neutral position, with hips, knees, and feet facing forward. Have the client hold the dumbbells at his or her sides, with arms fully extended and hands facing in. The client should perform the drawing-in maneuver to activate the core musculature and also to ready the gluteals. The client steps up with one foot, pushes upward, and balances on that foot

Copyright © Mometrix Media. You have been licensed one copy of this document for personal use only. Any other reproduction or redistribution is strictly prohibited. All rights reserved. This content is provided for test preparation purposes only and does not imply an endorsement by Mometrix of any particular political, scientific, or religious point of view.

while the other foot is brought up by fully bending the opposite leg. The second foot should never touch the step. Have the client balance for a beat then return to the original starting position.

To make this exercise easier, the client can use a lower step. To make this exercise more difficult, the client can step up in different planes of motion.

VERTICAL-LOADING: STRENGTH-LEVEL EXERCISES

FLAT DUMBBELL CHEST PRESS

For the flat dumbbell chest press, a weight bench and two dumbbells are used.

The client lies down flat on the weight bench with his or her knees hanging over the edge, bent at a right angle, toes pointed forward. Have the client hold the dumbbells straight in front of him- or herself, with arms fully extended at shoulder level. The hands should be facing down from the client's recumbent perspective. The client should perform the drawing-in maneuver, tightening the core musculature and making sure not to hyperextend the lower back.

Have the client bend the arms at the elbows, opening the arms, so the upper part is level with the body and the arms are bent at right angles. The client presses back up to the starting position. Be sure the arm muscles contract during the movement and the shoulders retract and press down.

BARBELL BENCH PRESS CHEST EXERCISE

For the barbell bench press, a weight bench and weighted barbell are used.

Have the client lie down flat on the weight bench with his or her knees hanging over the edge bent at a right angle; toes pointed forward. The client grips the barbell with the arms spaced wider apart than the shoulders. The client should perform the drawing-in maneuver, tightening the core musculature and making sure not to hyperextend the lower back. The client lifts the barbell from the stand, and then lowers it to the chest in a slow, controlled motion. Have the client press the bar back upward, fully straightening the arms.

SEATED CABLE ROW BACK EXERCISE

For the seated cable row, a cable machine is used.

The client sits facing toward the cable machine, placing the feet on the steps shoulder-width apart, knees slightly bent. Have the client grip the cables and fully extend the arms out front. The client should perform the drawing-in maneuver to activate the core musculature. Be sure the core muscles are in proper alignment to avoid unnecessary strain on the lower back. Have the client pull back on the cables, bending the elbows and pressing the shoulder blades down. Make sure no postural distortions occur, particularly the head-jutting-forward compensation, and have the client keep his or her torso stabilized and still. The client slowly releases the cables and returns to the starting position.

LAT PULL DOWN BACK EXERCISE

For the seated lat pull down, the client must use a lat machine.

Have the client sit facing in toward the lat machine. Hips, knees, and feet should face forward. The client should perform the drawing-in maneuver to activate the core musculature. The client grips the handles of the machine at a point wider than the shoulders; the hands should face forward, toward the machine. Leaning back just slightly, have the client pull the handles down in a slow, controlled manner so the arms are completely bent at the elbow, and the bar is in front of the chest. Have the client slowly release and return to the original position.

Copyright © Mometrix Media. You have been licensed one copy of this document for personal use only. Any other reproduction or redistribution is strictly prohibited. All rights reserved. This content is provided for test preparation purposes only and does not imply an endorsement by Mometrix of any particular political, scientific, or religious point of view.

Make sure the client maintains proper posture to avoid placing unnecessary stress on the lower back. NASM recommends against lat exercises that pull the weight behind the head instead of in front of the head because these exercises add stress to the upper back and neck musculature.

SEATED SHOULDER PRESS EXERCISE

For the seated shoulder press, a shoulder press machine is used.

The client sits on the shoulder press machine in a neutral position, with hips, knees, and feet facing forward. Knees are bent at a right angle, and feet are flat on the floor. Have the client grip the handles, with hands positioned wider than shoulder-width apart.

The client should perform the drawing-in maneuver to activate the core musculature. Make sure the client keeps proper posture to avoid unnecessary stress to the lower back. Have the client pull down slowly on the handles, bending at the elbow, until reaching the lowest point the handles will go. The client slowly releases and returns to the starting position.

Watch postural compensations, especially the head protruding forward; correct this immediately.

BICEPS CURL EXERCISE

For the biceps curl, a curl machine will be needed. Be sure the machine is calibrated to fit the client.

The client sits at the curl machine in a neutral position, with the hips, knees, and feet facing forward. Have the client grip the handles of the machine with the palms facing forward. The client should perform the drawing-in maneuver to activate the core musculature; make sure proper posture is maintained to avoid unnecessary strain on the lower back.

The client bends the arms at the elbow and brings the handle up in a full curl. Have the client slowly release and return to the original position. Be sure the client keeps the shoulder blades pressed down during the exercise and the movement is fully controlled all the way up and down to avoid strain on the elbow joint.

SEATED TWO-ARM DUMBBELL BICEPS CURL

For the seated two-arm dumbbell biceps curl, a weight bench and a set of dumbbells are used.

The client sits in a neutral position, with the hips, knees, and feet facing forward on the weight bench, which should be in the seat back position. The client holds the dumbbells in both hands in a low V formation, with arms fully extended; the palms are facing forward. The client should perform the drawing-in maneuver to activate the core musculature; make sure proper posture is maintained to avoid unnecessary strain on the lower back.

Have the client bend the arms at the elbow and bring the dumbbells up in a full curl. The client slowly releases and returns to the original position. Be sure the client keeps the shoulder blades pressed down during this exercise.

CABLE PUSHDOWN TRICEPS EXERCISE

For the cable pushdown, a cable machine is used.

The client stands in front of the cable machine in a neutral position, with hips, knees, and feet facing forward. Have the client grip the handles on the machine; the arms should be bent at right angles. The client should perform the drawing-in maneuver to activate the core musculature. The client pulls down on the handles, fully extending the arms, so they are in a straight line with the body. The

Copyright © Mometrix Media. You have been licensed one copy of this document for personal use only. Any other reproduction or redistribution is strictly prohibited. All rights reserved. This content is provided for test preparation purposes only and does not imply an endorsement by Mometrix of any particular political, scientific, or religious point of view.

client slowly releases and returns to the original position. Be sure the client fully controls motion, so the elbow is not strained.

SUPINE BENCH BARBELL TRICEPS EXTENSION EXERCISE

For the supine bench barbell triceps extension, a weight bench and a weighted barbell are used.

The client lies flat on the weight bench in a neutral position. The knees hang off the edge of the bench and bend at a right angle; knees and feet face forward. Have the client grip the barbell with both hands, spaced shoulder-width apart. The palms should face down, from the client's recumbent perspective. The client slowly bends the arms at the elbows, so the bar is being moved toward the face. The hands should face straight up. Have the client slowly release and return to the starting position.

Be sure that the client does not hold the barbell with too wide of a grip, because this can increase the stress on the elbow joint.

LEG PRESS EXERCISE

For this exercise, a leg press machine is needed.

The client sits on the leg press machine in a neutral position. Be sure the machine is calibrated for the client's height.

The client places the feet on the plate a shoulder-width distance apart, with knees and feet pointing forward. The client should perform the drawing-in maneuver to activate the core musculature and ready the gluteals then push the weight slowly away. Observe for kinetic-chain compensations and correct immediately. The client maintains the exercise for as long as the proper form can be maintained, and then slowly returns to the starting position.

BARBELL SQUAT

For the barbell squat, a weighted barbell is used.

The client stands in a neutral position, with feet evenly spaced under the shoulders. The hips, knees, and feet are pointing straight ahead. Have the client rest the barbell across the back of his or her shoulders. The hands should grip the barbell further apart than the shoulders.

The client should perform the drawing-in maneuver to activate the core muscles; be sure he or she maintains proper posture to avoid unnecessary strain on the lower back. The client squats by bending at the knee and slowly lowering down. Have the client continue to the point where postural compensations are seen, and then have the client slowly return to the original position.

As the client increases his or her strength and stability, he or she will be able to squat further without compensations.

VERTICAL-LOADING: POWER-LEVEL EXERCISES
TWO-ARM MEDICINE BALL CHEST PASS

For the two-arm medicine ball chest pass, a weighted medicine ball is used.

The client stands facing a wall that is about five to ten feet away. The shoulders, hips, and feet should face forward, with the knees slightly bent. The client holds the medicine ball in front of his or her chest, with the elbows slightly bent. The client should perform the drawing-in maneuver to activate the core musculature. Making sure the client's body maintains proper posture, have him or

173

Copyright © Mometrix Media. You have been licensed one copy of this document for personal use only. Any other reproduction or redistribution is strictly prohibited. All rights reserved.
This content is provided for test preparation purposes only and does not imply an endorsement by Mometrix of any particular political, scientific, or religious point of view.

her throw the ball at the wall by pushing it forward in an explosive motion, using the arm and chest muscles.

This exercise can also be performed on equipment if a medicine ball is not available.

TWO-ARM ROTATION CHEST PASS EXERCISE

For the two-arm rotation chest pass, a weighted medicine ball is used.

The client stands next to a wall that is about five to ten feet away. The shoulders, hips, and feet should face forward, with the knees slightly bent. The client holds the medicine ball in front of his or her chest, with the elbows slightly bent. The client should perform the drawing-in maneuver to activate the core musculature. Making sure the client's body maintains proper posture, have him or her twist sideways, pivoting the foot and inverting at the hip and knee joints as he or she throws the ball at the wall by pushing it forward in an explosive motion, using the arm and chest muscles, particularly using the arm farthest from the wall. This motion is much like a side pass in basketball.

MEDICINE BALL PULLOVER THROW-BACK EXERCISE

For the medicine ball pullover throw-back, a stability ball and weighted medicine ball are used.

Have the client lie on the stability ball with his or her mid-back pressed against the ball and legs hanging over the edge; knees bent at a right angle and feet pointing forward. The client should perform the drawing-in maneuver to activate the core musculature. Make sure the client maintains proper posture to avoid placing unnecessary stress on the lower back. The client holds the medicine ball in both hands; the arms should be fully extended over his or her head.

Focusing on using the abdominals, the client contracts up, bends forward, and throws the medicine ball forward in a strong, quick motion. Make sure the chin remains pressed into the chest during the exercise.

MEDICINE-BALL SCOOP PASS EXERCISE

For the medicine-ball scoop pass, a weighted medicine ball is used.

The client stands in a neutral position, with hips, knees, and feet facing forward. The feet are shoulder-width apart. The client should perform the drawing-in maneuver to activate the core musculature. Make sure the client keeps proper posture to avoid unnecessary stress to the lower back.

Have the client bend at the knees, keeping the back straight and core muscles pulled in, and hold the medicine ball with both hands on the outside of one knee. In a strong, explosive motion using the core muscles and gluteals, the client tosses the ball forward. The hands should be fully extended in front of the body at approximately shoulder level at the end of the movement. The client can toss the ball at a wall or work with a partner who tosses the ball back. Have the client repeat the exercise, alternating sides.

MEDICINE-BALL SIDE OBLIQUE THROW SHOULDER EXERCISE

For the medicine-ball side oblique throw, a weighted medicine ball is used.

The client stands in a neutral position, with hips, knees, and feet facing forward. The feet are shoulder-width apart. The client should perform the drawing-in maneuver to activate the core musculature. Make sure proper posture is maintained to avoid unnecessary stress to the lower back.

Copyright © Mometrix Media. You have been licensed one copy of this document for personal use only. Any other reproduction or redistribution is strictly prohibited. All rights reserved. This content is provided for test preparation purposes only and does not imply an endorsement by Mometrix of any particular political, scientific, or religious point of view.

Have the client bend at the knees, keeping the back straight and core muscles pulled in, and hold the medicine ball with both hands on the outside of one knee. In a strong, explosive motion using the core muscles and gluteals, the client tosses the ball sideways. The hands should be fully extended to the side of the body at approximately shoulder level at the end of the movement. The opposite hip, knee, and foot should fully rotate inward. The client can toss the ball at a wall or work with a partner who tosses the ball back. Have the client repeat the exercise, alternating sides.

SQUAT JUMP LEG EXERCISE

To perform the squat jump, the client stands in a neutral position with feet shoulder-width apart, and hips, knees, and feet are facing forward. The client bends slightly at the knees and pulls the arms straight down and back in alignment with the torso. The client should perform the drawing-in maneuver to activate the core muscles and maintain proper posture to avoid unnecessary strain on the lower back. In a quick, explosive movement, have the client bend even further in the squat, and then jump straight up, extending arms and legs straight. On landing, the client returns both arms and legs to the starting position.

Be sure the client keeps the body controlled and lands in a gentle manner to avoid unnecessary strain on the joints.

TUCK JUMP LEG EXERCISE

The client stands in a neutral position with feet shoulder-width apart and hips, knees, and feet facing forward. The client bends slightly at the knees and pulls the arms straight down and back in alignment with the torso. The client should perform the drawing-in maneuver to activate the core muscles and maintain proper posture to avoid unnecessary strain on the lower back. In a quick, explosive movement, have the client bend even further in the squat, and then jump up, pulling the knees into a tight tuck, but keeping the back straight. On landing, the client returns both arms and legs to the starting position.

Be sure the client keeps the body controlled and lands in a gentle manner to avoid unnecessary strain on the joints.

Copyright © Mometrix Media. You have been licensed one copy of this document for personal use only. Any other reproduction or redistribution is strictly prohibited. All rights reserved. This content is provided for test preparation purposes only and does not imply an endorsement by Mometrix of any particular political, scientific, or religious point of view.

Client Relations and Behavioral Coaching

Stages of Change Model

People naturally resist change. **Resistance to change** is one of the biggest obstacles preventing clients from achieving their fitness goals. A trainer can help a client overcome their resistance to change by using NASM's **stages of change model**. There are five stages in the model, each with defining characteristics and strategies for success. When a trainer identifies the client's location in the change model, they can apply the appropriate strategy to help the client reach their goal.

The first stage is **pre-contemplation**, defined by an unwillingness to change. These people rarely seek out a trainer. The best strategy for working with a prospective client in this stage is supportive myth dispelling. When a client is considering exercise but not actively exercising, they are in the **contemplation stage**. Education is the best tool for a client in this stage. In the **preparation stage**, a client exercises infrequently but would like to begin a more rigorous and consistent program. Designing a realistic program and setting SMART goals are important methods used to help clients in this stage. The fourth stage is the **action stage**. In this stage, the client is exercising, but has not reached the six-month mark. It is important to identify any obstacles to success and develop a strategy to overcome the barrier. The last stage is the **maintenance stage**. When a client has exercised for six months or more they are in this stage. The best way to assist a client in this stage is to help them evaluate their progress and set new goals.

> **Review Video: 4 Tips for Setting Great Client Goals**
> Visit mometrix.com/academy and enter code: 175935

Copyright © Mometrix Media. You have been licensed one copy of this document for personal use only. Any other reproduction or redistribution is strictly prohibited. All rights reserved. This content is provided for test preparation purposes only and does not imply an endorsement by Mometrix of any particular political, scientific, or religious point of view.

Client Goal Setting

POSITIVE VISION

When a person has **direction and purpose**, activities focus on attaining those goals. When a person only has a vague idea of what he or she may want to accomplish, actions may likewise be vague and meandering, never really adding up to any forward progress. These people are much more likely to have **negative effects** and to:

- Spend too much time thinking about what he or she wants to accomplish
- Spend less time working toward accomplishing these goals
- Be distractible and put things off
- Be less satisfied with life
- Be unhappy or depressed
- Have a higher incidence of illness

CLARITY AND DETAIL

A health and fitness professional must take responsibility in guiding the client's overall experience in the fitness setting. This starts with helping the client come up with a **specific vision** instead of a vague goal to set sights on a solid target and to avoid letdowns from the perception of not accomplishing a too-general goal.

For example, if a person says they want to lose weight, the health and fitness professional should press further for a more-specific vision. A person can work out with a great deal of success, lose inches from the waistline and build muscle, which weighs more than fat, thus revealing no actual weight loss. If the client's goal is merely to lose weight, he or she may perceive the efforts to have failed.

Instead, the trainer should inquire further as to what the client's underlying goals and motivations are and set more specific targets, such as losing inches from the waistline or reducing BMI.

ROOT CAUSE ANALYSIS

Root cause analysis is the process of continuing to ask a person "Why?" until the most basic **motivation** for an action is uncovered. When asking a client their goal or goals in the fitness setting, simply ask "Why?" when he or she gives a response. For example, if a client says she wants to lose weight, ask why. Her response may be that she wants to fit into her old jeans. Then ask why. Her response may be that she has a high school reunion coming up. It is always helpful to you and the client to understand the underlying motivation.

NASM also has a short list of alternative questions that help accomplish the same goal. Clients may find these queries unusual, so encourage the client to remain open minded as you create goals together. These questions include:

- The lottery scenario: What would you do if you won?
- The superman scenario: If you could do anything well, what would it be?
- Who do you admire and why?
- What are your favorite activities?

Copyright © Mometrix Media. You have been licensed one copy of this document for personal use only. Any other reproduction or redistribution is strictly prohibited. All rights reserved. This content is provided for test preparation purposes only and does not imply an endorsement by Mometrix of any particular political, scientific, or religious point of view.

PSYCHOLOGICAL ASPECT

A **vision** is an overarching picture of the goal or set of goals a client wants to achieve. However, just having this picture in mind will not put him or her on the road to achieving it. For that, there must be a **strategy**, or a defined method, of working toward those goals.

Developing a strategy is essential because a client can become discouraged if he or she feels the goals are not being met. By defining steps, the client can engage in activities and measure success in smaller increments. This allows the client to see that progress is being made; although the ultimate goals may not be realized right away, they are attainable.

NASM uses the acronym SMART to help the health and fitness professional and the client come up with a specific strategy for achieving fitness goals.

For many clients, fitness goals are not difficult because of the physical challenges they present, but because a person has **behavioral issues** that must be changed or negative attitudes about fitness, nutrition, or his or her own body that must be addressed to succeed.

As a health and fitness professional, it is important to know how to help a person accomplish their fitness goals not only from a training standpoint, but also from a psychological standpoint. This is necessary because trainers must continually motivate the client not only for the client's own good but also to help themselves achieve goals and retain clients.

MAXIMIZING PSYCHOLOGICAL APPROACH

There are five steps recommended by NASM to motivate clients, outline realistic goals, and put the client in the right frame of mind to overcome barriers and accomplish their goals:

1. **Vision**—encompasses looking at the big picture and creating an ideal scenario that the client is working toward
2. **Strategy**—breaks down exactly how the vision will be achieved, using measurable goals and methods
3. **Belief**—focuses on overcoming nonphysical barriers to success—specifically fear, uncertainty, and doubt (FUD)
4. **Persistence**—details how to maintain focus and determination even when the actions are difficult.
5. **Learning**—deals with tweaking the overall approach to learn from the good and the bad. Positive steps should be further explored, while missteps or negative aspects can be curtailed.

SMART

SMART is an acronym used by NASM to guide health and fitness professionals and assist in creating a strategy for each client to achieve his or her fitness goals. The letters stand for the following:

- **Specific**—A specific goal clearly identifies what is to be achieved. Specific goals offer clear direction and level set expectations.
- **Measurable**—Measurable goals can be quantified and tracked. Without the ability to track goals, it is difficult to determine success or failure.
- **Attainable**—An attainable goal follows the Goldilocks principle (not too easy not too hard). It is challenging enough that the client must work hard to achieve it, but not so difficult that the client loses hope. Clients do not progress when goals are too easy and lose motivation when goals are not attainable.

Copyright © Mometrix Media. You have been licensed one copy of this document for personal use only. Any other reproduction or redistribution is strictly prohibited. All rights reserved. This content is provided for test preparation purposes only and does not imply an endorsement by Mometrix of any particular political, scientific, or religious point of view.

- **Realistic**—A goal is realistic if a client is willing and able to achieve it.
- **Timely**— Time-bound goals have clearly defined time frames which provide structure and set priorities.

BELIEF

Belief is essential when working toward goals. No matter how specific a person's vision is and what strategy is undertaken to accomplish it, it will never come to fruition if the client does not believe that it is possible to accomplish the goals. Sometimes, a person may say they want something, but he or she will have an underlying fear of achieving it. These conflicting attitudes can lead to apathy or self-sabotage.

As a health and fitness professional, it is important to work toward minimizing what NASM refers to as **FUD**: fear, uncertainty, and doubt. Identifying these elements with the client is the first step. Small, achievable goals should be used to build the client's confidence. Any negative feelings can also be indulged in a controlled manner; for example, the client may be allowed one minute in the locker room to verbalize his or her fears or impediments and then leave these feelings at the door for the duration of the workout.

RESEARCH

There is a great deal of scientific information available relating to how a sense of believing in oneself can have a great positive impact on a person's life. These impacts include:

- Having a better work ethic
- Being more content
- Tackling problems in a positive manner
- Recovering from setbacks more easily
- Coping better and learn from mistakes
- Having better goal-setting skills

FEARS AND ANXIETIES

NASM encourages several different methods to help a client overcome fears and doubts. These include:

- **Making time for the negative**—Sometimes clients have a hard time keeping the voice quiet within that tells them they can't. Instead of forcing this noise to be quiet, allow the client to indulge, but only at a set time and place. By verbalizing fears, the client may be able to leave these feelings behind when beginning a workout.
- **Visualizing success**—Instead of picturing failure, the client visualizes success. This positive visualization is linked to better performance.
- **Take it one step at a time**—Even though a big-picture vision has been set, it is essential for clients to remember that goals are achieved one step at a time. Define some of these small steps, and work toward them to bolster confidence.

PERSISTENCE

Long-term success requires **persistence**, or the ability to continue on a path even in the face of problems or challenges. This holds true for fitness goals as well—not only accomplishing the goals in the first place but also maintaining the results over time. By addressing this reality with clients, it

Copyright © Mometrix Media. You have been licensed one copy of this document for personal use only. Any other reproduction or redistribution is strictly prohibited. All rights reserved. This content is provided for test preparation purposes only and does not imply an endorsement by Mometrix of any particular political, scientific, or religious point of view.

increases the likelihood that they will be able to accept that setbacks are part of a realistic journey toward the goal, and will help the client realize their ultimate goals.

Research has shown that even among people who can keep their annual resolutions for two years, they admit to more than a dozen cheats in that period. However, instead of becoming completely demoralized, they viewed this as a realistic part of life and resumed their drive to maintain the goal.

BOLSTERING LEVELS OF PERSISTENCE

When it comes to achieving fitness goals, it is important that a client is able to persevere through minor setbacks in pursuit of the ultimate goal. NASM recommends three different approaches to promoting perseverance:

1. **Plan for challenges**—When developing a strategy for accomplishing goals, account for occasional setbacks. If a client anticipates potential setbacks and there is a strategy in place for handling them, they may be easier to cope with.
2. **Give rewards**—NASM espouses the deposit-and-refund technique, where the client gives money to a friend and gets a partial refund for each increment of success (for example, losing a pound). This works very well in group training, too.
3. **Build a support group**—Help the client build a network of friends, family, and workout buddies who can act as a support system. Not only will this inspire high performance but these people can also help the client get through challenging times with love and encouragement.

> **Review Video: Achieving Success**
> Visit mometrix.com/academy and enter code: 152134

LEARNING

Learning deals with how a client can gain knowledge from the positives and negatives he or she has experienced on the road to meeting goals. NASM advocates **self-monitoring**, which simply means that the client monitors his or her progress, honestly viewing and recording the good and the bad. Studies have shown that people who engage in self-monitoring are better able to meet their goals.

Recording helps the client see progress or slipups more clearly. Once the client sees progress objectively, corrective action can be taken. The client should make adjustments to strategy and execution, tweaking the routine to incorporate what works and to eliminate things that are not working.

METHODS OF LEARNING

It is vitally important for a client to identify actions or activities that are not conducive to accomplishing a goal. Once the potential **detractors** are identified, the client must make the necessary **changes** to correct them. If a client continues with activities that are contrary to accomplishing a goal, progress may be slow or nonexistent, and the client may become discouraged or feel like they are failing. NASM recommends the following:

- **Change what you can**—It is important to work on things that can be changed and let go of what cannot. Look at actions, not measurements, when beginning a fitness regimen.
- **Look at the record**—When habits are examined, patterns (positive and negative) emerge. Use this information as a tool to develop improved strategies.

Copyright © Mometrix Media. You have been licensed one copy of this document for personal use only. Any other reproduction or redistribution is strictly prohibited. All rights reserved. This content is provided for test preparation purposes only and does not imply an endorsement by Mometrix of any particular political, scientific, or religious point of view.

- **Rate it**—Have clients rate their daily progress on a 0–10 scale.
- **Look at progress**—Review clients' training records with them to monitor progress toward fitness goals.

Copyright © Mometrix Media. You have been licensed one copy of this document for personal use only. Any other reproduction or redistribution is strictly prohibited. All rights reserved.
This content is provided for test preparation purposes only and does not imply an endorsement by Mometrix of any particular political, scientific, or religious point of view.

Customer Service

Instead of viewing personal training solely as a source of income, a health and fitness professional should focus on **improving people's lives** and **promoting healthy lifestyles**. This viewpoint helps underscore the main goal of a trainer's business—to maintain a happy, healthy clientele. When the trainer focuses on the client, better service (and the resulting benefits) is provided. Continued education with a focus on the ability to offer a wide array of tools to the client is part of the client-focused approach. NASM recommends continuing education through its **certification training**, which includes its Foundations for the Health and Fitness Professional course, the Certified Personal Trainer certification course, and numerous continuing education courses that give trainers tools to work with special populations or with specialized exercise techniques.

UNCOMPROMISING CUSTOMER SERVICE

Fitness training is a very competitive business. Thousands of gyms offer personal training sessions with independent trainers. This means that it is essential for a trainer to build an excellent reputation based not only on skill as a trainer and ability to get results, but also on the level of customer service offered.

Uncompromising customer service encompasses not only the quality of the training but also the level of attention and how valued the client feels. This can come from such features as promptly returned calls, timeliness of workouts, and professional billing practices. It is also important for the trainer to make sure the client feels comfortable in the workout environment—whether it is a health club or other locale. A trainer should remember that spending decisions are in large part emotional. By offering the very best customer service, a trainer improves the way a client feels about the entire training experience.

SIX GUIDELINES FOR CUSTOMER SERVICE

A health and fitness professional should act in a manner that reflects the idea that his or her entire business could depend on how each person he or she interacts with rates that interaction. Some **guidelines** for extending the best customer service are:

1. Present oneself professionally, consider appearance and in manner.
2. Speak to everyone at a health club and work toward making positive contacts.
3. Speak in a professional, educated manner that elicits confidence.
4. Answer and encourage all questions and respond respectfully.
5. Work to promote professional work relationships.
6. Learn from mistakes or complaints.

Maintaining positive relationships with coworkers and potential clients, continuing to educate oneself, increasing the services offered, and behaving in a professional manner are all essential components of excellent customer service.

Copyright © Mometrix Media. You have been licensed one copy of this document for personal use only. Any other reproduction or redistribution is strictly prohibited. All rights reserved. This content is provided for test preparation purposes only and does not imply an endorsement by Mometrix of any particular political, scientific, or religious point of view.

Acquiring Clients

POTENTIAL CUSTOMERS

Nearly everyone is a potential customer. As people consume foods laden with calories and lead increasingly sedentary lifestyles, adding daily fitness activities is crucial for improving health and wellness. Research has shown that people in special populations can benefit from regular exercise, making children, seniors, pregnant women, and even those with heart and lung problems potential clients in need of health and fitness trainers with specific and specialized knowledge.

In the past, personal training was viewed as a luxury, in modern life, it is becoming a **necessity**. Personal trainers are needed to help people stay fit and to prevent potential health problems that result from postural distortions and sedentary living.

There are a variety of **motives** driving people to seek a trainer. Motives may include a desire to look and feel better, a need to perform physical tasks more effectively, and improved overall health. Because nearly everyone wants to accomplish at least one of these goals, the number of potential customers is substantial.

APPROACH POTENTIAL CUSTOMERS

When a trainer is not working with a client, the focus should be on building clientele, making **approach techniques** essential. Adopting a policy of saying hello to every person, sprucing up the gym area, and offering water or towels to members, are examples of simple customer service gestures that will help the trainer build a reputation as a conscientious professional and attract potential clients.

Approach the client in a very friendly, neutral manner the first time. Introducing yourself or asking the client's name and leaving it at that until a future encounter is a good move. Upon meeting that person again, calling them by name will help you stick out in the customer's mind.

BUILDING RAPPORT

After breaking the ice, you may feel more comfortable offering a small bit of **advice** to a client who is working out independently. Proceed tactfully; focus on maximizing the exercise rather than correcting the client, and use the opportunity to share information, rather than offer instruction.

Many people have firm ideas about how to exercise and may perceive corrective language as admonishing or even rude. A negative approach may rub the client the wrong way, which is not the intent. Avoid correcting or offering a better way. Even the seemingly innocuous "can I suggest something?" can come off as offensive.

INCREASING VALUE OF SERVICES

Just because a person wants to get in shape or lose weight does not mean that he or she will. Before a person commits to working with a trainer, he or she must feel that there is adequate **value** for the money and time invested.

It is extremely helpful for a trainer to be well versed in all NASM's systematic tools to demonstrate that the services offered have a high value. These include performing assessments, programming the Optimum Performance Training (OPT) template, having a wide knowledge of different exercises that target various muscle groups, the ability to help a client achieve performance goals, and being able to discuss fluently the OPT model and how it can benefit a specific client.

Copyright © Mometrix Media. You have been licensed one copy of this document for personal use only. Any other reproduction or redistribution is strictly prohibited. All rights reserved. This content is provided for test preparation purposes only and does not imply an endorsement by Mometrix of any particular political, scientific, or religious point of view.

Being able to show clients that you are proficient with many specific **tools for success** gives them confidence that working with you will provide the value that they are seeking for their money.

READ SYSTEM

NASM teaches CPTs to employ a specific system to acquire new clients. To help describe the steps in a memorable way, NASM uses the acronym **READ**. The letters stand for the following:

- **Rapport**—the essential relationship building that a trainer must establish with a new client.
- **Empathy**—the sense of understanding that must go hand in hand with physical training skills, in which the trainer learns to uncover and cater to the emotional reasons a person seeks training.
- **Assessment**—the process of determining what the client is trying to accomplish.
- **Development**—the ability of the trainer to build a plan for success.

RAPPORT

Rapport is the first step required for trainers to obtain new clients; it is the foundation of a professional relationship based on communication, pleasant interaction, and commonality of purpose. This foundation is essential to establish trust and build common ground from which to work.

It is necessary to maximize **communication** to build rapport with a potential client. This comes not only in the form of verbal communication but also in actions and nonverbal cues, such as body language. These communications convey an overall impression to potential clients that reflects positively on the trainer and the training environment. Because people make decisions based on how they feel about a certain situation, establishing rapport in these subtle interactions is vital.

Developing a presence: Developing rapport with a potential client is an essential first step to eventually closing the sale. To maximize the level of positive nonverbal communication, a trainer can work on developing a certain **presence** that inspires confidence and respect.

According to NASM, presence is typified by three elements: professionalism, enthusiasm, and confidence.

- **Professionalism** can be conveyed by the style of dress and appearance, friendliness, and manner of behavior (never gossiping or bad-mouthing the health club, its staff, or other clients).
- **Enthusiasm** is displaying a positive outward attitude about training and clients. This shows that the trainer is happy to be working with clients and values their goals and business.
- **Confidence** is necessary to build the trust of a potential client and show that the trainer is competent and can deliver the results he or she promises.

EMPATHY

Empathy is being able to understand someone else's point of view and the emotions that result. This is important because it is a potential client's motivation—not his or her goals—that is key to gaining them as a client. The trainer must understand the client's motivation to build empathy.

Motivation is why someone does something, feels a certain way, or acts in a particular manner. It is essential for a trainer to understand motivation not only to develop a rapport with a potential client but also to understand how to inspire a current client to stick with his or her training program by encouraging them based on these emotional triggers.

184

Copyright © Mometrix Media. You have been licensed one copy of this document for personal use only. Any other reproduction or redistribution is strictly prohibited. All rights reserved. This content is provided for test preparation purposes only and does not imply an endorsement by Mometrix of any particular political, scientific, or religious point of view.

Empathizing with a client helps the trainer navigate the psychology associated with helping people accomplish fitness goals. If a trainer can understand where a person is coming from and what negative associations, fears, or doubts the person is dealing with, the trainer can be more sensitive and tactful while helping the person accomplish his or her goals.

Building empathy: People behave in large part based on how they feel about things, not necessarily on what they think. This is based on a person's life experiences and observations. To build empathy and understanding with a client, the trainer must ask four questions:

1. What is your goal?
2. When did you set this goal?
3. Why is this goal important to you?
4. What have been prior roadblocks to accomplishing this goal?

The answers will help the trainer uncover how the client feels about fitness, working out, and his or her body. Once a trainer knows the answers to the four questions, he or she can establish whether the person is motivated by the **positive** (feeling healthy or looking good) or the **negative** (avoiding illness or being fat). This will allow the trainer to empathize with the client and provide insight into how to motivate that particular person.

ENTHUSIASM

Once a health and fitness professional understands why a person wants to achieve certain fitness goals, he or she can tailor **motivational efforts** to match the person's specific needs. Clients can be motivated by the positive (feeling healthy or looking good), or the negative (avoiding illness or being fat).

To build enthusiasm among those who are motivated by the **positive**, trainers should:

- Remind the client that working out today will pay off in the future.
- List the potential benefits of each exercise for the client.
- Give praise that emphasizes accomplishment, pride, and noticing small improvements.

To build enthusiasm among those who are motivated by the **negative**, trainers should:

- Remind the client that skipping a workout today will have negative effects in the future.
- List the negative aspects of not performing a certain exercise for the client.
- Speak to the client's emotional issues: fear, being fat, and not being accepted.

ASSESSMENT

In the assessment phase of closing a sale with a potential client, the health and fitness professional puts the technical aspects of his or her NASM training into action. The trainer has already established a relationship of trust (rapport) and gotten to understand why the client wants to achieve certain goals (empathy).

Now is the time to find ways to accomplish those goals, utilizing the OPT model and all of the other assessment tools contained in the NASM CPT course. By detailing some ideas and concrete techniques to accomplish these fitness goals, the trainer will make the **value** of his or her services clear to the client, making it easier to close the sale. This will be accomplished by asking the right questions, and then making the features and benefits of a training program clear.

Copyright © Mometrix Media. You have been licensed one copy of this document for personal use only. Any other reproduction or redistribution is strictly prohibited. All rights reserved. This content is provided for test preparation purposes only and does not imply an endorsement by Mometrix of any particular political, scientific, or religious point of view.

Asking questions: To assess how to help a client achieve goals, it is vital to engage in a question-based dialogue. This not only helps identify what the client is trying to accomplish, but it also engages the client in the process. NASM recommends following these steps:

1. Ask directive and nondirective questions.
2. Engage closely when listening to the client's response.
3. Rephrase the response to show you understood and to clarify.
4. Jot things down to refer to later.

Directive questions result in short answers, preferably yes or no. **Nondirective questions** are leading in nature, resulting in a more detailed response.

DEVELOPMENT

The last step in closing a sale with a potential client is **development**. The health and fitness professional applies the knowledge gained from that particular client and crafts an action plan using techniques from NASM's CPT course.

This is the opportunity for the trainer to use his or her technical skills by showing the client the features of the program and its ultimate benefits. **Features** of a program include the number of workouts, the specific exercises that will be used, the set of assessments that will be employed, and any other technical aspects. **Benefits** refer to the positive results that come from using the features.

Clients tend to be more interested in benefits than in features. While it is good to discuss features to show proficiency in training techniques, don't go overboard just to hear yourself talk. Clients are more interested in how the features translate into benefits.

OPT FEATURES

IMPROVING OVERALL FITNESS

If a client's main goal is to improve general conditioning to improve **daily function**, incorporate the following features:

- Balance will improve through better neuromuscular control and efficiency.
- Core strength is increased; therefore, external forces will be guided away from the spine.
- Synergistic dominance is decreased.
- Flexibility will increase through improved arthrokinematics.
- Relative flexibility and reciprocal inhibition will be lessened.
- The OPT model is used to increase stability and functional strength, progressing through to the power stage: high-velocity strength training.

The program will focus on flexibility, stability, and increased strength. The benefits to the client (which they're more concerned with) will include the ability to accomplish daily tasks effectively and stave off chronic injury cycles. There will be a lower risk for injury and chronic illness, which translates into less time lost from work and more time for healthy engagement with loved ones. There will also be less pain resulting from sedentary work and lifestyle habits.

CHANGING BODY COMPOSITION

If a client's main goal is to improve his or her **general body tone**, incorporate the following features:

- The balance stage will focus on higher motor unit communication.
- The core strength phase will focus on building the transversus abdominis.

Copyright © Mometrix Media. You have been licensed one copy of this document for personal use only. Any other reproduction or redistribution is strictly prohibited. All rights reserved. This content is provided for test preparation purposes only and does not imply an endorsement by Mometrix of any particular political, scientific, or religious point of view.

- Strength aspects will start first with stabilization, then core strength, and then endurance.
- The client will build a base that will lead to a more-responsive neuromuscular system that is prepared for power training.
- Flexibility training will lower reciprocal inhibition and arthrokinematic inhibition.

The program will focus on improving flexibility and target tight areas that prevent major muscle groups from working properly (such as the gluteals). The benefit to the client (which they're more concerned with) will include better overall muscle tone.

BUILDING MUSCLE MASS

If a client's main goal is to improve his or her **level of strength and muscle size**, incorporate the following features:

- Increased **neuromuscular efficiency**, which increases balance and stabilization.
- **Core exercises** maximize the efficiency of the kinetic chain.
- **Strength exercises** first stabilize, then provide more everyday strength, and ultimately progress into optimal strength through muscle hypertrophy.
- **Power exercises** focus on neuromuscular improvement to target prime mover and synergist muscle function.

The program will focus on stabilizing the kinetic chain and getting the muscles and nervous system to communicate more efficiently, making it easier for those muscles to get a workout. The benefits to the client (which they're more concerned with) will include building joint strength so the joints can handle the stress necessary to build larger muscles.

MAXIMIZING CLIENT PERFORMANCE

The benefits of an OPT program aimed at improving **performance** for a specific sport or athletic activity is easy to describe to a client: Work will be aimed at better performance and reducing injury risk by improving speed, strength, and control over the body.

The features of such a program are more technical:

- The **core musculature** will be maximized and the kinetic chain balanced and strengthened.
- **Flexibility** will be enhanced through better tissue extensibility.
- **Balance** will be improved by stabilizing joints and by training on the neuromuscular level (mechanoreceptors and proprioceptors).
- All levels of **strength training** will be used to improve function, protect joints under higher levels of work and strain, and build muscle mass.
- **Power levels** will be explored to maximize the explosive power necessary in sporting events and athletic endeavors.

LOSING FAT AND DECREASING BMI

The benefits of a **fat-loss program** are easy for a potential client to understand. The main purpose is to lose fat while building lean muscle. These activities will increase the body's base metabolism level, burn more calories, and result in visible changes to the figure, including lost inches and slimmer appearance.

Copyright © Mometrix Media. You have been licensed one copy of this document for personal use only. Any other reproduction or redistribution is strictly prohibited. All rights reserved. This content is provided for test preparation purposes only and does not imply an endorsement by Mometrix of any particular political, scientific, or religious point of view.

The features of such a program are more technical:

- The **OPT model** will first focus on stabilizing the core musculature and increasing the neuromuscular communication throughout the body. This is necessary so that exercises will target the correct muscle groups. If these muscles are worked properly, muscle mass and metabolism will increase.
- **Flexibility exercises** will aim at increasing neuromuscular efficiency.
- **Strength training** will aim to increase lean muscle mass and rev up metabolism.

SELLING SERVICES

Health and fitness professionals must be highly proficient in the technical aspect of what they do, and they must also possess **business acumen** to make a living. For some, the selling aspect of the job can be challenging because selling might be perceived as being pushy, or it might open the trainer up for personal rejection that he or she finds unpalatable. To be successful, the trainer will have to deal with these aspects of the job and find a way to view them positively.

The best way to approach selling is by developing a **positive attitude** about the service that is being provided. If the trainer is competent, there is an absolute value in the service. By approaching customers with care and concern for their health and goals, a trainer can feel that he or she is sincerely providing a beneficial service and not attempting to sell a person something without value.

10 STEPS TO SUCCESS FORMULA

NASM developed a list of 10 Steps to Success designed to help a health and fitness professional understand what is necessary to handle the business side of a training practice:

1. **Annual income**—What is the trainer's annual income goal?

   This should be based on actual personal expenses, not some lofty number. It should reflect what other successful trainers in the area make, and be sufficient to provide a reasonable lifestyle.

2. **Weekly income**—How much income is needed per week to meet the annual goal?

   This is simply the annual income figure divided by 52 (or a lower number of weeks to reflect either an annual vacation or a slow period that may occur at holiday time).

3. **Weekly sessions**—How many sessions are needed per week to earn the weekly income goal?

   Once weekly income is figured, the number of sessions needed to accomplish this income goal can be deduced. The weekly income is divided by the cost of a training session. For example, if the weekly goal is $500, and the trainer charges $50 per hour, then 500 ÷ 50 = 10 one-hour training sessions per week.

4. **Closing percentage**—What percentage of client interactions result in a completed sale?
   The closing percentage refers to how many sales are made out of how many are attempted. For example, if a trainer speaks to 100 people and signs 10 up for training sessions, the closing percentage is 10%.

5. **Time frame**—What are some time goals?

Copyright © Mometrix Media. You have been licensed one copy of this document for personal use only. Any other reproduction or redistribution is strictly prohibited. All rights reserved.
This content is provided for test preparation purposes only and does not imply an endorsement by Mometrix of any particular political, scientific, or religious point of view.

To determine how to build a clientele to meet the ultimate annual income goals, there must be reasonable time frames built in. The time frame must be attainable and provide a sense of urgency.

6. **People contacted**—How many potential clients must be approached to meet the closing percentage goals?

   Divide the desired number of clients by the closing percentage to determine how many clients must be approached to retain the desired number of clients. Divide the total number of clients to be contacted by the desired time frame to determine the number of contacts per week.

7. **People contacted daily**—How many people must be communicated with every day to reach this closing percentage goal?

   Divide the weekly target by the number of days worked to get the daily goal. As an example, if a trainer must speak to 90 people over three weeks and works five days a week, this works out to six potential clients each day: $90 \div (3 \times 5) = 6$

8. **People contacted hourly**—How many people must be communicated with every hour to reach this closing percentage goal?

   Divide the daily goal by the number of hours worked to calculate the hourly goal. As an example, if the trainer works a six-hour shift, at least one potential client must be spoken to every hour.

9. **Contact information**—Has the trainer obtained the person's contact information?

   After a certain level of rapport has been established, the trainer should make an effort to get a potential client's contact information. The trainer could offer to design a few specific exercises for that person and contact the person to implement these in the future.

10. **Follow up**—Has the trainer contacted the person after the initial communication?

    Following up is extremely important when selling one's training services. Not only does it help to build rapport but it also develops relationships with people who may not be in a position to hire a trainer at the present but may want to do so in the future. It also creates a positive impression among people who may recommend others to the trainer.

LOSING SALES

Most trainers who struggle with sales do so because they are reluctant to ask for the sale. The primary reason a sale is not made is there is no direct attempt to ask for the sale. To overcome this hesitation, the trainer should **practice** making it a part of every dialogue with potential clients. With practice, a comfort level will be developed, and the aversion to sales will fade.

At times, the sale is asked for prematurely. There may not be enough rapport with the potential client for him or her to feel comfortable saying yes. Work on developing **rapport** before trying to sell the person.

It is also important to effectively communicate level of **value** of the service. If the potential client is unsure about the benefits of training, the trainer must educate him or her for a true understanding of value received.

Copyright © Mometrix Media. You have been licensed one copy of this document for personal use only. Any other reproduction or redistribution is strictly prohibited. All rights reserved.
This content is provided for test preparation purposes only and does not imply an endorsement by Mometrix of any particular political, scientific, or religious point of view.

Sometimes the client may not be able to **afford** a trainer. This situation cannot be changed by the trainer. The trainer can follow up and foster the relationship so that if the person's financial circumstances change trainer will be well positioned to make the sale.

The sale is not complete when a trainer closes a new client. The time immediately following a sale is vital for the trainer. The trainer must back up the sales talk and actively **demonstrate** the value of the service to the client.

The first meeting should be scheduled within **two days** of closing the sale. Send the client a thank-you via mail or email, to show your appreciation for their time and to confirm the time of the appointment. Call before the appointment to confirm and take a moment to review to avoid cutting into workout time. Sincerely congratulate the client on taking action to accomplish his or her goals.

DECLINING SERVICES

A potential client who resists signing up for training today is not a lost cause, and may be a **future client** or a **source** of other clients. Always maintain a high level of professionalism and friendliness. Thank the individual for his or her time, and get that person's contact information to check in with them at a later date.

Become a **resource** for that person. Place a follow-up phone call in 10-14 days to ask if he or she has any questions regarding the fitness regimen that you may be able to help with. Send an article or Web link that might be of interest to the person after approximately one month. Record each interaction in a daily journal or day planner.

Communication will help demonstrate your professionalism, commitment to your work, and convey the value of your services. Effective communication may eventually turn a no answer into a yes response.

Copyright © Mometrix Media. You have been licensed one copy of this document for personal use only. Any other reproduction or redistribution is strictly prohibited. All rights reserved.
This content is provided for test preparation purposes only and does not imply an endorsement by Mometrix of any particular political, scientific, or religious point of view.

Professional Development and Responsibility

Code of Ethics

A code of ethics represents some basic guidelines for behavior that members of a given profession adhere to. All major professions maintain ethical guidelines and require some manner of compliance to ensure the quality of practitioners in the field, and to keep the profession in good repute among the general public. This helps all members of the profession deliver the best services to its clients.

NASM has a **fourfold approach** to its code of ethics. This includes a section on general standards of professionalism, some tenets of confidentiality, legal and ethical aspects of fitness training, and a section on general business practices.

> **Review Video: Ethical and Professional Standards**
> Visit mometrix.com/academy and enter code: 810679

PROFESSIONALISM SECTION

The professionalism section of NASM's code of ethics contains 11 tenets:

1. To abide by the code
2. To conduct oneself professionally
3. To treat clients and colleagues with respect
4. To not be judgmental of clients and colleagues
5. To communicate professionally
6. To provide a safe environment for clients:
   a. By not making medical diagnoses or treating nonemergency conditions when not licensed to do so
   b. By ensuring clients see a physician before undertaking a workout regimen
   c. By reviewing a medical history form filled out by the client
   d. By holding emergency certifications
7. To tell the client to seek medical attention when:
   a. The client's health significantly changes
   b. You discover the client has an illness, injury, or risk factor
   c. The client is in unexpected, unusual, or unwarranted pain
8. To recommend the services of a nutritionist or dietitian and to not offer advice without training
9. To maintain personal hygiene
10. To maintain professional dress
11. To maintain certification and continuing education

Copyright © Mometrix Media. You have been licensed one copy of this document for personal use only. Any other reproduction or redistribution is strictly prohibited. All rights reserved. This content is provided for test preparation purposes only and does not imply an endorsement by Mometrix of any particular political, scientific, or religious point of view.

CONFIDENTIALITY SECTION

Three code of ethics tenets pertain to **confidentiality**. Clients provide a great deal of personal and medical information to health and fitness professionals, and it is imperative that trainers protect the clients' privacy. Trainers should follow these ethical guidelines:

1. Keep **all confidences** of the client, and do not discuss the client with others. Do not mention clients in promotional materials advertising the trainer's services unless there is express permission to do so. Only divulge information when it is necessary for professional or emergency medical reasons.
2. Remember that **minors** do not have the legal capacity to consent to how their personal information is being used, so seek permission from their legal guardian.
3. Protect **client records** and make sure they are not accessible to others.

> **Review Video: Ethics and Confidentiality in Counseling**
> Visit mometrix.com/academy and enter code: 250384

LEGAL AND ETHICAL SECTION

Four code of ethics tenets describe the **legal and ethical responsibilities** of CPTs. By following all applicable laws and rules, trainers protect themselves and keep the profession in good repute. NASM's rules include:

1. Follow **all applicable laws** for each jurisdiction in which the trainer resides (federal, state, and local).
2. Accept **responsibility** for everything he or she does.
3. Keep **records** that are true and complete. It is also important to keep these records in a secure place to maintain client confidentiality.
4. Make sure to respect **copyrights** and trademarks as they apply to the trainer's practice.

BUSINESS PRACTICES SECTION

Seven code of ethics tenets pertain to **business practices and responsibilities** of its CPTs. NASM's rules include:

1. Obtain appropriate insurance
2. Keep accurate notes about each client's work and progress
3. Represent services and capabilities honestly to the general public
4. Represent training and certifications honestly
5. Advertise in a professional way without using prurient images or language
6. Keep meticulous financial and tax records
7. Keep current with all laws on sexual harassment

COMPLIANCE WITH NASM'S CODE OF ETHICS

NASM members, whether currently certified or not, are expected to conform to the **code of ethics** to maintain the highest level of personal conduct and to keep the health and fitness professional profession in excellent repute.

Members that fail to comply with the code of ethics will be subject to a list of progressive **disciplinary actions**. Punishment range from minor sanctions to expulsion from the National Academy of Sports Medicine. Other punishments include temporary suspension and revocation of current certifications.

Copyright © Mometrix Media. You have been licensed one copy of this document for personal use only. Any other reproduction or redistribution is strictly prohibited. All rights reserved. This content is provided for test preparation purposes only and does not imply an endorsement by Mometrix of any particular political, scientific, or religious point of view.

Additionally, all members are ethically bound to **report** instances of breaches of the code of ethics by other members.

Copyright © Mometrix Media. You have been licensed one copy of this document for personal use only. Any other reproduction or redistribution is strictly prohibited. All rights reserved.
This content is provided for test preparation purposes only and does not imply an endorsement by Mometrix of any particular political, scientific, or religious point of view.

Emergency Aid

CPR is an acronym that stands for **cardiopulmonary resuscitation**. This is an emergency aid procedure given when a person has stopped breathing and has gone into cardiac arrest. Adult CPR is appropriate for people older than eight years old.

Be sure any immediate danger to oneself or the unconscious person is removed before commencing CPR. Call 911 to summon help, and follow instructions given by the dispatcher.

The ABCs of CPR stand for: **Airway**, **Breathing**, and **Circulation**. Clear the airway, and make sure there are no obstructions that might be causing the person to choke. Check for breathing; if there is no respiration, mouth-to-mouth must be given to introduce air into the body manually. Air must circulate through the body, which must also be done manually, by compressing the chest to get the heart to pump oxygenated air. These compressions can pump around 30 percent of the blood that the heart can normally.

MUSCLE STRAIN, BONE FRACTURE OR DISLOCATION, OR LIGAMENT STRAIN OR SPRAIN

It is not uncommon for a health and fitness professional to see **strains or sprains** in his or her line of work. Symptoms will include an immediate pain to the area, difficulty putting weight on that muscle or joint, swelling, and bruising. Immobilize the affected area, and apply ice packs to help reduce inflammation. If the person loses feeling to the area or has any indication of reduced blood flow, it will be necessary to get the person immediate medical attention.

If it is suspected that a person has **broken a bone**, it will be necessary to get immediate medical attention. Depending on the severity of the injury, an ambulance can be summoned, or the person can be driven by car. Immobilize the affected area, and watch for signs of shock. If there is a **spinal injury**, move the person only if there is an absolute need to get out of harm's way, and then call for emergency assistance.

BLEEDING

When a person bleeds, it can be as minor as a paper cut or as serious as a life-threatening emergency, depending on the situation. If a person begins to bleed, apply direct pressure to the wound to encourage the body's clotting response. If this does not stanch the blood flow, a pressure dressing should be used. If this does not work, try putting the injured area above the heart while continuing to apply pressure. If this doesn't work, apply a tourniquet.

Use precautions for your health when dealing with someone who is bleeding. Avoid touching the blood directly, and use gloves to minimize the chance of contracting a blood-borne illness.

SHOCK

When a person goes into shock, it is a serious medical emergency. Shock can occur for a variety of reasons, including blood loss, sudden stress, or cardiac or lung problems. The person will become clammy, fatigued, light-headed, possibly sick to his or her stomach, and might lose consciousness.

Help the person to a comfortable, prone position, with the feet higher than the heart. Bundle the person up to keep him or her warm. Watch the person carefully for signs of unconsciousness. Give cardiopulmonary resuscitation (CPR) if needed. If the person is breathing but loses consciousness, roll him or her onto the side to prevent choking due to potential vomiting.

Seek medical attention while carefully monitoring the person's condition.

Copyright © Mometrix Media. You have been licensed one copy of this document for personal use only. Any other reproduction or redistribution is strictly prohibited. All rights reserved. This content is provided for test preparation purposes only and does not imply an endorsement by Mometrix of any particular political, scientific, or religious point of view.

SEIZURES

A seizure can be a sudden and frightening episode in which a person loses control of his or her body. For many seizure sufferers, a single seizure is part of a long-term problem, such as epilepsy, that he or she manages on a regular basis. If this is the case, a health and fitness professional should be made aware of this condition. Have a physician-approved workout regimen and an emergency plan for a seizure episode.

If a person has a seizure, immediately make sure that he or she is in the safest position—on the floor and away from anything that he or she could hit with the body, especially the head. Do not put anything in the person's mouth.

Note when the seizure started, how long it lasts, and when it ends. If the person loses consciousness and begins to seize again, call 911 right away.

INSULIN SHOCK

Insulin shock is a problem that can occur for people with diabetes, which is a condition that the trainer should be made aware of if it exists in his or her clients. Symptoms can include irritability and irrational behavior, extreme and sudden fatigue up to unconsciousness, and clammy skin. Insulin shock is extremely serious and can lead to death if not attended to.

To help correct insulin shock, a health and fitness professional can provide something to eat that is high in sugar: juice, a sugary soda, a piece of candy, or the like. Do not give the person anything if he or she is unconscious, but do call for help immediately.

Unlike many other emergency conditions, insulin shock can in large part be avoided by careful monitoring of the blood sugar. If a client has diabetes, be sure that you and the client have a physician-approved workout regimen and an emergency plan for blood sugar issues that may occur.

ASTHMA ATTACKS

An asthma attack is an umbrella term for several lung problems that result in difficulty breathing. This can be as mild as a general wheezing or as serious as a life-threatening inability to breathe. Symptoms can include difficulty breathing, loud breathing (wheezing), turning purple or blue, and anxiety or a feeling of claustrophobia. The person's ability to speak can be a good indicator of how distressed the person is—an inability to speak or to only be able to speak a word or two at a time indicates serious trouble breathing.

Make sure the person is not choking or having an allergic reaction. Then put the person in a comfortable position. Call for help and follow the instructions given by the dispatcher. If the person has taken any medication, do not allow them to exceed the recommended dose without further instruction.

HEART ATTACK

A heart attack is a very serious medical condition that occurs when the heart muscle malfunctions, causing a lack of blood, and therefore oxygen, to the heart muscle. The damage can range from mild and self-correcting to that which requires immediate medical intervention.

Symptoms of a heart attack include pain and pressure in the chest that may also be felt in the arms, especially the left arm, or the jaw. The person may be cold and clammy, may sweat profusely, have trouble catching his or her breath, and may become ill.

Copyright © Mometrix Media. You have been licensed one copy of this document for personal use only. Any other reproduction or redistribution is strictly prohibited. All rights reserved.
This content is provided for test preparation purposes only and does not imply an endorsement by Mometrix of any particular political, scientific, or religious point of view.

If a heart attack is suspected, put the person in a safe, relaxed position and administer aspirin if possible to thin the blood so it can travel through restricted arteries. Help keep the person calm and breathing as normally as possible, and ask if he or she took nitroglycerin, as this information may be relevant to emergency personnel later.

STROKE

A stroke is a serious medical condition with effects that range from mild and temporarily debilitating, to fatal. If a client is having a stroke, it is important to recognize it as soon as possible and get the person medical attention.

A stroke is the result of a problem with a blood vessel in the brain; the vessel could have a blockage, it could leak, or it could burst. Symptoms include a sudden and serious headache, slurring when speaking, paralysis on one side of the body, hallucinations, becoming delirious, or passing out.

Put the person in a safe position and call for medical assistance immediately, or take the person to an emergency room if practicable.

CHOKING

Choking is a highly serious situation in which a person cannot take in oxygen because something is blocking the airway. A person who is choking will not be able to speak or cough, so they must be observed for physical cues. A person may wave their arms, point to their throat, clutch their throat, and, in the absence of oxygen, may even turn purple or blue.

Perform the **Heimlich maneuver** to remove the airway obstruction. Standing behind the person, place a fist over the belly button and below the rib cage, with the other hand resting on top of the fist. Quick, upward motions should be made to force air from the lungs up to dislodge the obstruction.

If the person passes out, lay him or her on the floor, try to open the mouth, look in for an obstruction, and remove it. If this doesn't work, a flat variation of the Heimlich can be tried by straddling the person's waist and placing the heel of the hand above the belly button and pressing down rapidly several times.

HEAT STROKE/EXHAUSTION

Heat exhaustion and heat stroke are two very serious medical conditions that must be monitored in hot outdoor environments as well as in cooler indoor settings, given that the rigors of a workout can raise body temperature, especially in people with known risk factors.

Heat exhaustion is characterized by clammy skin that is cool or normal in temperature. The person may be extremely fatigued, sweating profusely, and experience lightheadedness and a lowered pulse rate. Cramping may also be an issue. Get the person into a cooler environment, put his or her head between the knees if dizzy, and loosen any restricting garments. Fan the person and allow him or her to drink water or an electrolyte beverage.

Heat stroke is characterized by very hot skin. The person may feel extremely fatigued, but will likely have no sweating and an elevated pulse rate. They may even seem delirious. The person should be taken to a cool environment and cooled down slowly. Remove restricting clothing and apply cool (but not cold), wet cloths and cold packs in the armpits.

Copyright © Mometrix Media. You have been licensed one copy of this document for personal use only. Any other reproduction or redistribution is strictly prohibited. All rights reserved. This content is provided for test preparation purposes only and does not imply an endorsement by Mometrix of any particular political, scientific, or religious point of view.

AEDs

A **defibrillator** is a device that can be used to jump-start the heart when it is in cardiac arrest. It is only to be used in an emergency situation, but it can be very effective in restoring a heartbeat with an electrical charge.

A **manual defibrillator** is a complex piece of equipment meant for emergency personnel with more qualifications for handling the machine and the circumstances under which it might be necessary. Other, less-qualified, people may use an **automated defibrillator**, which may be fully automated or partially automated. A fully automated machine needs only to be attached properly to work, while a partially automated machine may require the operator to activate it.

An **adult automated external defibrillator (AED)** is not appropriate for small children (younger than 8 years old or less than 60 pounds). It should only be used for a person who is in cardiac arrest—that is, someone with no heartbeat and who is not breathing.

CARDIAC ARRHYTHMIAS:

The body has an **electrical impulse system** that controls the brain's communication with the muscles (via the nerves) as well as the efficient pumping of the heart. When the electrical pattern is disrupted or not working properly, it can lead to the heart stalling out, so to speak. This is referred to as cardiac arrhythmia or abnormal rhythm.

Several issues can lead to problems with the heart pumping:

- Ventricular fibrillation
- Pulseless ventricular tachycardia
- Pulseless electrical activity
- Asystole

The first two, **ventricular fibrillation** and **pulseless ventricular tachycardia**, will respond to the electrical current provided by an AED; the other two, **pulseless electrical activity** and **asystole**, will not respond to AED treatment.

Copyright © Mometrix Media. You have been licensed one copy of this document for personal use only. Any other reproduction or redistribution is strictly prohibited. All rights reserved. This content is provided for test preparation purposes only and does not imply an endorsement by Mometrix of any particular political, scientific, or religious point of view.

NASM Practice Test

Want to take this practice test in an online interactive format?
Check out the bonus page, which includes interactive practice questions and
much more: **https://www.mometrix.com/bonus948/nasm**

1. Which of the following is NOT required as a minimum to reduce additional risks in a fitness facility setting?

    a. Clean water or drinking supply
    b. Adequate lighting
    c. Staffing and supervision
    d. Member training for use of equipment

2. Which is the only type of stretching that does NOT need to follow the warm-up component of an exercise program?

    a. Dynamic stretching
    b. Proprioceptive neuromuscular facilitation (PNF)
    c. Static stretching
    d. Passive stretching

3. During an Overhead Press exercise the primary mover is the deltoid. Which muscle type can the deltoid be classified as?

    a. Synergist
    b. Antagonist
    c. Stabilizer
    d. Agonist

4. All of the following are reasons that a personal trainer should never recommend supplements to a client EXCEPT

    a. that supplement manufacturing companies usually do not carry insurance, leaving the personal trainer 100 percent liable for monetary compensation should either be sued.
    b. that supplements are not regulated by the Food and Drug Administration (FDA).
    c. that underlying and/or unknown medical conditions may be exacerbated by supplement use.
    d. that a trainer should always review a client's 3-day food log before recommending nutrient supplementation.

5. After a particularly difficult exercise, you look your client in the eye, acknowledge the effort he put in to the work, and compliment his form. What training tactic are you communicating?

    a. Stimulus control
    b. Positive reinforcement
    c. Shaping
    d. Behavior chains

Copyright © Mometrix Media. You have been licensed one copy of this document for personal use only. Any other reproduction or redistribution is strictly prohibited. All rights reserved. This content is provided for test preparation purposes only and does not imply an endorsement by Mometrix of any particular political, scientific, or religious point of view.

6. You are working with a new client, and you have asked her to write down her weight loss goals using the SMART guidelines. Which is an example of a SMART goal?

    a. To lose 20 lbs, in the next 30 days by increasing participation in cardio exercise and playing sports with friends

    b. To lose 10 lbs, over the next 2 months by performing 30 minutes of cardiovascular activity three times a week and weight training one time a week so that she can prepare to try out for the local soccer team

    c. To lose 10 lbs, so that the client may purchase the new swimsuit

    d. To lose weight by increasing cardiovascular activity to three times week and lifting weights two times a week

7. Which form is considered an agreement between the client and personal trainer and works in conjunction with the informed consent?

    a. Physical Activity Readiness Questionnaire (PARQ)

    b. Medical history form

    c. Self-assessment

    d. Release of liability

8. How many positive risk factors must a client have to be considered a moderate risk?

    a. 0

    b. 1

    c. 2

    d. Any known cardiovascular, pulmonary, or metabolic disease

9. What key coping strategy is most important for relapse prevention?

    a. Social support

    b. Assertiveness

    c. Self-regulation

    d. Intrinsic motivation

10. You meet a client who has been exercising on her own for the past 3 months. She has a plan of action and a steady routine at the local gym. Which stage of change is this client in, per the Transtheoretical Model?

    a. Contemplation

    b. Preparation

    c. Action

    d. Maintenance

11. Which model of behavior change is dependent on the weighing of barriers to change and the perceived benefits of change?

    a. Transtheoretical Model

    b. Theory of Planned Behavior

    c. The Health Belief Model

    d. Social Cognitive Theory

Copyright © Mometrix Media. You have been licensed one copy of this document for personal use only. Any other reproduction or redistribution is strictly prohibited. All rights reserved. This content is provided for test preparation purposes only and does not imply an endorsement by Mometrix of any particular political, scientific, or religious point of view.

12. The most important predictors for behavior change, according to Social Cognitive Theory, are the expectations of results and what other principle?

    a. Motivation

    b. Self-efficacy

    c. Goal setting

    d. Extrinsic motivation

13. What is the name of the plane of motion that divides the body into right and left sides?

    a. Frontal

    b. Sagittal

    c. Axial

    d. Transverse

14. Which is true of a client who has been determined to have moderate risk during risk classification?

    a. Doctor supervision during submaximal testing is required.

    b. The client has one risk factor.

    c. The client requires a medical exam prior to moderate exercise.

    d. A medical exam is required before vigorous exercise.

15. Which of the following choices is an example of a synovial bicondylar joint?

    a. Elbow

    b. Ankle

    c. Knee

    d. Hip

16. What muscles of the scapulothoracic joint are the major agonists when performing a push-up?

    a. Serratus anterior, pectoralis minor, trapezius, levator scapulae, and rhomboids

    b. Anterior deltoid, pectoralis minor, supraspinatus, and rhomboids

    c. Serratus anterior, pectoralis major, biceps, and triceps

    d. Anterior deltoid, biceps, levator scapulae, and trapezius

17. Which of the following is a physiological benefit of beginning an exercise program?

    a. Improvement in bone health

    b. Enhanced feeling of well-being

    c. Better cognitive function

    d. Decreased anxiety and depression

18. What is the baseline recommendation for cardiorespiratory programming of moderate intensity?

    a. At least 30 minutes per day on at least 5 days per week

    b. At least 15 minutes per day on at least 5 days per week

    c. At least 45 minutes per day on at least 3 days per week

    d. At least some moderate activity at least 4 days per week

Copyright © Mometrix Media. You have been licensed one copy of this document for personal use only. Any other reproduction or redistribution is strictly prohibited. All rights reserved. This content is provided for test preparation purposes only and does not imply an endorsement by Mometrix of any particular political, scientific, or religious point of view.

19. During the initial consultation with a new client, he states his current activity consists of training with resistance bands at home to a workout DVD and an occasional run in the evenings when he has time after work. What is this client's aerobic activity status and the associated training focus?

a. Beginner: no prior activity
b. Beginner: minimal activity
c. Intermediate: minimal activity
d. Intermediate: fair to average fitness

20. Which of the following is NOT a major type of hypoperfusion?

a. Obstructive
b. Hypovolemic
c. Destructive
d. Cardiogenic

21. You have a client who is male, 47 years old, who is looking to increase his range of motion (ROM) and decrease tightness in his joints. What is the most beneficial flexibility programming for this client?

a. At least 5 minutes after each training session
b. At least 10 minutes for a minimum of 1 day per week
c. At least 10 minutes daily
d. At least 5 minutes for a minimum of 3 days per week

22. Flexibility and resistance training for pregnant women in which position should be avoided after what point in pregnancy?

a. Supine; after the second trimester
b. Prone; after 6 weeks
c. Supine; after the first trimester
d. Prone; as soon as the client knows she is pregnant

23. Each of these are a special precaution a personal trainer should take when working with a client with diabetes EXCEPT

a. keeping a vigilant eye out for the warning signs or hypo- and hyperglycemia.
b. having the client eat 1 to 2 hours prior to exercise.
c. having fruit juice available.
d. having the client eat a snack if blood glucose reads more than 100mg/dl.

24. What types of training are the most effective way to improve an athlete's stride rate and frequency?

a. Sprint, plyometric, strength, and ballistic training
b. Cardiovascular, plyometric, and ballistic training
c. Resistance, ballistic, cardiovascular, and plyometric training
d. Sprint, plyometric, and strength training

Copyright © Mometrix Media. You have been licensed one copy of this document for personal use only. Any other reproduction or redistribution is strictly prohibited. All rights reserved. This content is provided for test preparation purposes only and does not imply an endorsement by Mometrix of any particular political, scientific, or religious point of view.

25. Effective programming will be different for each client based on his or her fitness level and goals. However, program progression follows what important rule for all clients?

    a. Increase repetitions for faster improvements in strength and technique.

    b. Single sets are more beneficial than super sets.

    c. Increase weight loads for faster improvements in strength and technique.

    d. Always begin with a light weight when teaching a new skill.

26. What is the appropriate length of time for the cool-down phase of a training session?

    a. 2–4 minutes

    b. 5–10 minutes

    c. 10–15 minutes

    d. 3–5 minutes

27. The anatomical position can be described as which of the following?

    a. The body is erect, feet together, arms at the sides with palms facing forward, thumbs pointed away from the body, and fingers extended.

    b. The body is erect, feet hip width apart, arms at the sides with palms facing forward, thumbs pointed away from the body, and fingers extended.

    c. The body is erect, feet together, arms at the sides with palms facing forward, thumbs pointed away from the body, and fingers flexed.

    d. The body is erect, feet hip width apart, arms at the sides with palms facing rear, thumbs pointed toward the body, and fingers extended.

28. A client who suffers from a hernia may be further injured by any activity that increases pressure in the abdominal cavity. Which breathing technique should never be used with one of these clients?

    a. Timed breathing

    b. Pranayama

    c. Valsalva maneuver

    d. Yogic

29. In terms of reversibility of resistance training, what is the rate at which an individual will lose his or her strength if the client completely stops resistance training at any point?

    a. One-third the rate it was gained

    b. One-half the rate it was gained

    c. One-fourth the rate it was gained

    d. One-third total mass in the same time it was gained

30. Proprioceptive neuromuscular facilitation (PNF) is the type of stretching that has what specific advantage?

    a. It stretches the muscles using strong momentum.

    b. It activates the stretch reflex.

    c. It stimulates the Golgi tendon, allowing a deep, second, passive stretch.

    d. It closely mimics the activities of daily living and emphasizes functional movements.

Copyright © Mometrix Media. You have been licensed one copy of this document for personal use only. Any other reproduction or redistribution is strictly prohibited. All rights reserved.
This content is provided for test preparation purposes only and does not imply an endorsement by Mometrix of any particular political, scientific, or religious point of view.

31. Each of the following are signs of overtraining and should signal to the trainer to decrease intensity and/or frequency of training EXCEPT

    a. decreased resting hear rate.
    b. increased resting heart rate.
    c. disturbed sleep.
    d. decreased hunger.

32. A client who is incorrectly performing a resistance training movement would likely benefit most from which cues to correct form?

    a. Imagery, affirmational, and visual
    b. Alignment, safety, and tactile
    c. Visual, wrong/right, and tactile
    d. Breathing, visual, and motivational

33. Which key movement would best help a client improve his or her functional rotational movement?

    a. Unilateral rows
    b. Hay balers
    c. Thoracic matrix
    d. Bilateral presses

34. Which is NOT a characteristic of proper weight lifting technique?

    a. Use the correct grip.
    b. Keep the abdominals tight.
    c. Use distinct, segmented motions.
    d. Keep the weight close.

35. The dietary guidelines recommend that general population adults reduce their daily sodium intake to less than what amount?

    a. 2500 mg
    b. 1500 mg
    c. 1300 mg
    d. 2300 mg

36. The most successful goals are those that are all of the following EXCEPT

    a. client selected.
    b. SMART.
    c. self-monitored.
    d. flexible.

37. During the initial consultation with a new client, she informs you that her main goal will be training for a marathon. As a fitness professional, you design a program that progresses in stages that mimic the physical demands of a marathon. The specific exercises you chose to train her with will stimulate the adaptations she will need to complete a marathon. Which principle of specificity should you use to design this client's program?

    a. Prioritization
    b. Specific Adaptations to Imposed Demands (SAID)
    c. Resistance training
    d. Cardiovascular prioritization

Copyright © Mometrix Media. You have been licensed one copy of this document for personal use only. Any other reproduction or redistribution is strictly prohibited. All rights reserved. This content is provided for test preparation purposes only and does not imply an endorsement by Mometrix of any particular political, scientific, or religious point of view.

38. A regular member of your gym approaches you asking for advice for pain that is running along the outside of his thigh to his knee, and you recommend myofascial release. What overuse injury is he likely suffering from?

a. Lateral epicondylitis
b. Tendinitis
c. Iliotibial band syndrome (ITBS)
d. Bursitis

39. As a client's abilities increase and his or her body adapts to the stimulus of training, it will be necessary to increase the intensity of the stimulus to continue to see increased results. What is this principle known as?

a. Progressive overload
b. Prioritization of training
c. Variation in training
d. Overload

40. You are working with a client whose goal is muscle hypertrophy. Despite proper training, muscle hypertrophy has been limited in the prime movers of the right shoulder, and the imbalance has been significant. The client has complained of pain in that shoulder in the past but no actual injury has been identified after a referral to a physician. What concept is most likely responsible for the hypertrophy imbalance experienced by your client?

a. Reciprocal inhibition
b. Morphological adaptation
c. Motor unit recruitment
d. Arthrokinetic inhibition

41. What are the primary, functional movements?

a. Bend-and-lift, single-leg, pushing, pulling, and rotational
b. Bend-and-lift, single-leg, jumping, and pushing/pulling
c. Single-leg, jumping, pushing, and pulling
d. Jumping, pushing, rotational, and multidirectional

42. Stress management is an important part of any good program. As a trainer, you should encourage clients to participate in stress-reducing activities such as massage therapy or guided imagery, which decreases catecholamine and cortisol production from which gland?

a. Apocrine
b. Eccrine
c. Sebaceous
d. Adrenal

43. During an evaluation of the lower body's kinetic chain, you notice an abduction of the client's knees between the femur and tibia, and the ankles are collapsed medially. This client has which postural deviation?

a. Pronation with external rotation of the knee
b. Supination with internal rotation of the knee
c. Neutral subtalar position
d. Pronation with internal rotation of the knee

Copyright © Mometrix Media. You have been licensed one copy of this document for personal use only. Any other reproduction or redistribution is strictly prohibited. All rights reserved. This content is provided for test preparation purposes only and does not imply an endorsement by Mometrix of any particular political, scientific, or religious point of view.

44. What is the only negative risk factor in the American College of Sports Medicine (ACSM) risk stratification criteria?

    a. High-serum HDL cholesterol ≥ 60 mg/dl (1.55mmol/L)
    b. Total serum cholesterol ≥ 200 mg/dl (5.18 mmol/L)
    c. Prescribed antihypertensive medication
    d. Quit smoking cigarettes within the past 6 months

45. Which of the following is responsible for initiating the stretch reflex during active and passive stretching?

    a. Muscle spindles
    b. Ligaments
    c. Golgi tendon
    d. Tendons

46. What is the average amount of hip flexion required to perform a correct squatting motion?

    a. 95 percent
    b. 135 percent
    c. 95 degrees
    d. 135 degrees

47. Which is true of proper spotting technique during resistance training?

    a. Keep hands as far from the weights as possible as to not obstruct the movement.
    b. Remove the weight collars and clips when a client is exceeding his or her personal maximum.
    c. Allow the client to count his or her own repetitions and signal to you when he or she is finished.
    d. Assist any time the predetermined speed decreases.

48. What is the purpose of the hip hinge motion when teaching the correct way to perform a squat?

    a. To promote quad dominance over glute dominance
    b. To promote glute dominance over quad dominance
    c. To promote hip alignment over the knees and feet
    d. To promote alignment between the trunk and tibia

49. Which communication form requires trust, attention, and understanding to be effective?

    a. Rapport
    b. Active listening
    c. Periphrasis
    d. Facial expressions

50. During a 6-month review with your client, he has decided that his current gains in strength are substantial enough that he would like to move to a maintenance program. What term best describes the close of this portion of his program?

    a. Variable goals
    b. End review
    c. Capping
    d. Evaluation

Copyright © Mometrix Media. You have been licensed one copy of this document for personal use only. Any other reproduction or redistribution is strictly prohibited. All rights reserved.
This content is provided for test preparation purposes only and does not imply an endorsement by Mometrix of any particular political, scientific, or religious point of view.

51. All the following are characteristics of a SMART goal EXCEPT

    a. specific.
    b. measurable.
    c. affordable.
    d. time-bound.

52. Which activities would you recommend for training children with the goal of bone strengthening?

    a. Hopscotch, skipping, and jumping
    b. Tug-of-war and tree climbing
    c. Walking and bicycle riding
    d. Swimming, skiing, and running

53. Which endocrine system hormonal response to exercise reduces the urinary secretion of water to counteract the dehydration effects of sweating?

    a. Growth hormone (GH) is secreted by the anterior pituitary gland.
    b. Antidiuretic hormone (ADH) is released by the posterior pituitary gland.
    c. Catecholamines are released by the adrenal medulla.
    d. Glucagon is secreted by the pancreas.

54. Which functional exercise improves thoracic extension?

    a. Supine 90-90
    b. Rocking quadrupeds
    c. Shoulder bridge
    d. Spinal extensions and spinal twists

55. What is the proper progression when teaching and performing bilateral and unilateral chest presses?

    a. Standing press, single-arm press with contralateral stance, and single-arm press with ipsilateral stance
    b. Seated press, standing press, single-arm press with contralateral stance, and single-arm press with ipsilateral stance
    c. Seated press, seated single-arm press, seated double-arm press, and standing press with wide leg stance
    d. Seated press, standing press with staggered leg stance, and standing press with wide leg stance

56. What is the proper progression of the wood chop, rotational movement, exercise?

    a. Long moment arm, standing short moment arm, standing long moment arm, hip hinge/squat, long moment arm, and full chop
    b. Standing long moment arm, hip hinge/squat, and full chop
    c. Long moment arm, short moment arm, hip hinge/squat, and full chop
    d. Long moment arm, standing long moment arm, hip hinge/squat, and full chop

Copyright © Mometrix Media. You have been licensed one copy of this document for personal use only. Any other reproduction or redistribution is strictly prohibited. All rights reserved. This content is provided for test preparation purposes only and does not imply an endorsement by Mometrix of any particular political, scientific, or religious point of view.

57. Which of the following is the only form to identify coronary heart disease (CHD) risk factors in potential clients?

  a. Medical history
  b. Physical Activity Readiness Questionnaire (PARQ)
  c. Informed consent
  d. Physician's clearance

58. A decreased risk of falls and what other benefit of exercise are specific to older adults?

  a. Increased metabolic rate
  b. Positive effect on stress
  c. Improved cognitive function
  d. Weight loss and reduced obesity

59. Which of the following is NOT one of the four elements of active listening?

  a. Listening to spoken statements
  b. Identifying statements that indicate learning opportunities
  c. Observing nonverbal cues
  d. Exhibiting understanding through the use of local expressions and industry terminology

60. During the initial consultation with a new client, you learn that she is being treated for stable coronary artery disease (CAD). She has no ongoing issues and has been stable for more than six months. What is the best course of action for this client?

  a. Begin regular programming with the client.
  b. Schedule a second session with the client and ask that she speak with her physician between now and then.
  c. Require the client complete Release of Liability and Informed Consent forms.
  d. Obtain a physician's medical clearance.

61. What kind of learner is the majority of the population?

  a. Kinesthetic
  b. Auditory
  c. A combination of visual, auditory, kinesthetic
  d. Visual

62. In reference to behavioral strategies, which of the following is the process of gradually achieving a desired behavior by using reinforcements?

  a. Observational learning
  b. Shaping
  c. Stimulus control
  d. Extinction

Copyright © Mometrix Media. You have been licensed one copy of this document for personal use only. Any other reproduction or redistribution is strictly prohibited. All rights reserved.
This content is provided for test preparation purposes only and does not imply an endorsement by Mometrix of any particular political, scientific, or religious point of view.

63. Which of the following would be the most effective way to teach a client a new movement?

    a. Identify the movement, detail the exercise, demonstrate the movement, and have the client attempt the exercise.

    b. Demonstrate the movement, have the client begin the movement, and detail the exercise while cueing client corrections.

    c. Identify the movement, demonstrate the movement, detail the exercise, and demonstrate the movement again.

    d. Demonstrate the movement, identify the movement, detail the movement, and demonstrate the movement again.

64. A potential client is referred to you by a doctor and calls to schedule the initial consultation. During your meeting, he informs you that he does not want to schedule the first session just yet, and he is merely gathering information. Per the Transtheoretical Model of behavior change, this client is at which stage of change?

    a. Precontemplation

    b. Contemplation

    c. Preparation

    d. Action

65. The exercise continuum is a scale from left (1) to right (6) that is used to rate the difficulty of an exercise. Which way would the trainer be moving an exercise if he or she must modify it for an unconditioned client?

    a. Left

    b. Right

    c. Up

    d. Down

66. A client is showing signs of overuse from additional training she has been performing separate from personal training sessions. She complains of pain in the anterior lower leg. She is most likely suffering from which injury?

    a. Iliotibial band syndrome (ITBS)

    b. Shin splints

    c. Bursitis

    d. Lateral epicondylitis

67. The exercise continuum is a scale from left (1) to right (6) that is used to rate the difficulty of an exercise. When giving your client an exercise to perform, you notice she moves the weight with ease. You decide to move the exercise from a 4 to a 5 on the exercise continuum. What is this called?

    a. Modification

    b. Engagement

    c. Progression

    d. Conditioning

Copyright © Mometrix Media. You have been licensed one copy of this document for personal use only. Any other reproduction or redistribution is strictly prohibited. All rights reserved. This content is provided for test preparation purposes only and does not imply an endorsement by Mometrix of any particular political, scientific, or religious point of view.

68. What type of joint is the glenohumeral?

a. Ball-and-socket
b. Ellipsoidal
c. Bicondylar
d. Hinge

69. A person who is exercising at a moderate to high altitude must reduce the intensity of a workout to keep the heartrate in its target zone. This is a result of what characteristic of blood at a high altitude?

a. Density
b. Oxygenation
c. Pressure
d. Temperature

70. You have completed the initial consultation with a new client. Given the information provided, you have set appropriate goals and designed a 12-week program. You prepared your client for a certain level of self-monitoring and prepped a schedule for the upcoming weeks. What important part of physical activity behavior change is missing?

a. Positive reinforcement
b. Feedback
c. Intervention
d. Customization

71. Which resistance training progression technique utilizes the micro-cycle as the timing basis for intervals and intensity?

a. Reverse linear programming
b. Nonlinear periodized programs
c. Linear periodization programming
d. Progressive overload

72. Which of the following is likely NOT a factor that plays into behavior change?

a. Readiness for change
b. Perceived self-efficacy
c. Scheduling
d. Cost

73. What is the process of weighing the pros and cons of behavior change with a client during intervention called?

a. Decisional balance
b. Transtheoretical modeling (TTM)
c. Cognitive strategies
d. Behavioral strategies

74. Which model of behavior change states that self-efficacy and expectations are the most important factors for behavior change?

a. Health Belief Model
b. Goal Setting Theory
c. Social Cognitive Theory
d. Theory of Planned Behavior

Copyright © Mometrix Media. You have been licensed one copy of this document for personal use only. Any other reproduction or redistribution is strictly prohibited. All rights reserved.
This content is provided for test preparation purposes only and does not imply an endorsement by Mometrix of any particular political, scientific, or religious point of view.

75. Which is NOT true of relapse?

    a. It is an inevitable part of the work of a personal trainer.

    b. Talking to clients about relapse before it occurs may prevent it.

    c. Regulating the schedule of a client with poor time-management skills can help prevent relapse.

    d. A personal trainer should prepare a client for relapse from Day 1 of the training program.

76. What is another name for the whole-part-whole teaching method?

    a. Demo-detail-demo

    b. Tell, show, do

    c. Demo-show-demo

    d. Tell, show, cue

77. A client who has dyslipidemia has what?

    a. Lowered HDL

    b. Elevated LDL

    c. Elevated LDL and total cholesterol

    d. Elevated total cholesterol

78. What is considered a normal level for triglycerides?

    a. <150

    b. <500

    c. 150–199

    d. 200–499

79. Your 16-year-old female client is experiencing energy imbalances, menstrual disturbances, and a decrease bone mineral density. What disorder is she likely suffering from?

    a. Anorexia nervosa

    b. Bulimia nervosa

    c. Female Athlete Triad

    d. Binge-eating disorder

80. How many kcals are in 1 gram of carbohydrates?

    a. 9

    b. 7

    c. 5

    d. 4

81. Clients wishing to increase muscle mass should perform muscle-building exercises and consume how many more calories per day?

    a. 300–400 kcals

    b. 250–350 kcals

    c. 350–500 kcals

    d. 250–400 kcals

Copyright © Mometrix Media. You have been licensed one copy of this document for personal use only. Any other reproduction or redistribution is strictly prohibited. All rights reserved. This content is provided for test preparation purposes only and does not imply an endorsement by Mometrix of any particular political, scientific, or religious point of view.

82. Which is NOT a result of eating smaller, more frequent meals?

a. Lower body fat
b. Increase of metabolic rate
c. Maintenance of muscle mass
d. Lower stress hormone levels

83. Which of the following is NOT a chest stabilization exercise?

a. Ball two-arm dumbbell chest press
b. Ball push-up
c. Two-arm dumbbell chest press
d. Single-leg one-arm cable chest press

84. What is the lean mass percentage of a client with a body fat percentage of 17 percent?

a. 83 percent
b. 17 percent
c. 5.88 percent
d. 1.2 percent

85. Which principle of strength training states that the body will adapt to the imposed demands placed upon it?

a. Specificity
b. Overload
c. Variation
d. Progression

86. A client weighs 210 lbs. and has a body fat percentage of 21 percent. What is the weight of his or her lean body mass?

a. 166 lbs.
b. 44 lbs.
c. 189 lbs.
d. 171 lbs.

87. Each of the following is a major sign or symptom suggestive of pulmonary, metabolic, or cardiovascular disease EXCEPT

a. syncope.
b. fatigue.
c. ankle edema.
d. orthopnea.

88. Under which theories of law would a personal trainer be liable to training a client in an unsafe environment?

a. Malpractice
b. Tort
c. Negligence
d. Liability

Copyright © Mometrix Media. You have been licensed one copy of this document for personal use only. Any other reproduction or redistribution is strictly prohibited. All rights reserved.
This content is provided for test preparation purposes only and does not imply an endorsement by Mometrix of any particular political, scientific, or religious point of view.

89. As a personal trainer, obtaining your cardiopulmonary resuscitation **(CPR), automated external defibrillator (AED), and first aid training, creating an emergency response plan, and having written emergency procedures are all part of what part of business?**

  a. Risk management
  b. Initial public offering (IPO)
  c. Accountability structure
  d. Audits

90. The American Heart Association (AHA) dictates there will be what maximum interval between trainings to maintain a cardiopulmonary resuscitation **(CPR) qualification?**

  a. 12 months
  b. 3–12months
  c. 24 months
  d. 36 months

91. A first aid kit containing a cardiopulmonary resuscitation **(CPR) micro-shield is stocked for what emergency procedure?**

  a. Mouth-to-mouth resuscitation
  b. Mouth-to-mask ventilations
  c. Automated external defibrillation
  d. Mask-to-mouth defibrillation

92. While training a client on the facility's main floor, you observe another member trying to operate a machine, but the machine is malfunctioning. What should you do?

  a. Excuse yourself from your client, and remove the machine or have it removed, from the gym floor until it can be repaired.
  b. Place an "out of order" sign on the machine.
  c. Do not leave your client. After the session, take steps to have the machine repaired and/or replaced.
  d. Apologize to the member, and unplug the machine to prevent further inconveniences.

93. The primary role of which ligament is to prevent medial valgus on the knee?

  a. Medial collateral ligament (MCL)
  b. Anterior cruciate ligament (ACL)
  c. Posterior cruciate ligament (PCL)
  d. Meniscus

94. How many vertebrae make up the lumbar curve of the spine?

  a. 8
  b. 5
  c. 12
  d. 7

Copyright © Mometrix Media. You have been licensed one copy of this document for personal use only. Any other reproduction or redistribution is strictly prohibited. All rights reserved.
This content is provided for test preparation purposes only and does not imply an endorsement by Mometrix of any particular political, scientific, or religious point of view.

95. Your client just finished a 60-minute workout with you in which she consumed 8 ounces of water every 15 minutes, and she has lost 1 kilogram of body weight. How much fluid should she drink?

    a. 800 mL
    b. 1000 mL
    c. 1400 mL
    d. 675 mL

96. Which of the following is the ability of the neuromuscular system to allow motor unit recruitment and synchronization within a single muscle?

    a. Intermuscular coordination
    b. Speed strength
    c. Intramuscular coordination
    d. Reactive strength

97. A nutrition label states the food contains 104 calories per each ¼ cup serving, and there are six servings in the package. It also states that there are 14 grams of carbohydrates per serving. What percentage of calories are from carbohydrates per serving?

    a. 54%
    b. 13%
    c. 45%
    d. 31%

98. Which of the following is NOT true in terms of flexibility?

    a. Exercise sessions should be preceded by a dedicated warm-up, regardless of time constraints.
    b. Clients must practice maximum flexibility to reduce the chance of injury.
    c. A client who has been diagnosed with hyperlaxity should not be encouraged to stretch to the joint's full possible range of motion (ROM).
    d. Flexibility is joint specific, allowing for movement beyond ROM in some joints and a below-average range in others.

99. What percentage of total calorie consumption should be from fat?

    a. 10–35 percent
    b. 20–35 percent
    c. 10–25 percent
    d. 20–30 percent

100. At the close of your initial conversation with a new client, he tells you that he feels he is ready to change his unhealthy behaviors and wants your help. What type of communication did you most likely use to help him achieve that emotional state?

    a. Verbal
    b. Kinesthetic
    c. Touch
    d. Visual

Copyright © Mometrix Media. You have been licensed one copy of this document for personal use only. Any other reproduction or redistribution is strictly prohibited. All rights reserved. This content is provided for test preparation purposes only and does not imply an endorsement by Mometrix of any particular political, scientific, or religious point of view.

101. Which of the following is NOT a type of flexibility training?

a. Resistance
b. Proprioceptive neuromuscular facilitation (PNF)
c. Ballistic
d. Static

102. Which muscle is stretched by turning the head to look left and turning the head to look right?

a. Piriformis
b. Splenae
c. Suboccipitals
d. Sternocleidomastoid

103. When engaging in a static stretching practice, what is the ideal number of seconds to hold each stretch?

a. 15
b. 30
c. 45
d. 60

104. Which of the following is NOT true in regard to static stretching?

a. Clients are least flexible in the morning.
b. Small muscle groups should be stretched first.
c. Stretching should be preceded with a warm-up intense enough to produce a light sweat.
d. Stretching should be done at least three times per week.

105. Which injury is defined as a stop in continuation of bone continuity?

a. Sprain
b. Strain
c. Hypoxia
d. Fracture

106. Which muscles are stretched by pressing the hands, while clasped together, behind the back in the "hands-behind-back" stretch?

a. Erector spinae and piriformis
b. Sternocleidomastoid and splenae
c. Triceps brachii and latissimus dorsi
d. Anterior deltoids and pectoralis major

107. What resistance training benefit is eliminated if a client is only using body weight exercises in his or her resistance training programming?

a. Maximal strength and power development
b. Increase muscle mass
c. Muscular endurance
d. Substantial caloric expenditure

Copyright © Mometrix Media. You have been licensed one copy of this document for personal use only. Any other reproduction or redistribution is strictly prohibited. All rights reserved. This content is provided for test preparation purposes only and does not imply an endorsement by Mometrix of any particular political, scientific, or religious point of view.

108. What is the correct size of a stability ball to be used with a client who suffers from low back pain?

a. The client can sit on the ball with thighs parallel to the floor.
b. The client can sit on the ball with thighs slightly above parallel and knees lower than the hips.
c. The client can sit on the ball with thighs slightly below parallel and knees higher than the hips.
d. The fully inflated ball should reach the client's mid-thigh.

109. Which resistance training system typically includes one to three sets of eight to 15 repetitions with 15 to 60 seconds of rest between exercises?

a. The pyramid system
b. Vertical loading
c. The multiple-set system
d. Compound sets

110. What is the term used to describe the consumption of recovery oxygen?

a. VO2
b. EPOC
c. O2
d. HRmax

111. What are the three training parts that make up stabilization training?

a. Core, neuromuscular, and skeletal
b. Balance, core, and strength
c. Power, core, and balance
d. Neuromuscular, strength, and core

112. Which of the following is NOT considered to be part of the core?

a. Lumbar spine
b. Lumbo-pelvic-hip complex (LPHC)
c. Thoracic spine
d. Cervical spine

113. Which of the following exercises is NOT one included in the power level of balance training?

a. Box jump up with stabilization
b. Single-leg windmill
c. Multiplanar hops with stabilization
d. Squat jump with stabilization

114. Which of the following are NOT variables for the concept of variation?

a. Volume
b. Muscle action
c. Neural demand
d. Rest interval

Copyright © Mometrix Media. You have been licensed one copy of this document for personal use only. Any other reproduction or redistribution is strictly prohibited. All rights reserved.
This content is provided for test preparation purposes only and does not imply an endorsement by Mometrix of any particular political, scientific, or religious point of view.

115. Which of the following is not a FITTE factor?

    a. Frequency
    b. Intensity
    c. Type
    d. Equipment

116. According to the criteria set by American College of Sports Medicine (ACSM), all of the following are positive risk factors on a Medical Health Screening EXCEPT

    a. myocardial infarction before the age of 55 in father or male first-degree relative.
    b. body mass index $\geq$ to 30 kg/m2.
    c. systolic blood pressure $\geq$ 135 mmHg.
    d. impaired fasting glucose (IFG).

117. What is the maximum daily caloric deficit recommended for weight loss?

    a. 500 kcals
    b. 300 kcals
    c. 400 kcals
    d. 350 kcals

118. A client's food log reveals she ate 40 grams of carbohydrates, 16 grams of protein, and 9 grams of fat for lunch yesterday. How many calories did your client consume during that meal?

    a. 260 calories
    b. 305 calories
    c. 385 calories
    d. 297 calories

119. As a personal trainer, it is important to integrate different forms of cardiovascular training into your client's programming. What is the primary reason for implementing this specific method?

    a. Reduce adaptation
    b. Increase endurance
    c. Reduce vertical loading
    d. Minimize excess post-exercise oxygen consumption (EPOC)

120. You are working with a new client. She is inexperienced with resistance training and considered a beginner-level client. You decide to implement a single-set system in her training program. Per this method, your client will perform how many repetitions of each exercise and with what frequency?

    a. Three to six repetitions one time each week
    b. Six to eight repetitions three times each week
    c. Eight to 12 repetitions two times each week
    d. Repetitions until failure two times each week

Copyright © Mometrix Media. You have been licensed one copy of this document for personal use only. Any other reproduction or redistribution is strictly prohibited. All rights reserved. This content is provided for test preparation purposes only and does not imply an endorsement by Mometrix of any particular political, scientific, or religious point of view.

Answer Key and Explanations

1. D: Clean drinking water, adequate lighting, adequate staffing and supervision, and nonslip surfaces are among the many steps a facility must take to minimize risk. Caution signs must be posted near machines, but the facility does not need to provide training to each new member. Many facilities offer new member orientation classes, but these are considered far above the minimum requirements.

2. A: Dynamic stretching is appropriate for use during the, and as a form of, warm-up because it involves the movement of body parts through their full range of motion by gradually increasing intensity. PNF, static, and passive stretching are only appropriate after a thorough warm-up of at least 5 to 10 minutes of light to moderate multi-joint, large muscle group movements. PNF should also only be performed by certified fitness professionals if they have been properly educated on the technique.

3. D: Primary movers of muscle movements are classified as agonists. During the overhead press the triceps are the synergists muscle.

4. D: A personal trainer should never recommend supplements to a client; any nutritional advice beyond the scope of practice of a personal trainer should be referred to a licensed nutritionist. Supplements are not regulated by the FDA, and supplement manufacturing companies usually do not carry insurance, leaving the trainer liable to any implications of supplement recommendation or misuse. Additionally, underlying medical conditions such as heart disease or diabetes can be worsened by supplement use; use in these cases could lead to severe injury or death.

5. B: Positive reinforcement is communicated using verbal (praise) and nonverbal (eye contact and empathy) cues that create a positive experience for the client. Stimulus control and shaping are also operant conditioning tools. Shaping is the process of gradually increasing the demands of a skill the client already has to help him or her achieve a desired behavior. Stimulus control refers to the altering of the cause of an action to change the outcome of the situation. Behavior chains are series of responses to stimuli that can either lead to or avoid desired behaviors.

6. B: A SMART goal must be specific, measurable, attainable, relevant, and time-bound. Choice A is not attainable as it is unrealistic to expect to lose 20 lbs. in 1 month of training. Choice C is nonspecific and is not measurable. Choice D is specific but not measurable.

7. D: The release of liability is an added level of liability protection and is an agreement between the client and trainer and/or facility that the participant relinquishes his or her rights to collect damages in the case of injury. Both the PARQ and medical history forms are used as screening tools, and a self-assessment quiz is used to help clients understand their own levels of wellness.

8. C: Individuals who have two or more risk factors are considered to be a moderate risk. Clients with zero or one risk factor are considered low risk, and any client with a known cardiovascular, pulmonary, or metabolic disease is automatically high risk.

9. A: Social support has been shown to be a key element in program adherence and is an important coping strategy in preventing relapse. Individuals with a strong support network, and whose family and friends are involved in their program, have greater success than those who do not. Assertiveness is the straightforward and honest expression of thoughts. Self-regulation is a client's ability to control his or her own behaviors, schedules, priorities, and so on. Intrinsic motivation is

Copyright © Mometrix Media. You have been licensed one copy of this document for personal use only. Any other reproduction or redistribution is strictly prohibited. All rights reserved.
This content is provided for test preparation purposes only and does not imply an endorsement by Mometrix of any particular political, scientific, or religious point of view.

not a coping strategy but is the internal motivation of a person to adhere to the program for the sake of personal satisfaction and not because of the positive response of an external stimuli.

10. C: This client is at the action stage of change. During the action stage, a person has a plan of action and is actively making behavior changes; however, he or she has been doing so for less than 6 months. The contemplation stage is during the time when a client is thinking about change and plans to do so in the future (within 6 months). During the preparation stage, the client has decided on a plan of action and will be beginning changes in behavior within the next 30 days. A client has reached the maintenance stage when he or she has been participating in behavior change for at least 6 months.

11. C: The Health Belief Model is a theoretical approach in which the client must believe he or she can change, and the benefits of change are not outweighed by the barriers to change. Clients can be predicted to change based on their perceived seriousness of the negative consequences of their current state and their belief in a decreased risk of consequences as a result of change.

12. B: Self-efficacy, an individual belief in one's own success, and the expectation of outcomes are the principles of the Social Cognitive Theory. Motivation is a person's mental drive toward behavior change, and extrinsic motivation is the drive coming from an outside source such as a change in appearance. Goal setting is a separate behavioral change theory that depends on the defining of personal goals and creating a plan to reach them.

13. B: The sagittal plane divides the body into right and left sides. The frontal plane divides the body in posterior and anterior portions and is also called the coronal plane. The transverse plane, also called the axial, cross-sectional, or horizontal plane, divides the body into superior and inferior portions.

14. D: Clients who are deemed to be moderate risk require a medical exam prior to vigorous exercise. Doctor supervision during submaximal testing and a medical exam before moderate exercise are required only for high risk clients. Clients with one risk factor are considered low risk.

15. C: The knee is an example of a bicondylar joint. The elbow is a hinge joint. The talocrural ankle joint is a hinge, and the subtalar ankle is a gliding joint. The hip is a ball-and-socket joint.

16. A: The serratus anterior, pectoralis minor, trapezius, levator scapulae, and rhomboids are the major agonist muscles, found in the scapulothoratic joint, that allow the body to perform a push-up. The anterior deltoid, supraspinatus, and pectoralis major are all found in the glenohumeral joint. The biceps and triceps are agonists of the elbow joint.

17. A: Exercise, specifically weight-bearing and impact activities, promote bone health and strengthening. Enhanced feeling of well-being, improved cognitive function, and a decrease in anxiety and depression are all psychological benefits of exercise.

18. A: The baseline recommendation for moderate intensity cardiorespiratory training is at least 30 minutes per day on at least 5 days per week for a total of at least 150 minutes each week. Although any activity is better than none, it is recommended that an apparently healthy person participate in aerobic exercise between 3 to 5 days each week, with a combination of moderate and vigorous intensity levels.

19. D: A client who has sporadic bouts of activity but no clear training plan are assigned the "Intermediate" activity status. The aerobic training plan for an intermediate client is to focus on moderate activity and aim for 200 to 300 minutes per week (fair to average fitness). The beginner

Copyright © Mometrix Media. You have been licensed one copy of this document for personal use only. Any other reproduction or redistribution is strictly prohibited. All rights reserved. This content is provided for test preparation purposes only and does not imply an endorsement by Mometrix of any particular political, scientific, or religious point of view.

status with either no prior or minimal activity is assigned to those who are completely inactive or deconditioned.

20. C: The four major types of shock (hypoperfusion) are obstructive, hypovolemic, distributive, and cardiogenic.

21. C: Daily flexibility exercise is most the most effective for adults and at least 10 minutes of stretching is recommended. At a minimum, stretching exercises should be included in exercise programming 2 to 3 days each week.

22. C: Because of the risk of orthostatic hypotension due to the possible obstruction of venous return in the supine position, pregnant women should avoid resistance and flexibility training in this position after the first trimester. The prone position is safe for pregnant women up until and after 6 weeks.

23. D: A client with diabetes should always check his or her blood glucose level prior to exercise and eat a snack if the reading is less than 100 mg/dl.

24. A: Sprint, plyometric, strength, and ballistic training are the best ways to improve an athlete's stride rate and frequency. This comprehensive approach helps the trained athlete to increase acceleration, enhance maximal speed and endurance, and strengthen the lower body.

25. A: An increase in repetitions, even for beginners, will create faster improvements in technique and strength. While single sets may be enough for the most inexperienced clients to see results, they are not the most efficient way to progress at any level. A client should always increase repetitions and reach a maximum number of repetitions and sets before increasing weight loads. When teaching a new skill to a client, a trainer should always begin with no additional weight added until the client has mastered the balance and achieve the strength needed to complete the weighted exercise safely.

26. B: The cooldown portion of the training session should be between 5 and 10 minutes in length, depending on the client and the intensity of the active phase of training. It begins with a slow decrease in activity and concludes prior to the final flexibility and abdominal work.

27. A: The universally accepted body position, for reference, is the anatomical position. It is described as the body being erect with the arms at the sides, palms facing forward with thumbs pointed away from the body, and fingers extended.

28. C: The Valsalva maneuver is performed by trying to forcefully push inhaled air out through a closed mouth and obstructed nasal passage. It is essentially the "bearing down" of one's breath such as techniques used to "pop" a person's ears during an airplane descent, and it works by decreasing the preload pressure to the heart. As a result, however, it increases pressure in the abdominal cavity, which can further injure a client suffering from a hernia. Times breathing is a typical strategy used in exercise and is safe for all individuals. Pranayama and yogic breathing are the same technique, both used in yoga as slow, controlled inhalations and exhalations.

29. B: A client will lose strength and changes in muscle size at a rate of one-half the rate it was gained. For example, a client who increases his or her bench press by 50 percent over the course of 10 weeks will lose half that strength gain in 10 weeks and all of that gain in 20 weeks.

30. C: PNF is an effective form of stretching because it is specifically designed to activate the Golgi tendon, using the body's own reflexes to allow a deeper stretch on a second, more passive, attempt.

Copyright © Mometrix Media. You have been licensed one copy of this document for personal use only. Any other reproduction or redistribution is strictly prohibited. All rights reserved. This content is provided for test preparation purposes only and does not imply an endorsement by Mometrix of any particular political, scientific, or religious point of view.

Ballistic stretching is the type that uses momentum to move muscles through their range of motion, stretching them to the limit. Static stretching focuses on the stretch reflex; however, the reflex is to be avoided by moving through a slow stretch only to the point of minor discomfort. Dynamic stretching uses movements that mimic those of daily living.

31. A: Increased resting heart rate, disturbed sleep, and decreased hunger are all signs of overtraining. A client exhibiting these symptoms should be encouraged to provide more time for recovery and decrease frequency and/or decrease intensity of training sessions.

32. C: A client who has improper form during a certain movement would most benefit from visual cues (shown on your own body), wrong-right cues (moving your own body in and out of the correct position), and tactile cues (using a hands-on method) to correct the form. Imagery is best used in yoga or meditation to elicit an emotion or thought in the client. Safety cues are informational but would not be the best way to describe a corrective motion. Affirmational or motivational cues are used as encouragement and to energize.

33. B: Hay balers require stabilization of the core in all three planes of motion, and the weight transference through the hips and legs help gain leverage and maintain balance. Unilateral rows perform the pull motion, and bilateral presses perform the push motion. A thoracic matrix also performs a push motion but through the entire kinetic chain.

34. C: Weight lifting should be performed in smooth, continuous motions using the correct grip, with a tight, engaged core, proper body positioning, and the weight held close to the body to avoid injury.

35. D: The dietary guidelines at ChooseMyPlate.org state that average adults should intake less than 2300 milligrams of sodium per day with less than 1500 milligrams of sodium for high-risk populations.

36. D: The most successful goals are those that are self-monitored by the client, follow the goal-setting strategies of SMART goals, and client-selected. Goals should not be flexible; they should be specific, measurable, attainable, realistic, and time oriented to ensure accurate monitoring.

37. B: SAID is a common specificity principle that calls for programming that causes adaptations within the body that will be specific to the demands of the goal. Prioritization is often used opposite a competitive season schedule and trains one aspect of muscular fitness at a time, and resistance training refers to a combination of consecutive training sessions. Cardiovascular prioritization is not a specificity principle.

38. C: ITBS is an overuse injury that causes pain along the outside of the thigh down to the knee. Lateral epicondylitis is another name for "tennis elbow"; tendinitis is an inflammatory response in the tendons caused by a new, increased level of demand on tendons.

39. A: Progressive overload is the continual increase of stimuli to encourage growth, strength, and endurance. Prioritization and variation in training are other principles of specificity but do not consist of any specific level of intensity or frequency; they are differentiated by timing of stimuli and organization of the training program. Overload is specifically applying beyond the current adaptations of the body.

40. D: Arthrokinetic inhibition is the decrease in muscle recruitment surrounding a joint that is working improperly or experiencing pain. This leads to a muscular imbalance in the joint and synergistic dominance of one muscle group over another. Reciprocal inhibition is a muscle

Copyright © Mometrix Media. You have been licensed one copy of this document for personal use only. Any other reproduction or redistribution is strictly prohibited. All rights reserved. This content is provided for test preparation purposes only and does not imply an endorsement by Mometrix of any particular political, scientific, or religious point of view.

inhibition caused by a tight agonist. Morphological adaptation is another way to describe hypertrophy, and motor unit recruitment is the means by which the nervous system moves muscles to perform work.

41. A: The five primary functional movements are bend-and-life, single-leg, pushing, pulling, and rotational. These should be taught and evaluated prior to teaching clients any movement patterns or progressing to weight-bearing exercises.

42. D: The adrenal gland is responsible for production of cortisol, also known as the stress hormone. Mind-body exercise such as yoga as well as stress reducing activities help reduce the cortisol produced by the adrenal gland, therefore lowering stress levels. The apocrine, eccrine, and sebaceous glands are all located on the skin and are sweat glands.

43. D: Pronation of the foot causes the ankles to collapse inward, and abduction of the knee is an internal rotation between the femur and tibia. This causes valgus stress and increases strain on the anterior cruciate ligament (ACL).

44. A: The only negative risk factor in the ACSM risk stratification is a high-serum HDL cholesterol of ≥ 60 mg/dl. The three other available choices are all positive risk factors when listed on the medical history form.

45. A: The muscle spindle is responsible for initiating the stretch reflex, counteracted by the Golgi tendon, to reduce injury during passive and active stretching. Ligaments and tendons are connective tissues.

46. C: The amount of hip flexion required to perform the squat averages approximately 95 degrees. The hips typically flex between 100 and 135 degrees with a full range of motion.

47. D: A spotter should always assist any time the client's speed decreases. The spotter should also always keep hands as close to the weights as possible while not obstructing the movement, always use collard or clips on an evenly loaded bar, and communicate to the client how many repetitions remain in each set.

48. B: The hip hinge is an exercise in a functional training progression that promotes glute dominance over quad dominance when performing a squat. A lower-extremity alignment and bend-and-lift screen would promote hip alignment over the hips, knees, and feet and determine if the client requires hip abductor or adductor strengthening and/or stretching. The figure-four position is one that promotes alignment between the tibia and truck.

49. B: The success of active listening hinges on both verbal and nonverbal feedback from the listener to portray understanding and attention. During active listening, the listener accepts what the speaker is saying at face value and trusts it to be true. Rapport is a positive result of effective communication. Facial expressions are a form of nonverbal communication and can be used to express feedback to the speaker.

50. C: Capping is a term used to describe the cease of a program prior to reaching the end goal. This may be done because the end goal has been deemed unrealistic, the current gains have been good enough, or the small gains between a current ability and the goal are not necessary for success. For example, a client with an original goal that was a very high 1RM on the bench press but who has decided to focus more effort on lower extremity training, even though he or she has not reached the 1RM goal.

Copyright © Mometrix Media. You have been licensed one copy of this document for personal use only. Any other reproduction or redistribution is strictly prohibited. All rights reserved. This content is provided for test preparation purposes only and does not imply an endorsement by Mometrix of any particular political, scientific, or religious point of view.

51. C: SMART goals are specific, measurable, attainable, relevant, and time-bound.

52. A: Hopscotch, skipping, and jumping are activities that encourage bone strengthening because of the force they place on the developing bones of children. Tug-of-war and tree climbing are examples of muscle-strengthening activities. Walking and bicycle riding are moderate-intensity aerobic activities for children, and swimming and skiing are vigorous-intensity aerobic activities.

53. B: Antidiuretic hormone (ADH), also known as vasopressin, is secreted by the posterior pituitary gland to reduce urinary excretion during exercise. GH, or growth hormone, is released by the anterior pituitary gland to facilitate protein synthesis. The catecholamines epinephrine and norepinephrine are released by the adrenal medulla to stimulate the fight-or-flight response to exercise. Glucagon is secreted by the pancreas to balance the effects of insulin.

54. D: Spinal twists and spinal extensions are thoracic spine (T-spine) mobilization exercises. The supine 90-90 hip rotator stretch improves hip mobility in the transverse plane, the shoulder bridge improves hip mobilization with glute activation, and rocking quadrupeds are for posterior mobilization.

55. B: The correct progression for performing bilateral and unilateral chest presses is seated press, standing press, single-arm press with contralateral stance, and single-arm with ipsilateral stance

56. A: The correct progression of the wood chop exercise when training rotational movement is the long moment arm, standing short moment arm, standing long moment arm, hip hinge/squat, long moment arm, and full chop.

57. A: The medical history form is used for screening purposes and identifies metabolic, cardiovascular, pulmonary, musculoskeletal, or other client problems. Although the PARQ is another medical screening tool, it does not identify CHD risk factors. The informed consent form is a signed acknowledgement of the possible risks involved in participating in the activity, and the physician's clearance form is used after risks have been identified and assists in program design.

58. C: An older adult who follows a regular exercise program can expect to have a decreased risk of falls and experience an improvement of cognitive function. Both aerobic and resistance training has been shown to reduce the risk of dementia and other age-related declines in cognitive function. An increased metabolic rate, positive effect on stress, and weight loss are all benefits of exercise; however, they are not specific to any special population.

59. D: An effective communicator should always avoid using metaphors or slang. The fourth element of active listening is to understand contextual anxiety.

60. D: A physician's medical clearance is required for any client with CAD. A personal trainer should not work with a client who has a preexisting condition until receiving input from the client's physician, and the trainer will follow the guidelines set by the physician. Regular programming cannot continue with a person who has CAD until clearance is given by a qualified physician. It is imperative that a personal trainer obtains the clearance in writing, along with the Release of Liability and Informed Consent.

61. D: About 65 percent of the population is visual learners and will benefit most from first being shown how to perform a movement. The most effective trainers use a combination of all three learning types along with the proper cuing.

Copyright © Mometrix Media. You have been licensed one copy of this document for personal use only. Any other reproduction or redistribution is strictly prohibited. All rights reserved. This content is provided for test preparation purposes only and does not imply an endorsement by Mometrix of any particular political, scientific, or religious point of view.

62. B: Shaping is the behavioral change tactic that uses reinforcements to achieve a target behavior. Observational learning is the influence a person's environment has on his or her ability to make a change, and stimulus control is adjustments made to a person's environment that either increase or decrease the likelihood of healthy behaviors. Extinction is the removal of a positive stimulus that once existed following a behavior, and it decreases the likelihood that the behavior will be repeated.

63. C: The whole-part-whole teaching method helps the trainer give clear and specific instructions on how to perform a new movement. The trainer should identify the movement, demonstrate the movement (whole), detail the exercise by breaking down the parts of the movement, and demonstrate it a second time (whole) before cuing the client to begin.

64. A: This client is at the precontemplation stage of change, per transtheoretical modeling (TTM) of behavior change. During the precontemplation stage, the client is not yet ready to make change and is not motivated by the benefits of change now. During the contemplation stage of change, the client is aware of the negative effects of the behavior and is considering change within the next 6 months. Both the preparation and action stages of change come after the client has a relationship with a personal trainer and a plan of action.

65 A: The exercise continuum is a scale from left (1) to right (6) that is used to rate the difficulty of an exercise. A client who cannot perform a given movement must have the exercise moved to the left (modified) to decrease difficulty.

66. B: Shin splints are an overuse injury causing pain in the lower, anterior leg. ITBS is shown along the outside of the knee and thigh. Bursitis is caused by inflammation of the bursa sac, and lateral epicondylitis is the medical term for "tennis elbow."

67. C: Movement to the right on the exercise continuum, or increasing the difficulty of a given exercise, is called "progression" and is done when a given movement becomes too easy. Progression is achieved by increasing repetitions, increasing weight, increasing the speed of an exercise, or any combination of progressions.

68. A: The glenohumeral (shoulder) joint is a synovial ball-and-socket joint.

69. B: At higher altitudes, air contains less oxygen than at sea level. Because there is less pressure to force the reduced oxygen into the blood, it is unable to deliver as much oxygen to the lungs as it would with higher levels of oxygen. While the pressure, density, and temperature are all different at various altitudes, the lightheadedness experienced by the exerciser is a direct result from a lack of oxygen.

70. B: Feedback is an essential part of goal setting and an important component of behavior change. Feedback is defined as two-way communication, is imperative for effective self-monitoring, and should be strongly encouraged at the onset of a new program, especially with a new, unfamiliar client. Positive reinforcement is a motivational tactic, intervention is used with a person who has not yet decided on a behavior change, and customization is completed on an ongoing basis through any normal programming.

71. C: The linear periodization is a classic method that uses a 1- to 4-week micro-cycle to time an increase in intensity and volume. A reverse linear program is beneficial to clients looking to achieve muscular endurance, but it follows the linear periodization in reverse order. A nonlinear program deviates from the classic periodization and usually uses a 12-week mesocycle. Progressive overload refers only to the increase in weight during resistance training.

Copyright © Mometrix Media. You have been licensed one copy of this document for personal use only. Any other reproduction or redistribution is strictly prohibited. All rights reserved. This content is provided for test preparation purposes only and does not imply an endorsement by Mometrix of any particular political, scientific, or religious point of view.

72. D: Behavior change is hindered by many things; the ability to change, scheduling, readiness, self-efficacy, scheduling, peer influence, and motivation are just a few. The cost, however, is a secondary conflict as changing one's behavior does not cost any money. The cost of a personal trainer, the cost of a gym membership, and so on, may be influences in the decision to change, but the cost itself is usually used to mask a lack of motivation, low self-efficacy, or insufficient readiness.

73. A: A decisional balance exercise helps a client determine the positives and negatives of behavior change and is used in conjunction with the TTM. Cognitive and behavioral strategies are used to combine stages of change and the process of change in the TTM.

74. C: The Social Cognitive Theory is based on the Health Belief Model and states that what a person thinks may happen (expectations) and self-efficacy are the most important factors in behavior change. The Health Belief Model states that a client must believe the health benefits of behavior change outweigh the barriers to change. Goal Setting Theory is moderated by the level of commitment to change, and the Theory of Planned Behavior states that a person's intention to engage in a certain behavior will ultimately lead to that behavior.

75. C: Despite the fact that unorganized or busy clients, or those with poor time-management skills, are more prone to relapse, regulating that client's schedule eliminates the important lapse deterrent of self-regulation. Clients should be taught to self-monitor and make their own behavioral changes to maximize success in fitness programming.

76. A: The whole-part-whole teaching method follows the same procedure as the demo-detail-demo teaching method.

77. C: Dyslipidemia is the elevated measurements of LDL cholesterol and total cholesterol.

78. A: A normal reading for triglycerides is <150 mg/dl; 150 to 199 is borderline high; 200 to 499 is high; and ≥500 is considered very high.

79. C: Female Athlete Triad is characterized by a decrease in bone mineral density with or without osteoporosis, energy imbalances with or without eating disorders, and menstrual disturbances.

80. D: One gram of carbohydrates is 4 kcals, or 4 calories. One gram of protein is also 4 kcals, and 1 gram of fat is 9 kcals.

81. A: A client who wishes to increase his or her muscle mass should consume 300 to 400 kcals more per day and perform muscle-building exercises.

82. B: Eating smaller, more frequent meals has been shown to maintain metabolic rate, but it does not cause a change to the metabolic rate such as an increase or decrease. This style of eating also helps lower body fat and lower weight on high caloric intakes, maintain muscle mass and better glucose tolerance, improve physical performance, and lower stress hormone production.

83. C: The two-arm dumbbell chest press is a chest strength exercise. Chest stabilization exercises include the ball push-up, ball two-arm dumbbell chest press, ball alternate arm dumbbell chest press, ball one-arm dumbbell chest press, ball seated cable chest press, flat bench one-arm dumbbell chest press, incline bench alternate-arm dumbbell chest press, single-leg two-arm cable chest press, single-leg alternate arm cable chest press, and the single-leg one-arm cable chest press.

Copyright © Mometrix Media. You have been licensed one copy of this document for personal use only. Any other reproduction or redistribution is strictly prohibited. All rights reserved. This content is provided for test preparation purposes only and does not imply an endorsement by Mometrix of any particular political, scientific, or religious point of view.

84. A: The lean mass percentage of a client with a body fat percentage of 17 percent is 83 percent: 100 − 17% = 83%.

85. A: The principle of specificity, also known as specific adaptation to imposed demands (SAID), states that the kinetic chain within the body will adapt specifically to the demand placed upon it.

86. A: A client whose weight is 210 lbs. with 21 percent body fat has a lean body mass weighing 166 lbs.: 210 × 0.21 = 44.1 lbs. (body fat); 210 − 44.1 lbs. = 165.9 lbs. (lean mass).

87. B: Fatigue is a normal result of exertion, especially at the start of an exercise program. Unusual fatigue or shortness of breath, syncope (dizziness), ankle edema, and orthopnea are all major signs or symptoms that suggest the presence of more serious diseases. Clients who exhibit these symptoms should be referred to a physician.

88. B: Tort law is the theory of law that regulates civil wrongdoing. There is an area of tort law called "premises liability," which states it is the trainer's responsibility to maintain a safe premise and ensure the safety of the client while training. Malpractice refers to wrongdoing by licensed professionals such as doctors and surgeons. Negligence is the law itself that is upheld by the theory of tort law, and liability is the responsibility the trainer accepts in keeping clients safe.

89. A: Risk management is a process through which a business uses foreseeability to minimize health risks and liability issues. As a personal trainer, this includes CPR, AED, and first aid training, the creation of an emergency response plan, and written emergency procedures that include when to call 911 and the use of automated defibrillators. An IPO is the initial public offering of company shares to potential, public shareholders. The accountability structure is a defined list of responsibilities and to whom each responsibility falls. Audits are a common business practice that involves the testing and evaluating of company procedures and, more commonly, bookkeeping.

90. C: Although the AHA recommends training refreshers every 3 to 12 months after initial CPR qualification, they state that there will be a maximum of 2 years between training sessions to maintain the certification; after the 2-year mark, the qualification will no longer be valid.

91. B: A CPR micro-shield is a pliable, plastic shield designed to cover the victim's mouth while performing mouth-to-mask ventilation, also known as protected mouth-to-mouth resuscitation. Mouth-to-mouth resuscitation should be avoided in the public setting to avoid direct contact with the victim's mouth. Automated external defibrillation is performed using an automated external defibrillator in the emergency procedures of cardiac arrest.

92. A: Removing the machine from the gym floor is the only way to completely remove the additional risk of harm or injury from attempting to use a malfunctioning machine. When it is safe, excuse yourself from your client to remove the machine, or recruit other staff members to remove it. An "out of order" sign does not remove the risk from attempting to use the broken machine. It also allows for the sign to be removed, moved, or unable to be read during daily tasks around the machine. Although you should never leave a client mid-exercise and should wait until he or she has finished performing the movement, you should not wait until after the session is complete to remove the risk. Unplugging the machine creates the additional risk of the loose cord.

93. A: The MCL is responsible for preventing medial bending on the knee. The ACL's primary purpose is to prevent anterior glide of the tibia, separating it from the femur. The PCL is the posterior cruciate ligament, and the meniscus is a soft layer of cushion protecting the femur and tibia.

Copyright © Mometrix Media. You have been licensed one copy of this document for personal use only. Any other reproduction or redistribution is strictly prohibited. All rights reserved.
This content is provided for test preparation purposes only and does not imply an endorsement by Mometrix of any particular political, scientific, or religious point of view.

94. B: The lumbar curve is made up of five vertebrae. The cervical curve consists of seven vertebrae, and the thoracic curve is 15 vertebrae.

95. B: The recommendation for fluid intake following exercise is 450 to 675 milliliters for every 0.5 kilograms of body weight lost. One thousand milliliters falls between the recommended range of 900 and 1350 milliliters after losing 1 kilogram of body weight.

96. C: Intramuscular coordination is the neuromuscular system's ability to allow the optimum motor recruitment and synchronization levels within a single muscle. Conversely, intermuscular coordination is the same ability but through all muscles working together. Speed, strength, or power is the ability of the body to produce the greatest possible force in the shortest possible time. Reactive strength, or elastic strength, is the ability to efficiently switch between force reduction and force production.

97. A: Each serving contains 54% carbohydrate (14 g carbohydrate × 4 calories per gram = 56 calories per serving, so 56/104 calories total per serving = 0.54 or 54%).

98. B: A common misconception about flexibility is that clients must reach extreme levels for the practice to be effective in reducing injury. In fact, flexibility is unique to everyone and is simply the free movement of a joint through its normal range of motion for that person, whatever that may be.

99. B: It is recommended that 20 to 35 percent of total calorie consumption should be from fats; 45 to 65 percent of total calories should be carbohydrates; and 10 to 35 percent should be protein.

100. B: Kinesthetic communication refers to how the communicator makes the listener feel. Effective motivation uses kinesthetic communication to help the person receiving the information achieve the optimal emotional state for behavior change. Verbal and visual are forms of communication but do not help achieve an emotional connection as well as kinesthetic. Touch is a type of nonverbal communication.

101. A: Resistance training is not a type of flexibility training. The four types of flexibility training are ballistic, static, dynamic, and proprioceptive neuromuscular facilitation (PNF).

102. D: The sternocleidomastoid is the muscle in the neck stretched by turning the head left and right, looking in each direction. The suboccipitals and splenae are both muscles in the neck but are stretched during neck flexion and extension (looking up and down). The piriformis is a muscle of the lower body, stretched in the pretzel position.

103. B: During static stretching, each position is held and stretched for at least 30 seconds with a slow, constant, controlled pressure. Clients who are just beginning a flexibility program may have difficulty holding a stretch for this length of time, so personal trainers should work with the client, gradually increasing stretch time until each position can be held for the minimum of 30 seconds.

104. B: When static stretching, large muscle groups should be stretched first, and clients should move through the same routine during each stretching session.

105. D: A fracture is a break or disruption in the continuation of bone; they are deemed either "open" or "closed" depending on whether the broken bone pushes through the skin after injury. A sprain is an injury caused by the twisting of a body joint. A strain is a stretch or tear in muscle fibers, such as a tendon or fascia. Hypoxia is an injury caused by when a person stops breathing during a seizure.

Copyright © Mometrix Media. You have been licensed one copy of this document for personal use only. Any other reproduction or redistribution is strictly prohibited. All rights reserved.
This content is provided for test preparation purposes only and does not imply an endorsement by Mometrix of any particular political, scientific, or religious point of view.

106. D: The "hands-behind-back" stretch lengthens the front of the chest: the anterior deltoids and pectoralis major muscles. The erector spinae and piriformis are both stretched in the pretzel position, and the sternocleidomastoid and splenae are lengthened by neck flexion and extension. The triceps brachii and latissimus dorsi are specifically targeted in the "behind-neck stretch," reaching one arm over the shoulder and pushing at the elbow with the opposite hand.

107. A: Personal trainers must be aware that if a client is only performing body weight exercises in resistance training programming, that client will never reach maximal power and strength because these movements will not create the intensity necessary to develop these adaptations. Body weight exercises will, however, provide an increase in muscle mass, increase muscular endurance, and create a substantial caloric expenditure if performed correctly.

108. B: When sized correctly, a client should be able to sit on a stability ball with the thighs parallel to the floor. If the client suffers from low back pain, however, he or she should be seated on the ball with thighs slightly above parallel, with the knees lower than the hips.

109. B: Vertical loading, also known as the circuit training system, consists of a series of exercises performed one right after the other with minimal rest between them. The typical circuit consists of one to three sets of eight to 15 repetitions.

110. B: Excess post-exercise oxygen consumption (EPOC) is the raised metabolism and increased oxygen consumption in recovery following exercise.

111. C: Core, balance, and power training are the three parts of stabilization training.

112. A: The core, in terms of stabilization training, is defined as the lumbo-pelvic-hip complex (LPHC), thoracic, and cervical spine.

113. B: The single-leg windmill is an exercise in the stabilization level of balance training. The power level includes multi-planar hops with stabilization, box jump-ups and jump-downs with stabilization, and squat jumps with stabilization.

114. B: Muscle action is an acute variable for the concept of overload. The variables for variation include volume, movement pattern, repetition tempo, rest interval, and neural demand.

115. D: The FITTE factors, used by the National Academy of Sports Medicine (NASM) and supported by the American College of Sports Medicine (ACSM) are frequency, intensity, time, type, and enjoyment.

116. C: Systolic blood pressure ≥ 140 mmHg is a positive risk factor, not the listed reading of 135 mmHg. All other choices are positive health risk factors according to the guidelines set forth by ACSM.

117. C: A person whose goal is to lose weight and decrease body fat should decrease his or her daily caloric intake by no more than 300 to 400 kcals.

118. B: Forty grams of carbohydrate at 4 calories per gram, 16 grams of protein at 4 calories per gram, and 9 grams of fat at 9 calories per gram equal a total of 305 calories: $(40 \times 4) + (16 \times 4) + (9 \times 9) = 305$.

119. A: As a client continues to perform the same training routine, his or her body will adapt to the stimulus, and it will require less energy to complete the same tasks. Because of this, personal trainers should alter the training stimuli to reduce the body's adaptations, and the client will see

227

Copyright © Mometrix Media. You have been licensed one copy of this document for personal use only. Any other reproduction or redistribution is strictly prohibited. All rights reserved. This content is provided for test preparation purposes only and does not imply an endorsement by Mometrix of any particular political, scientific, or religious point of view.

better results in less time. Any resistance and/or cardiovascular training will increase endurance; this is not a specific reason to integrate various training modalities but is a mere by-product of any additional activity. Vertical loading is an effective training modality that has altered training forms as part of its base, making it very effective in reducing adaptation. EPOC is the post-exercise consumption of oxygen.

120. C: The single-set system is a beneficial method for training beginning-level clients. This system dictates that each exercise is performed for a single set consisting of eight to 12 repetitions, two times each week.

Copyright © Mometrix Media. You have been licensed one copy of this document for personal use only. Any other reproduction or redistribution is strictly prohibited. All rights reserved.
This content is provided for test preparation purposes only and does not imply an endorsement by Mometrix of any particular political, scientific, or religious point of view.

NASM Image Credits

LICENSED UNDER CC BY 4.0 (CREATIVECOMMONS.ORG/LICENSES/BY/4.0/)

Muscles: "The Three Connective Tissue Layers" by Openstax Anatomy & Physiology Chapter 10.2 (https://cnx.org/contents/FPtK1zmh@8.25:bfiqsxdB@3/Skeletal-Muscle)

Muscle Fibers: "Muscle Fibers" by Openstax Anatomy & Physiology Chapter 10.2 (https://cnx.org/contents/FPtK1zmh@8.25:bfiqsxdB@3/Skeletal-Muscle)

Human skeleton: "Human skeleton front en" by Mariana Ruiz Villarreal (https://commons.wikimedia.org/wiki/File:Human_skeleton_front_en.svg)

Cardiovascular System: "Circulatory System en edited" by Mariana Ruiz Villarreal (https://commons.wikimedia.org/wiki/File:Circulatory_System_en_edited.svg)

Respiratory System: "Respiratory system complete en" by Mariana Ruiz Villarreal (https://commons.wikimedia.org/wiki/File:Respiratory_system_complete_en.svg)

Muscular System: "Overview of Muscular System" by Openstax Anatomy & Physiology Chapter 11.2 (https://cnx.org/contents/FPtK1zmh@8.25:FL6Dj0EF@3/Naming-Skeletal-Muscles)

Respiratory System and Heart: "Pulmonary Circuit" by Openstax Anatomy & Physiology Chapter 20.5 (https://cnx.org/contents/FPtK1zmh@8.25:GqYHW4Z4@3/Circulatory-Pathways)

LICENSED UNDER CC BY-SA 3.0 (CREATIVECOMMONS.ORG/LICENSES/BY-SA/3.0/DEED.EN)

Heart: "Heart diagram blood flow en" by Wikimedia user ZooFari (https://commons.wikimedia.org/wiki/File:Heart_diagram_blood_flow_en.svg)

Planes of Movement: "Human anatomy planes" by YassineMrabet (https://commons.wikimedia.org/wiki/File:Human_anatomy_planes.svg)

Copyright © Mometrix Media. You have been licensed one copy of this document for personal use only. Any other reproduction or redistribution is strictly prohibited. All rights reserved. This content is provided for test preparation purposes only and does not imply an endorsement by Mometrix of any particular political, scientific, or religious point of view.

How to Overcome Test Anxiety

Just the thought of taking a test is enough to make most people a little nervous. A test is an important event that can have a long-term impact on your future, so it's important to take it seriously and it's natural to feel anxious about performing well. But just because anxiety is normal, that doesn't mean that it's helpful in test taking, or that you should simply accept it as part of your life. Anxiety can have a variety of effects. These effects can be mild, like making you feel slightly nervous, or severe, like blocking your ability to focus or remember even a simple detail.

If you experience test anxiety—whether severe or mild—it's important to know how to beat it. To discover this, first you need to understand what causes test anxiety.

Causes of Test Anxiety

While we often think of anxiety as an uncontrollable emotional state, it can actually be caused by simple, practical things. One of the most common causes of test anxiety is that a person does not feel adequately prepared for their test. This feeling can be the result of many different issues such as poor study habits or lack of organization, but the most common culprit is time management. Starting to study too late, failing to organize your study time to cover all of the material, or being distracted while you study will mean that you're not well prepared for the test. This may lead to cramming the night before, which will cause you to be physically and mentally exhausted for the test. Poor time management also contributes to feelings of stress, fear, and hopelessness as you realize you are not well prepared but don't know what to do about it.

Other times, test anxiety is not related to your preparation for the test but comes from unresolved fear. This may be a past failure on a test, or poor performance on tests in general. It may come from comparing yourself to others who seem to be performing better or from the stress of living up to expectations. Anxiety may be driven by fears of the future—how failure on this test would affect your educational and career goals. These fears are often completely irrational, but they can still negatively impact your test performance.

> **Review Video: 3 Reasons You Have Test Anxiety**
> Visit mometrix.com/academy and enter code: 428468

Copyright © Mometrix Media. You have been licensed one copy of this document for personal use only. Any other reproduction or redistribution is strictly prohibited. All rights reserved. This content is provided for test preparation purposes only and does not imply an endorsement by Mometrix of any particular political, scientific, or religious point of view.

Elements of Test Anxiety

As mentioned earlier, test anxiety is considered to be an emotional state, but it has physical and mental components as well. Sometimes you may not even realize that you are suffering from test anxiety until you notice the physical symptoms. These can include trembling hands, rapid heartbeat, sweating, nausea, and tense muscles. Extreme anxiety may lead to fainting or vomiting. Obviously, any of these symptoms can have a negative impact on testing. It is important to recognize them as soon as they begin to occur so that you can address the problem before it damages your performance.

> **Review Video: 3 Ways to Tell You Have Test Anxiety**
> Visit mometrix.com/academy and enter code: 927847

The mental components of test anxiety include trouble focusing and inability to remember learned information. During a test, your mind is on high alert, which can help you recall information and stay focused for an extended period of time. However, anxiety interferes with your mind's natural processes, causing you to blank out, even on the questions you know well. The strain of testing during anxiety makes it difficult to stay focused, especially on a test that may take several hours. Extreme anxiety can take a huge mental toll, making it difficult not only to recall test information but even to understand the test questions or pull your thoughts together.

> **Review Video: How Test Anxiety Affects Memory**
> Visit mometrix.com/academy and enter code: 609003

Effects of Test Anxiety

Test anxiety is like a disease—if left untreated, it will get progressively worse. Anxiety leads to poor performance, and this reinforces the feelings of fear and failure, which in turn lead to poor performances on subsequent tests. It can grow from a mild nervousness to a crippling condition. If allowed to progress, test anxiety can have a big impact on your schooling, and consequently on your future.

Test anxiety can spread to other parts of your life. Anxiety on tests can become anxiety in any stressful situation, and blanking on a test can turn into panicking in a job situation. But fortunately, you don't have to let anxiety rule your testing and determine your grades. There are a number of relatively simple steps you can take to move past anxiety and function normally on a test and in the rest of life.

> **Review Video: How Test Anxiety Impacts Your Grades**
> Visit mometrix.com/academy and enter code: 939819

Copyright © Mometrix Media. You have been licensed one copy of this document for personal use only. Any other reproduction or redistribution is strictly prohibited. All rights reserved. This content is provided for test preparation purposes only and does not imply an endorsement by Mometrix of any particular political, scientific, or religious point of view.

Physical Steps for Beating Test Anxiety

While test anxiety is a serious problem, the good news is that it can be overcome. It doesn't have to control your ability to think and remember information. While it may take time, you can begin taking steps today to beat anxiety.

Just as your first hint that you may be struggling with anxiety comes from the physical symptoms, the first step to treating it is also physical. Rest is crucial for having a clear, strong mind. If you are tired, it is much easier to give in to anxiety. But if you establish good sleep habits, your body and mind will be ready to perform optimally, without the strain of exhaustion. Additionally, sleeping well helps you to retain information better, so you're more likely to recall the answers when you see the test questions.

Getting good sleep means more than going to bed on time. It's important to allow your brain time to relax. Take study breaks from time to time so it doesn't get overworked, and don't study right before bed. Take time to rest your mind before trying to rest your body, or you may find it difficult to fall asleep.

> **Review Video: The Importance of Sleep for Your Brain**
> Visit mometrix.com/academy and enter code: 319338

Along with sleep, other aspects of physical health are important in preparing for a test. Good nutrition is vital for good brain function. Sugary foods and drinks may give a burst of energy but this burst is followed by a crash, both physically and emotionally. Instead, fuel your body with protein and vitamin-rich foods.

Also, drink plenty of water. Dehydration can lead to headaches and exhaustion, especially if your brain is already under stress from the rigors of the test. Particularly if your test is a long one, drink water during the breaks. And if possible, take an energy-boosting snack to eat between sections.

> **Review Video: How Diet Can Affect your Mood**
> Visit mometrix.com/academy and enter code: 624317

Along with sleep and diet, a third important part of physical health is exercise. Maintaining a steady workout schedule is helpful, but even taking 5-minute study breaks to walk can help get your blood pumping faster and clear your head. Exercise also releases endorphins, which contribute to a positive feeling and can help combat test anxiety.

When you nurture your physical health, you are also contributing to your mental health. If your body is healthy, your mind is much more likely to be healthy as well. So take time to rest, nourish your body with healthy food and water, and get moving as much as possible. Taking these physical steps will make you stronger and more able to take the mental steps necessary to overcome test anxiety.

Copyright © Mometrix Media. You have been licensed one copy of this document for personal use only. Any other reproduction or redistribution is strictly prohibited. All rights reserved. This content is provided for test preparation purposes only and does not imply an endorsement by Mometrix of any particular political, scientific, or religious point of view.

Mental Steps for Beating Test Anxiety

Working on the mental side of test anxiety can be more challenging, but as with the physical side, there are clear steps you can take to overcome it. As mentioned earlier, test anxiety often stems from lack of preparation, so the obvious solution is to prepare for the test. Effective studying may be the most important weapon you have for beating test anxiety, but you can and should employ several other mental tools to combat fear.

First, boost your confidence by reminding yourself of past success—tests or projects that you aced. If you're putting as much effort into preparing for this test as you did for those, there's no reason you should expect to fail here. Work hard to prepare; then trust your preparation.

Second, surround yourself with encouraging people. It can be helpful to find a study group, but be sure that the people you're around will encourage a positive attitude. If you spend time with others who are anxious or cynical, this will only contribute to your own anxiety. Look for others who are motivated to study hard from a desire to succeed, not from a fear of failure.

Third, reward yourself. A test is physically and mentally tiring, even without anxiety, and it can be helpful to have something to look forward to. Plan an activity following the test, regardless of the outcome, such as going to a movie or getting ice cream.

When you are taking the test, if you find yourself beginning to feel anxious, remind yourself that you know the material. Visualize successfully completing the test. Then take a few deep, relaxing breaths and return to it. Work through the questions carefully but with confidence, knowing that you are capable of succeeding.

Developing a healthy mental approach to test taking will also aid in other areas of life. Test anxiety affects more than just the actual test—it can be damaging to your mental health and even contribute to depression. It's important to beat test anxiety before it becomes a problem for more than testing.

> **Review Video: Test Anxiety and Depression**
> Visit mometrix.com/academy and enter code: 904704

Copyright © Mometrix Media. You have been licensed one copy of this document for personal use only. Any other reproduction or redistribution is strictly prohibited. All rights reserved.
This content is provided for test preparation purposes only and does not imply an endorsement by Mometrix of any particular political, scientific, or religious point of view.

Study Strategy

Being prepared for the test is necessary to combat anxiety, but what does being prepared look like? You may study for hours on end and still not feel prepared. What you need is a strategy for test prep. The next few pages outline our recommended steps to help you plan out and conquer the challenge of preparation.

STEP 1: SCOPE OUT THE TEST

Learn everything you can about the format (multiple choice, essay, etc.) and what will be on the test. Gather any study materials, course outlines, or sample exams that may be available. Not only will this help you to prepare, but knowing what to expect can help to alleviate test anxiety.

STEP 2: MAP OUT THE MATERIAL

Look through the textbook or study guide and make note of how many chapters or sections it has. Then divide these over the time you have. For example, if a book has 15 chapters and you have five days to study, you need to cover three chapters each day. Even better, if you have the time, leave an extra day at the end for overall review after you have gone through the material in depth.

If time is limited, you may need to prioritize the material. Look through it and make note of which sections you think you already have a good grasp on, and which need review. While you are studying, skim quickly through the familiar sections and take more time on the challenging parts. Write out your plan so you don't get lost as you go. Having a written plan also helps you feel more in control of the study, so anxiety is less likely to arise from feeling overwhelmed at the amount to cover.

STEP 3: GATHER YOUR TOOLS

Decide what study method works best for you. Do you prefer to highlight in the book as you study and then go back over the highlighted portions? Or do you type out notes of the important information? Or is it helpful to make flashcards that you can carry with you? Assemble the pens, index cards, highlighters, post-it notes, and any other materials you may need so you won't be distracted by getting up to find things while you study.

If you're having a hard time retaining the information or organizing your notes, experiment with different methods. For example, try color-coding by subject with colored pens, highlighters, or post-it notes. If you learn better by hearing, try recording yourself reading your notes so you can listen while in the car, working out, or simply sitting at your desk. Ask a friend to quiz you from your flashcards, or try teaching someone the material to solidify it in your mind.

STEP 4: CREATE YOUR ENVIRONMENT

It's important to avoid distractions while you study. This includes both the obvious distractions like visitors and the subtle distractions like an uncomfortable chair (or a too-comfortable couch that makes you want to fall asleep). Set up the best study environment possible: good lighting and a comfortable work area. If background music helps you focus, you may want to turn it on, but otherwise keep the room quiet. If you are using a computer to take notes, be sure you don't have any other windows open, especially applications like social media, games, or anything else that could distract you. Silence your phone and turn off notifications. Be sure to keep water close by so you stay hydrated while you study (but avoid unhealthy drinks and snacks).

Also, take into account the best time of day to study. Are you freshest first thing in the morning? Try to set aside some time then to work through the material. Is your mind clearer in the afternoon or evening? Schedule your study session then. Another method is to study at the same time of day that

Copyright © Mometrix Media. You have been licensed one copy of this document for personal use only. Any other reproduction or redistribution is strictly prohibited. All rights reserved.
This content is provided for test preparation purposes only and does not imply an endorsement by Mometrix of any particular political, scientific, or religious point of view.

you will take the test, so that your brain gets used to working on the material at that time and will be ready to focus at test time.

STEP 5: STUDY!

Once you have done all the study preparation, it's time to settle into the actual studying. Sit down, take a few moments to settle your mind so you can focus, and begin to follow your study plan. Don't give in to distractions or let yourself procrastinate. This is your time to prepare so you'll be ready to fearlessly approach the test. Make the most of the time and stay focused.

Of course, you don't want to burn out. If you study too long you may find that you're not retaining the information very well. Take regular study breaks. For example, taking five minutes out of every hour to walk briskly, breathing deeply and swinging your arms, can help your mind stay fresh.

As you get to the end of each chapter or section, it's a good idea to do a quick review. Remind yourself of what you learned and work on any difficult parts. When you feel that you've mastered the material, move on to the next part. At the end of your study session, briefly skim through your notes again.

But while review is helpful, cramming last minute is NOT. If at all possible, work ahead so that you won't need to fit all your study into the last day. Cramming overloads your brain with more information than it can process and retain, and your tired mind may struggle to recall even previously learned information when it is overwhelmed with last-minute study. Also, the urgent nature of cramming and the stress placed on your brain contribute to anxiety. You'll be more likely to go to the test feeling unprepared and having trouble thinking clearly.

So don't cram, and don't stay up late before the test, even just to review your notes at a leisurely pace. Your brain needs rest more than it needs to go over the information again. In fact, plan to finish your studies by noon or early afternoon the day before the test. Give your brain the rest of the day to relax or focus on other things, and get a good night's sleep. Then you will be fresh for the test and better able to recall what you've studied.

STEP 6: TAKE A PRACTICE TEST

Many courses offer sample tests, either online or in the study materials. This is an excellent resource to check whether you have mastered the material, as well as to prepare for the test format and environment.

Check the test format ahead of time: the number of questions, the type (multiple choice, free response, etc.), and the time limit. Then create a plan for working through them. For example, if you have 30 minutes to take a 60-question test, your limit is 30 seconds per question. Spend less time on the questions you know well so that you can take more time on the difficult ones.

If you have time to take several practice tests, take the first one open book, with no time limit. Work through the questions at your own pace and make sure you fully understand them. Gradually work up to taking a test under test conditions: sit at a desk with all study materials put away and set a timer. Pace yourself to make sure you finish the test with time to spare and go back to check your answers if you have time.

After each test, check your answers. On the questions you missed, be sure you understand why you missed them. Did you misread the question (tests can use tricky wording)? Did you forget the information? Or was it something you hadn't learned? Go back and study any shaky areas that the practice tests reveal.

Copyright © Mometrix Media. You have been licensed one copy of this document for personal use only. Any other reproduction or redistribution is strictly prohibited. All rights reserved. This content is provided for test preparation purposes only and does not imply an endorsement by Mometrix of any particular political, scientific, or religious point of view.

Taking these tests not only helps with your grade, but also aids in combating test anxiety. If you're already used to the test conditions, you're less likely to worry about it, and working through tests until you're scoring well gives you a confidence boost. Go through the practice tests until you feel comfortable, and then you can go into the test knowing that you're ready for it.

Test Tips

On test day, you should be confident, knowing that you've prepared well and are ready to answer the questions. But aside from preparation, there are several test day strategies you can employ to maximize your performance.

First, as stated before, get a good night's sleep the night before the test (and for several nights before that, if possible). Go into the test with a fresh, alert mind rather than staying up late to study.

Try not to change too much about your normal routine on the day of the test. It's important to eat a nutritious breakfast, but if you normally don't eat breakfast at all, consider eating just a protein bar. If you're a coffee drinker, go ahead and have your normal coffee. Just make sure you time it so that the caffeine doesn't wear off right in the middle of your test. Avoid sugary beverages, and drink enough water to stay hydrated but not so much that you need a restroom break 10 minutes into the test. If your test isn't first thing in the morning, consider going for a walk or doing a light workout before the test to get your blood flowing.

Allow yourself enough time to get ready, and leave for the test with plenty of time to spare so you won't have the anxiety of scrambling to arrive in time. Another reason to be early is to select a good seat. It's helpful to sit away from doors and windows, which can be distracting. Find a good seat, get out your supplies, and settle your mind before the test begins.

When the test begins, start by going over the instructions carefully, even if you already know what to expect. Make sure you avoid any careless mistakes by following the directions.

Then begin working through the questions, pacing yourself as you've practiced. If you're not sure on an answer, don't spend too much time on it, and don't let it shake your confidence. Either skip it and come back later, or eliminate as many wrong answers as possible and guess among the remaining ones. Don't dwell on these questions as you continue—put them out of your mind and focus on what lies ahead.

Be sure to read all of the answer choices, even if you're sure the first one is the right answer. Sometimes you'll find a better one if you keep reading. But don't second-guess yourself if you do immediately know the answer. Your gut instinct is usually right. Don't let test anxiety rob you of the information you know.

If you have time at the end of the test (and if the test format allows), go back and review your answers. Be cautious about changing any, since your first instinct tends to be correct, but make sure you didn't misread any of the questions or accidentally mark the wrong answer choice. Look over any you skipped and make an educated guess.

At the end, leave the test feeling confident. You've done your best, so don't waste time worrying about your performance or wishing you could change anything. Instead, celebrate the successful

Copyright © Mometrix Media. You have been licensed one copy of this document for personal use only. Any other reproduction or redistribution is strictly prohibited. All rights reserved. This content is provided for test preparation purposes only and does not imply an endorsement by Mometrix of any particular political, scientific, or religious point of view.

completion of this test. And finally, use this test to learn how to deal with anxiety even better next time.

> **Review Video: 5 Tips to Beat Test Anxiety**
> Visit mometrix.com/academy and enter code: 570656

Important Qualification

Not all anxiety is created equal. If your test anxiety is causing major issues in your life beyond the classroom or testing center, or if you are experiencing troubling physical symptoms related to your anxiety, it may be a sign of a serious physiological or psychological condition. If this sounds like your situation, we strongly encourage you to seek professional help.

Copyright © Mometrix Media. You have been licensed one copy of this document for personal use only. Any other reproduction or redistribution is strictly prohibited. All rights reserved. This content is provided for test preparation purposes only and does not imply an endorsement by Mometrix of any particular political, scientific, or religious point of view.

Tell Us Your Story

We at Mometrix would like to extend our heartfelt thanks to you for letting us be a part of your journey. It is an honor to serve people from all walks of life, people like you, who are committed to building the best future they can for themselves.

We know that each person's situation is unique. But we also know that, whether you are a young student or a mother of four, you care about working to make your own life and the lives of those around you better.

That's why we want to hear your story.

We want to know why you're taking this test. We want to know about the trials you've gone through to get here. And we want to know about the successes you've experienced after taking and passing your test.

In addition to your story, which can be an inspiration both to us and to others, we value your feedback. We want to know both what you loved about our book and what you think we can improve on.

The team at Mometrix would be absolutely thrilled to hear from you! So please, send us an email at tellusyourstory@mometrix.com or visit us at mometrix.com/tellusyourstory.php and let's stay in touch.

Copyright © Mometrix Media. You have been licensed one copy of this document for personal use only. Any other reproduction or redistribution is strictly prohibited. All rights reserved. This content is provided for test preparation purposes only and does not imply an endorsement by Mometrix of any particular political, scientific, or religious point of view.

Additional Bonus Material

Due to our efforts to try to keep this book to a manageable length, we've created a link that will give you access to all of your additional bonus material:

mometrix.com/bonus948/nasm

Copyright © Mometrix Media. You have been licensed one copy of this document for personal use only. Any other reproduction or redistribution is strictly prohibited. All rights reserved. This content is provided for test preparation purposes only and does not imply an endorsement by Mometrix of any particular political, scientific, or religious point of view.

Made in the USA
Monee, IL
08 April 2023

31572903R00138